*The Temple Legend
and the Golden Legend*

GW00578170

THE TEMPLE LEGEND AND THE GOLDEN LEGEND

Freemasonry & Related Occult Movements

From the Contents of the Esoteric School

RUDOLF STEINER

Twenty Lectures given in Berlin between 23 May 1904 and 2 January 1906

RUDOLF STEINER PRESS

Translated by John M. Wood

Rudolf Steiner Press
Hillside House, The Square
Forest Row, East Sussex
RH18 5ES

www.rudolfsteinerpress.com

First edition 1985
This edition 1997
Reprinted 2002

Originally published in German under the title *Die Tempellegende und die Goldene Legende* (volume 93 in the *Rudolf Steiner Gesamtausgabe* or Collected Works) by Rudolf Steiner Verlag, Dornach. This authorized translation published by kind permission of the Rudolf Steiner Nachlassverwaltung, Dornach

Revised translation © Rudolf Steiner Press 1997

The moral right of the translator has been asserted under the Copyright, Designs and Patents Act, 1988

All rights reserved. No part of this publication may be reproduced, stored in a retrieval system, or transmitted, in any form or by any means, electronic, mechanical, photocopying, recording or otherwise, without the prior permission of the publishers

A catalogue record for this book is available from the British Library

ISBN 1 85584 041 3

Cover: art by Anne Stockton; design by Andrew Morgan
Typeset by DP Photosetting, Aylesbury, Bucks.
Printed and bound in Great Britain by Cromwell Press Limited, Trowbridge, Wilts.

CONTENTS

PART II

PART III

SYNOPSIS

PART I

1. *Whitsuntide—Festival of the Liberation of the Human Spirit*
Berlin, Whit Monday, 23 May 1904
Whitsuntide and its connection with world evolution, according to a manuscript in the Vatican Library and one in the possession of the Count of Saint-Germain. The two great world philosophies of the fifth Root Race: the Egypto-Indo-South European outlook depending on the intuition of the Devas; the Persian-Germanic world outlook connected with the intuition of the Asuras. The contrast between these two currents. The beginning of human reincarnation during Lemuria and the events connected therewith. The Fall of Man as prerequisite of freedom-seeking mankind. Prometheus as representative of man's striving for freedom. The reference to the Whitsuntide Mystery in St John's Gospel. Whitsuntide as a symbol of man's striving for freedom.

2. *The Contrast Between Cain and Abel*
Berlin, 10 June 1904
The occult core in the Mosaic story of Adam and Eve and their descendants; asexual and sexual propagation. Sexual propagation only since the time of Seth. The transition from Adam to Seth; Cain and Abel. Contrast between Cain (male spirit) and Abel (female spirit): the principle connected with the intellect and the principle of inspiration. The birth of egoism through the intellect. The struggle against the occult enemies of mankind; the race of the Rakshasas. The fulfilment of

Nostradamus's prophecy through the founding of the Theosophical Society and the re-establishment of the original
Mysteries. The doctrine of reincarnation and karma.

3. *The Mysteries of the Druids and the 'Drottes'*
Berlin, 30 September 1904 (Notes)
Drottes or Druids, the ancient Germanic initiates. The three
stages of initiation. The Edda as a description of what actually
took place in the ancient Drottic Mysteries. The Druid priest
as architect of the human race; a faint copy of that in the
beliefs of the Freemasons.

4. *The Prometheus Saga*
Berlin, 7 October 1904
The exoteric, allegorical and occult interpretation of sagas.
The Prometheus saga. Its interpretation as Mystery account of
the history of post-Atlantis. The Lemurian, Atlantean and
post-Atlantean times. The discovery of fire, and Prometheus
as representative of post-Atlantean times. The contrast of
kama-manasic thinking of Epimetheus and the manasic
thinking of Prometheus, the initiated leader, in wisdom and
deed, of post-Atlantean mankind.

5. *The Mystery Known to Rosicrucians*
Berlin, 4 November 1904
The myth of Cain and Abel and of Hiram and Solomon (the
Temple Legend) given by Christian Rosenkreutz to the
Rosicrucian Brotherhood in the fifteenth century. The legend
as a symbolic representation of the destiny of the third,
fourth and fifth Sub-Races of the fifth Root Race in connec-
tion with the development of Christianity. The Christian
principle of the equality of man in the sight of God and its
application in a worldly sense during the French Revolution.
The Count of Saint-Germain and the French Revolution.
The Christianity of the Crucified One and the future Chris-

festo of the Grand Orient of Memphis and Misraim Masonry in Germany. The meaning of the Temple Legend, of Operative Masonry; intuitive knowledge which had to disappear. Our epoch (fifth Sub-Race) as the true epoch of human understanding. The transmutation of the mineral world by human spirituality as the meaning of the Molten Sea. The speech of the English Prime Minister, Lord Balfour, about the meaning of electricity; a reference to a turning-point in human thinking. The very ancient origin of Freemasonry establishments.

9. *The Essence and Task of Freemasonry*
from the Point of View of Spiritual Science—III
Berlin, 16 December 1904
Freemasonry of the higher degrees. The Combined Rite of Memphis and Misraim. Cagliostro and the Higher Degrees. The Philosopher's Stone (immortality) and the Mystic Pentagram in the teaching of Cagliostro. The French Revolution and the Count of Saint-Germain. The difference between the step-by-step initiation in the higher degrees and the democratic administration of knowledge in Craft Masonry. The four teaching methods of the Memphis and Misraim Rites. The reality of the occult establishments; the significance of outer forms. The new knowledge about the atom, and future knowledge of the connection between the atom, electricity and human thought.

10. *Evolution and Involution*
as they are Interpreted by Occult Societies
Berlin, 23 December 1904
The significance of occult knowledge in promoting conscious prolongation of life, immortality. The universal law of the development of consciousness. The task of our epoch to permeate the mineral world with human spirit. Spiritualized natural kingdoms as future soul-content of man, resting on the

law of evolution and involution. Future penetration of man's spirit into the atom. Relationship of the atom, thought and electricity. The destruction of the fifth Root Race through the War of All Against All. The significance of forms in connection with future stages of development. Their correspondence with the higher degrees of Freemasonry. The fifth Sub-Race as epoch of pure intellect, as epoch of egoism and its necessary defeat.

PART II

of God (Abel-Seth Sons). The aim of the Rosicrucians, as continuators of the Order of the Knights Templar, was no different from that of theosophy; the building of the great temple of humanity.

13. *Concerning the Lost Temple
and How it is to be Restored—III*
Berlin, 29 May 1905
The Legend of the True Cross and the world historic significance of Solomon's temple. The contrast of the two currents within mankind: the Sons of God (descendants of Abel-Seth) and the Sons of Man (descendants of Cain). The uniting of the two streams in Christ Jesus. The construction of the three-stage world temple (corresponding to physical body, etheric body and astral body of man) throughout the time of the Old Covenant by the Sons of Cain, the servants of the world. Work performed in the service of the Divine World Order by the Sons of God, the servants of the Ark of the Covenant. Solomon's temple, an external expression of what the Ark of the Covenant should become. Man's earthly evolution in connection with the symbol of the Cross. The Pauline distinction between the law and grace. The connection of law and sin in the Old Covenant and law and love in the New Covenant.

14. *Concerning the Lost Temple
and How it is to be Restored—IV*
Berlin, 5 June 1905, Whit Monday
The Lost Word to be rediscovered—an allegory connected with the Whitsuntide festival. Whitsuntide, the festival of mankind's freedom. Freedom of choice between good and evil. The Fall of Man. The evolution of the world throughout the aeons: Rounds, Globes and Races or epochs. The seven kings of Solomon's Dynasty during the seven epochs of the Astral Globe. The construction of the macrocosmos by Spirit,

Son and Father; the inner working of man from the Spirit, through the Son, to the Father. Post-Atlantean culture until the time of the Christ event in its connection with the principles Father, Son and Spirit. The awakening of the Inner Word; the resurrection of the etheric body as the secret of the Whitsuntide festival.

PART III

or pillars of civilization: Wisdom, Beauty and Strength. Consideration of the twelfth century and the saga of the Holy Grail according to Masonic interpretation. Contrast between the male-Masonic and female-priestly principles; mastery over inanimate nature and acceptance of God-bestowed living forces. The sign of the Cross. The Holy Grail as a symbol of the mastery over the forces of life to be attained in the future; the Royal Art in a new form.

PRELIMINARY REMARKS BY THE EDITOR OF THE THIRD GERMAN EDITION

The lectures here presented, in so far as their content is concerned, really belong to the teaching material of Rudolf Steiner's Esoteric School.* In them a form of esoteric work was being prepared which was put into practice from 1906 onwards.

By means of explanations related to the esoteric content of the picture language of myths, sagas and legends, especially that of 'The Temple Legend' and 'The Legend of the True Cross' usually called 'The Golden Legend' by Rudolf Steiner, a 'basis was to have been created for the practice of a kind of cultic symbolism. It is only through everything pertaining to a cult,† not just the outward form of a cult, but the understanding of the world by means of pictures,' through meditating in pictures, that one is led to the true knowledge of man and of the world (Dornach, 27 April 1924, *Karmic Relationships*, Vol. II). It is through pictures, as they appear through imaginative thinking, that all things are created. 'Pictures are the real origin of things, pictures lie behind all that surrounds us . . . it is these pictures which are meant when people speak of primeval spiritual causes' (Berlin, 6 July 1915, 'Thoughts for the Times', lecture 12). These pictures were wrapped in myths and legends by the wise men of old. For modern consciousness the true effect depends upon the extent to which picture language can be penetrated by an understanding of the ideals.

---

* The Esoteric School from 1904 until the outbreak of the First World War in summer 1914 existed in three sections or classes (see GA 264, 265 and 266—the latter was previously 245).

† The word 'cult' is used here in the sense of ritual.

As the pictures belonging to the Temple Legend and the Golden Legend form an integral part of the section dealing with cult and symbolism, the present series of lectures deals mainly with their interpretation for present-day consciousness. Rudolf Steiner regarded it as a necessary preliminary to working with pictures—that is, with symbols—that one should first become acquainted with their esoteric content. That entailed the Rosicrucian training as given by him, of which the first step is study and only the second is imaginative thinking.

Concerning the remarks about Freemasonry, one thing is to be especially noted. Rudolf Steiner was at that time about to inaugurate the second section of his Esoteric School, dealing with cult and symbolism. As a new form of the 'Royal Art', created out of his own spiritual investigation, was to have been presented in the School, the preparatory lectures were concerned with clarifying its history and nature, and pointing out that mankind is standing at the threshold of a new phase of evolution, indicating what its future content would be.

When in later years he spoke in some of his lectures about what happened in connection with Freemasonry, it is because he always rigorously condemned the mixing of occultism and a striving after power, wherever it occurred. (Compare, for example, *The Karma of Human Vocation*, Dornach, 4–27 November 1916; *The Occult Movement in the Nineteenth Century*, Dornach, 10–25 October 1915; *The Challenge of the Times*, Dornach, 29 November–8 December 1918; *How Can Mankind Find the Christ Again?*, Dornach, 25–29 December 1918.)

The outbreak of the First World War had proved to him that 'certain pieces of knowledge' had been misused by particular occult brotherhoods of the West 'to stir up the necessary political atmosphere conducive to bringing about the world catastrophe and influencing world events'. Thus Rudolf Steiner saw himself obliged to draw attention to the fact that an originally good and necessary thing, which was intended to serve 'the whole of mankind without distinction of race or personal interests', must necessarily turn to something bad when used 'as a means of power in the hands of isolated groups of people' (from an unsigned foreword to Karl Heise's *Entente-Freimaurerei und Weltkrieg*, Basle 1918).

Regarding the connection which Rudolf Steiner made in a quite definite external form with the Symbolic-Cultic Section of the Misraim-Memphis Freemasonry of John Yarker, often deliberately misconstrued by his enemies, see Rudolf Steiner, *The Course of My Life*, Chapter 36, and also publications on the history of the Esoteric School, containing letters, circulars and other documents.*

As Rudolf Steiner still taught within the Theosophical Society when these lectures were given, he made use of the customary terminology of that time. For historical reasons we have forborne substituting the expression 'theosophy' for 'anthroposophy', as was usually done at the specific request of Rudolf Steiner after the German Section of the Theosophical Society had re-formed under the title Anthroposophical Society. The reader must be aware, however, that the theosophy taught by Rudolf Steiner—as represented in his fundamental book *Theosophy, an Introduction to the Supersensible Knowledge of the World and the Destination of Man*—has always been identical with what he later only referred to as 'anthroposophy' or 'anthroposophically-orientated spiritual science'.

Concerning the texts, it must be stressed that, in common

---

* See the following volumes from the collected works of Rudolf Steiner: GA 264—*Zur Geschichte und aus den Inhalten der ersten Abteilung der Esoterischen Schule 1904 bis 1914*; GA 265—*Zur Geschichte und aus den Inhalten der erkenntniskutischen Abteilung der Esoterischen Schule von 1904 bis 1914*; GA 266—*Aus den Inhalten der esoterischen Stunden: Band I, Stunden der Jahre 1904–1909; Band II, Stunden der Jahre 1910–1912; Band III, Stunden der Jahre 1913–1914*.

with most of the early transcripts, where professional steno-graphers were not employed, they are noticeably incomplete, sometimes only existing in the form of notes. Stylistic and logical imperfections must not, therefore, be laid at Rudolf Steiner's door. But even though we are not always dealing with a word-for-word transcript, the contents as they have been conveyed to us form a unique and indispensable part of the complete works of Rudolf Steiner. In order to guarantee as far as possible a text that is free from mistakes, all sources have been tested and compared, and where shorthand notes exist these too have been used in checking. In the notes at the end of the book the sources have been given for each lecture sepa-rately. Words and phrases in the text enclosed in square brackets are the insertions of the editor,* whereas those enclosed in ordinary brackets are original to the text. The copious notes are intended to compensate as far as possible for the deficiencies of the text. Pertinent books from Rudolf Steiner's own library were the chief source material used.

H.W.

---

* And in a few cases by the translator of the English edition.

PART I

Whitsuntide—Festival of the Liberation of the Human Spirit

Berlin, Whit Monday, 23 May 1904

It was to be expected[1] that only a small company would gather here today. I have nevertheless decided to hold our meeting this evening to talk to those of you who are present about something connected with Whitsuntide.

Before I start I would like to report to you one result of my latest visit to London, which is that in all likelihood Mrs Besant will be visiting us here[2] in the autumn. We shall have the opportunity then of hearing again one of the personalities belonging to the most powerful spiritual influences of our time. The next two public lectures[3] will be held in the Architektenhaus—on spiritualism a week hence, and on somnambulism and hypnotism the following week. Then the usual Monday arrangements will take place again regularly. On the coming Thursdays[4] I shall speak about theosophical cosmology, about theosophical ideas concerning the creation of the universe. Those of you who are interested in such things may hear much that is not already known from the usual theosophical literature. I wish to hold over till a later date the lectures on the rudiments of theosophy.[5]

What I wish to talk about today comes from an old occult tradition. The subject cannot, of course, be dealt with exhaustively today. Some of it may appear incredible. I would request, therefore, that today's lecture be treated as an episode in which nothing is to be proved, but only things related.

People celebrate their festivals today without having an

inkling of what is signified by them. In the newspapers, which constitute the main source of the education and enlightenment of most of our contemporaries, one can read many and various articles dealing with such festivals, the writers of which have not the slightest idea of the meaning of such a festival. But for theosophists it is necessary to look again at their inner meaning. And so I want today to direct your attention to the origin of such an age-old festival: the source of the Whitsuntide festival.

Whitsuntide is one of the most important festivals and one of the most difficult to understand. For Christian consciousness it commemorates the coming of the Holy Ghost. This event is described as a miracle: the Holy Spirit was poured out over the Apostles so that they started to speak in all manner of tongues. This means that they could enter into every heart and speak according to each one's understanding. That is *one* of the interpretations of Whitsuntide. If we wish to reach a more fundamental understanding of it, we must go still deeper into the matter. Whitsuntide—as symbolical festival—is connected with the most profound mysteries, with the holiest spiritual qualities of humanity; that is why it is so difficult to talk about it. Today I should like at least to touch on just a few things.

What the Whitsuntide festival symbolizes, the underlying principle from which it receives its deep inner meaning, is preserved in a single manuscript copy[6] which is to be found in the Vatican Library, where it is guarded with the greatest care. To be sure, no mention is made of Whitsuntide in this manuscript, but it certainly tells of that for which Whitsuntide is only the outer symbol. Hardly anyone has seen this manuscript, unless he has been initiated into the deepest secrets of the Catholic Church, or has been able to read it in the Astral Light.[7] One copy is possessed by a personality who has been very much misunderstood in the world, but who is beginning to interest today's historians. I could equally well have said 'was possessed' instead of 'is possessed', but it would thereby cause a lack of clarity. Therefore I say again: a copy *is* in the possession of the Count of Saint-Germain,[8] who is the only existing source of information about it.

I should like to give a few hints about this from a theosophical point of view. We shall be led thereby to something intimately connected with the evolution of mankind during the fifth Root Race. Man assumed his present-day form during the third Root Race (the time of ancient Lemuria), developed it further during the fourth Root Race (the time of ancient Atlantis), and then progressed to the fifth Root Race with what he had thus acquired. Whoever heard my Atlantis lectures[9] will remember that a vivid memory of those times still existed among the Greeks.

To find our bearings,[10] we must get a little insight into two currents belonging to our fifth Root Race, which are active as hidden powers in the souls of men and are often in conflict with one another. The one current is most clearly and best represented by what we call the Egyptian, Indian and South European outlook on life. Everything belonging later to Judaism and even to Christianity contains a little of that. But in our European culture, on the other hand, this has been intermingled with that other current which is to be found in ancient Persia and—if we disregard what the anthropologists and etymologists say and go deeper into the matter—we find it again stretching westwards from Persia to the regions of the Teutons.

Of these two currents[11] I would maintain that two mighty and important spiritual intuitions underlie them. The one was best understood by the ancient Rishis. To them was revealed the intuition of beings of a higher order, the so-called Devas.[12] He who has undergone occult training and can carry out investigations into these matters will know what Devas are. These purely spiritual beings, of the astral or mental plane, have a twofold inner nature, whereas man's nature is threefold. For man consists of body, soul and spirit, but the Deva nature—as far as can be investigated—consists only of soul and spirit. It may possess other members, but we are unable to find them, even by occult means. The Deva is an ensouled spirit. The impulses, emotions, desires and wishes that live invisibly within man, but are seen as light effects by the seer, these soul powers, this soul body, which constitutes man's inner being, supported by the physical body, is the lowest body that the Devas possess. We can regard it as their body. The intuitive faculty of the Indian was concerned mainly with the worshipping of these Devas. The man of India sees these Devas all around. He sees them as creating powers when he penetrates the veil of outward appearance. This intuition is fundamental to the outlook on life of the peoples of the Southern Zone.[13] It is expressed most powerfully in the Egyptians' conception of the world.

The other intuition was the basis upon which the ancient Persian mysticism was founded, and this led to the veneration of beings who were also only twofold in their nature: the Asuras. They, too, possessed what we call soul, but the soul organ was enclosed within a physical body developed in sublime and titanic fashion. The Indian view of the world, which clung to the Deva worship, looked upon the Asuras as something inferior, whereas those who inclined to the viewpoint of the Northern peoples[14] adhered to the Asuras,[15] to physical nature. Thus there developed in the Northern Zone more especially the impulse towards controlling the things of the sense world in a material way, towards an ordering of the world of realities by means of the highest technical advancement, through physical arts and so on. Nowadays there is nobody who still persists in Asura worship, but there are many among us who still have something of this within them. Thence comes the tendency towards the materialistic side of life and that is the basic tendency of the Northern peoples.[16] Whoever acknowledges purely materialistic principles can be sure that he has something of the Asuras in his nature.

Among the Asura adherents there then developed a strange undertone of feeling. It first made its appearance in the spiritual life of Persia. The Persians developed a kind of fear of the Deva nature. They experienced fear, apprehension and dread in face of what was of a purely soul-spirit nature. That was the reason for the great contrast which we now observe between the Persian and the Indian attitude. In the Persian attitude those things were often venerated which to the Indians were bad and inferior, and just those things were avoided by the Persians which the Indians held in veneration. The Persian experience of the world was steeped in a mood of soul that feared and avoided a being of the nature of a Deva. In short, it was the picture of Satan which arose in this view of the world. Lucifer, the being of Spirit and Soul, became an object of fear and dread. That is where we have to look for the origin of the belief in the Devil. This mood of soul has also been absorbed into the modern view of the world; Lucifer became a much feared and avoided figure in the Middle Ages. Lucifer was definitely shunned.

We learn particulars about it[17] in the manuscript already mentioned. If we follow in it the course of earth evolution we shall find that in the middle of the third Root Race, the Lemurian epoch, mankind was clothed in physical matter. It is a wrong conception when theosophists believe that reincarnation had no beginning and will have no ending. Reincarnation started in the Lemurian age and will cease again at the beginning of the sixth Root Race or age. It is only a certain period of time in earth evolution during which mankind reincarnates. It was preceded by a most spiritual condition that precluded any necessity for reincarnation, and there will follow again a spiritual state that will likewise obviate the necessity for reincarnation.

Simultaneously with its first incarnation in the Lemurian Age the untarnished human spirit, consisting of Atma-Buddhi-Manas, sought its primal physical incarnation. The physical development of the earth with its animal-like creatures had not evolved so far at that time, the whole of this animal-human organism was not so far advanced then that it could have incorporated the human spirit. But a part of it, a certain group of animal-like beings, had evolved so far that the seed of the human spirit could descend into it to give form to the human body.

Some of the individualities who incarnated at that time formed the small nucleus of those who later spread over the whole earth as the so-called Adepts. They were the original Adepts, not those whom we call initiates today. Those whom we call initiates today did not go through incarnation at that time. Not all incarnated at that time who would have been able to find human-animal bodies, only some of them. Some others were opposed to the process of incarnation for a particular reason. They delayed that until the time of the fourth age. The Bible hints at that in a concealed and profound way: 'The Sons of God saw the daughters of men[18] that they were fair and they took them wives of all which they chose.'

That is to say, the incarnation of those who had waited began at a later time. We call this group the 'Sons of Wisdom', and it almost appears as if there were a kind of arrogance, a sort of pride about them. We shall make an exception of the small group of Adepts. Had these other ones also incarnated at the earlier period, mankind would never have been able to acquire the clarity of consciousness that he possesses today. He would have been held fast in a dull trancelike state of consciousness. He would have developed that kind of consciousness which is to be found in people who have been hypnotized, sleepwalkers and the like. In short, man would have remained in a kind of dreamlike state. But one thing would have been lacking then, one thing of great importance if not of the utmost importance—he would have lacked a feeling of freedom, a capacity to exercise his individual discrimination with regard to good and evil by means of his own consciousness, his own human ego.

This postponement of incarnation—in the form it assumed in consequence of that feeling of dread of the Devas which I characterized—this is called in the Book of Genesis the 'Fall of Man'. The Devas delayed their incarnation and only descended to the earth to take possession of physical bodies when humanity had reached a further stage in its development. Through this they were able to evolve a more mature form of consciousness than would have been the case earlier.

Thus, you see, the cost of man's freedom was the deterioration of his nature, by waiting for his incarnation till he could descend into denser physical conditions. A deep understanding of this has been preserved in Greek mythology. Had man descended earlier into incarnation—so says the Greek myth—then that would have happened which Zeus wanted when man was still living in Paradise. He wished to make man happy, but as an unconscious being. Clear consciousness would have been possessed solely by the gods, and man would have been without a feeling of freedom. The rebellion of the Lucifer Spirit, the Deva Spirit within humanity, who wished to descend in order to rise up again out of his own freedom, is symbolized by the saga of Prometheus.[19] But Prometheus had to suffer for his endeavours by having an eagle—symbol of inordinate desire—gnawing at his liver and causing him the most deadly pain.

Man had thus descended more deeply and now had to achieve through his own free conscious activity what he would have attained by magical arts and powers. But because he had descended deeper he must suffer pains and torment. This is also indicated in the Bible with the words: 'In sorrow thou shalt bring forth children.[20] In the sweat of thy face shalt thou eat bread,' etc. That is no less than to say: mankind must raise itself again with the help of culture.

Through the figure of Prometheus, Greek mythology has

symbolized free humanity struggling towards culture. He is the representative of suffering mankind, but at the same time the giver of freedom. The one who sets Prometheus free is Heracles, of whom it is said that he underwent initiation in the Eleusinian Mysteries. Whoever descended to the underworld was an initiate, for the descent into the underworld is a technical term denoting initiation. This journey to the underworld is attributed to Heracles, Odysseus and to all who are initiates, who wish to lead man of his epoch to the source of primeval wisdom, to a life of the spirit.

Had mankind retained the attitude of Lemurian times we would have been dreamers today. Through his Deva nature, mankind fructified his lower nature. Out of his self-awareness, out of his awareness of freedom, man now has to reawaken that spark of awareness which he brought down from heaven in justified presumption; he has to reawaken that spiritual knowledge which he had received without his own striving when he was still unfree. There lies in human nature itself that satanic rebelliousness which, however, in the form of luciferic aspiration is the only safeguard of our freedom. And out of this freedom we shall again wrest spiritual life. It will be reawakened in the man of the fifth Root Race, our present epoch. This form of consciousness will again be conveyed through initiates. It will not be a dreamy, but a clear consciousness. It is the Heraclean spirits, the initiated ones, who will help mankind forward and reveal to him his Deva nature, his knowledge of the spirit. That was also the endeavour of all the great founders of religion, that they should restore to mankind the knowledge of the spirit which had been lost in physiological existence. The Atlanteans had a high physical civilization and our fifth epoch still contains much of the material life within it. This materialistic culture of the present time shows us how far man has become embedded in purely physical-physiological nature, as Prometheus was enmeshed in his chains. But it is equally certain that the vulture, the symbol of lust and craving, gnawing at our liver, will be thrust aside by spiritual men. That is the goal to which the initiates would lead mankind through consciousness of self, by means of such movements as the theosophical movement, so that it can raise itself up in full freedom.

The moment which we have to regard as the one in which spiritual life poured into the self-conscious human being is indicated precisely in the New Testament. It is alluded to in the profoundest of the Gospels, the one which is misunderstood by today's theologians, the St John's Gospel, when it speaks of the Feast of the Tabernacles which was attended by Jesus. The founder of Christianity there speaks of the outpouring of spiritual life with which humanity was to be endowed. It is a remarkable passage. For the Feast of the Tabernacles, the people had to visit a spring from which water flowed. There followed a festival which intimated to man that he should call to mind again his spiritual nature, his Deva and spiritual strivings. The water that flowed there was to remind him of the soul and spirit world. After repeated refusals Jesus finally went up to the feast. The following happened on the last day of the feast (John 7:37): 'In the last day, that great day of the feast, Jesus stood and cried saying, If any man thirst, let him come unto me and drink.' Those who drank celebrated a feast in which the spiritual life was brought to recollection. But Jesus connected something else with it, as can be seen in the following words of St John's Gospel: 'He that believeth on me, as the scripture hath said, out of his belly shall flow rivers of living water. (But this spake he of the Spirit, which they that believe on him should receive: for the Holy Ghost was not yet given; because that Jesus was not yet glorified).'

Here the Whitsuntide mystery is indicated. It is intimated that man has to wait for the coming of the Holy Spirit. When the moment arrives in which man is able to kindle the spark of spiritual life within him, when the physiological nature of man is able to attempt the ascent by means of its own forces, then will the Holy Spirit descend upon him and the time of spiritual awakening will be at hand.

Man descended as far as the physical body and so, in contrast to the nature of the Devas, he is built up out of three principles: spirit, soul and body. The Devas are at a higher stage than man, but they do not have to surmount physical nature as man does. This physical nature has to be transfigured so that it can absorb the life of the spirit. Man's consciousness in the body, his physiological consciousness of today, will itself be able to enkindle the spark of spiritual existence in freedom.

Christ's sacrifice is an example which shows that man will be able to unfold a higher form of consciousness out of his life on the physical plane. His lower individuality lives in the physical body, but it must be enkindled so that the higher personality can develop. Only then can the 'rivers of living water' flow from man's 'belly'. Then can the Holy Spirit appear and be poured forth upon humanity. Man, as an ego being, must be as though dead to physiological existence.

Herein lies what is truly Christian, and it also embodies the deeper mystery contained in the Whitsuntide festival. Man lives primarily in his lower organism, in his consciousness imbued with desires. It is right that this is so, because it is only this consciousness which can provide him with awareness of his true goal, to attain freedom. He should not remain there, however, but must raise his ego to the nature of a Deva. He must develop the Deva within him, bring it to birth so that it becomes a spirit of healing—a Holy Spirit. To that end he must consciously sacrifice his earthly body, he must experience that 'dying and becoming', so that he does not remain a 'gloomy guest'[21] on this dark earth.

Thus the Easter mystery is only revealed in its fullness when taken together with the Whitsuntide mystery. We see the human ego, exemplified in its Divine Representative, divesting itself of the lower ego and dying in order to be completely transfigured in its physical nature and offered up again to the Godhead. Ascension is the symbol of this. When man has become transfigured in the physical body, has offered it up again to the Spirit, he will be ripe to receive the outpouring of spiritual life, to experience what is called the 'coming of the Holy Spirit' according to the explanation of One who is mankind's greatest Representative. Therefore it is also said: 'And there are three that bear witness in earth,[22] the Spirit, the water and the blood.' Whitsuntide is the outpouring of the Spirit into man.

The highest goal of humanity is symbolically expressed by means of the Whitsuntide festival; that is, that mankind must progress once more from an intellectual to a spiritual life. Just as Prometheus was set free from his suffering by Heracles, so will mankind be set free by the power of the Spirit. By descending into matter, mankind has attained self-consciousness. Through the fact that he ascends again, he will become a self-aware Deva. Those who worshipped the Asuras and regarded the Devas as beings of a satanic nature, who did not wish to descend into the innermost depths, regarded this descent as something devilish.

That, too, is referred to in Greek mythology. The one whose state of consciousness is not free—the contemplator—the one who does not wish to win redemption in complete freedom, and therefore is the opponent of Prometheus, is Epimetheus. Zeus gives him Pandora's box, the contents of which—sufferings and plagues—fall on mankind when it is opened. The only gift that is left behind is hope—the hope that one day, in a future state, he will also progress to this higher, clear consciousness. He is left with the hope that he will be set free. Prometheus advises him against accepting this doubtful gift from the god Zeus. Epimetheus does not listen to his brother, but accepts the gift. The gift that Epimetheus receives is not worth as much as the one belonging to his brother Prometheus.

Thus we see that there are two ways of life open to men. Some of them cling to a feeling of freedom and—although it is dangerous to develop spirituality—they search for it in freedom nevertheless. The others are the ones who find their satisfaction in the dull round of life and in blind faith, and who suspect danger in the luciferic endeavours of their fellow men. The founders of the Church's outward doctrine have distorted the deeper meaning of luciferic striving. The ancient teachings on the subject are contained in hidden manuscripts[23] in undisclosed places, where they have hardly been seen by anyone. They are available to a few people who are able to see them in the Astral Light, and otherwise only to a few initiates. The path is fraught with danger, but it is the only one which leads to the sublime goal of spiritual freedom.

The spirit of man should be free and not dull. That is also the aim of Christianity. Health and healing are connected with holiness. A spirit that is holy is able to heal; it sets men free from sufferings and torments. Healthy and free is the human being who is released from the bondage of his physiological state. For only the free spirit is the healthy one, whose body is no longer gnawed by an eagle.

Thus Whitsuntide can be looked upon as the symbol of the freeing of the human spirit, as the great symbol of mankind's struggle for freedom, for consciousness of his own freedom.

If the Easter festival is the festival of resurrection in nature, then the Whitsuntide festival is the symbol of the becoming conscious of the human spirit, the festival of those who know and understand and—penetrated through and through by this—go in search of freedom.

Those spiritual movements of modern times which lead to a perception of the spiritual world in clear day consciousness—not in trance or under hypnosis—are the ones that lead to an understanding of such important symbols as this. The clear consciousness, which only the spirit can set free, is what unites us in the Theosophical Society. Not the word alone, but the spirit gives it its meaning. The spirit which emanates from the great Masters, which flows through a few people only who are able to say, 'I know they are there, the great Adepts, who are the founders of our spiritual movement, not our society,'[24] this spirit flows into our present civilization and bestows on it the impulse for the future.

Let a spark of understanding of this Holy Spirit flow again into the misunderstood Whitsuntide festival, then it will be revivified and gain meaning once more. We want to live in a world that makes sense. Whoever celebrates festivals without sparing them a thought is a follower of Epimetheus. Man must see what binds him to his surroundings and also to what is invisible in nature. We have to know where we stand. For we humans are not confined to a dull, dreamy, semi-existence, we are destined to develop a free, fully conscious unfolding of our whole being.

LECTURE 2

The Contrast Between Cain and Abel

Berlin, 10 June 1904

I mentioned already[1] last time that a great number of occult secrets lie hidden in the story of Cain and Abel. I wish to point out certain things today, but right at the beginning I would stress that the relationship between Cain and Abel—with regard to its deeper aspect, of course—is an allegory for very profound Mysteries,[2] which we will only be able to reveal in part on the basis of the conceptions we hold.

If we take the five books of the Pentateuch, we shall find therein many things that indicate the development of mankind since the Lemurian epoch. The story of Adam and Eve and their descendants is not simply to be taken literally, in a naive fashion. I would ask you to take into account that in the Pentateuch, in Enoch,[3] in the Psalms and some important chapters in the Gospels, in the Epistle to the Hebrews and some Epistles of Paul and in the Apocalypse, we are dealing wholly with the work of initiates, so that in these writings it behoves us to search for an occult meaning. In the occult schools this meaning was everywhere discussed. If the Bible is not just read thoughtlessly—thoughtlessly in a higher sense—many things will become apparent. And I should like to draw your attention to something which may easily be overlooked, but must be taken quite literally if we are to see that nothing is without a meaning in the Bible and that it is quite easy for this meaning to escape us.

Take the first sentence from the fifth chapter of Genesis:[4]

This is the book of the generations of man. In the days that

God created man, in the likeness of God made he him; male-female created he him; and blessed him, and called his name Adam, in the day when he was created. And Adam lived an hundred and thirty years, and begat a son in his own likeness, after his image; and called his name Seth:

One must take the literal rendering. Adam himself was simply called a man. Male-female created he him; not yet sexually defined, asexual. And how was he created? In the likeness of God.

And moreover, in the second sentence, 'In so and so many years'—that indicates a long span of time—'Adam begat a son Seth, after *his* likeness.' In the beginning of the time of Adam we have men in the likeness of God; at the end of Adam's time after the likeness of Adam, after a *human* likeness. Earlier, man was made in the likeness of God; later, in Adam's likeness.

We thus have, to start with, human beings who are all similar in appearance and all created after the image of God. They were propagated by asexual means. We must be clear about the fact that they all retained the same form which they had at the beginning, so that father looked like son and grandson also looked like son. What first caused mankind to change, to become differentiated? In what way did it change? Through the fact that two were engaged in propagation. The son or daughter looked like the father on the one hand, like the mother on the other.

Now just imagine you have a race of people that were originally similar to God in appearance and they were propagated not by sexual means, but asexually; the descendants are all similar in appearance to their forebears. There is no mixing of the race. The differentiation first came about in the Seth period. But between the times of Adam and Seth something else occurred. Namely, before the transition from Adam to Seth two others were born, who were important representatives: Cain and Abel. They came between and represent a transitional stage. They were not born at a time when propagation had already taken on a strongly marked character of sexuality. We can infer this from the meaning of the names Cain and Abel. Abel is the same as *pneuma* in Greek,[5] which means 'spirit', and if we look at that from the point of view of sexuality, it denotes a decidedly female character. Cain, on the other hand, means almost literally 'the masculine', so that in Cain and Abel the masculine and feminine principles confront one another. Not yet on an organic level: they tend to differentiate on a spiritual level.

Now I would ask you to hold that fast in your minds. Originally mankind was male-female. Later on it was divided into a male and a female gender. The male, the more material race, was represented in Cain, the female, the more spiritual, in Abel-Seth. A differentiation has occurred. That is symbolized in the words: 'Abel was a keeper of sheep, but Cain was a tiller of the ground' (Genesis 4:2).

'Ground' (*Boden*) has the significance of the 'physical plane' in all ancient languages and the three aggregate conditions of the physical plane are: the solid earth, the water and the air. 'Cain was a tiller of the ground' in its original sense means: he learnt to live on the physical plane, he became a man on the physical plane. That was the male characteristic. It consisted of being strong and robust in order to cultivate the soil and then retire again from the physical to the higher planes.

'Abel was a keeper of sheep.' As a shepherd one accepts life as the Creator has presented it. One does not cultivate the herds, one tends them. Therefore Abel is the representative of the sex that does not reach spirituality through its own individual effort of understanding, but only receives it as a revelation of the Godhead and then merely tends it. The keeper of flocks, the guardian of that which has been placed on the earth, that is Abel. The one who creates things for himself, that is Cain. Cain lays the foundation of zither playing and other arts (Genesis 4:21–2).

Now comes a contrast in their attitude towards the Godhead. Abel receives from the spirit and offers up the best, the highest fruits of the spirit. God regards the offering of Abel with satisfaction—of course, because it is what He Himself has bestowed on the earth. Cain makes a different claim. He turns to God with the products of his own intelligence. That is something quite foreign to the nature of God, because it is something that man has achieved out of his own freedom.

Cain is the type of man who aspires to the arts and sciences. That has nothing to do with the Deity to begin with. A profound truth is expressed here. He who has occult experience knows that the arts and sciences, in spite of having made man free, do not lead him to the spirit. Rather are they the things that lead him away from what is truly spiritual. The arts have sprung up from man's inner being, which have their roots in the earthly plane. That has no immediate appeal for the Deity. It produces the conflict that arises when the smoke of Abel's offering, the spirit implanted in the earth by God himself, is accepted by the divine worlds but the smoke from Cain's offering is rejected and remains on the earth. What is independently produced remains on the earth, like the offering of Cain.

That, too, is the same as the contrast between male and female. Female is inspired by what is received directly from God. *Pneuma* is achieved through conception. What Cain has to offer is human work on the physical plane itself. That is the contrast between female and male spirit. Here these two are fundamentally opposed to one another.

Man is not only a physical being but is spiritually both male and female at the same time; he is both the one who receives and allows himself to be inspired and the one who works upon the inspirations and combines them through his intellect. These two functions were now separated—we can regard male and female simply as a symbol from now on. From now on the principle of inspiration was transferred to those who were like Abel, who remained shepherds and priests. It was not transferred to the others. They dedicated themselves to the worldly things of science and the arts and confined themselves purely to earthly activities.

That could not have taken place without a change occurring in the human being. While man was still male-female, it was impossible for him to separate spiritual wisdom and scientific knowledge. Only through a definite separation into the two sexes could man's brain be brought to the pitch where it could function. The brain became male,[6] the deeper nature became female. Mankind can only be productive through his physical nature. Through that he produces something, namely, descendants. But a spirit, inasmuch as it is connected with the brain, is male and confined to productivity on the physical plane. Therefore Cain and Abel are the representative types of these two kinds of thinking.

Through this separation, it came about that in the propagation of the human species the offspring ceased to be merely identical copies of their parents and became differentiated. I would ask you to visualize the following. The greater the importance attached to sex, the more the differentiation that resulted. If we were dealing with purely asexual propagation then the new generation would look just like the one that had gone before. A variation would not occur in the sequence of the generations. Variation only comes about when a mixture occurs. And how was this mixture made possible? Through the fact that the masculine element committed itself to the earth. Cain was the one who became a tiller of the soil and transformed it. This outward difference in the generations would not have come about in man if a part of humanity had not descended onto the physical plane. It was no longer as it had been before when propagation had descended on mankind from the higher planes. Something was now introduced into man's make-up because he had extracted something from the physical earth. Now man takes on the likeness of what he has won for himself on the physical plane and he carries it up with him to higher planes. The physical is the mark of Cain. The physical plane and the effect it has on man is the mark set upon Cain.

Now man is fully united with the earth so that there is a contrast between Cain and Abel, a contrast between the Sons of God and the sons of the physical plane, between the Abel-Seth generation who are the Sons of God and the Cain generation, the sons of the physical plane.

You will now understand how it is that the episode of Cain and Abel falls into the period between Adam and Seth. A new principle entered into mankind, the principle of heredity, the original sin consisting of being dissimilar to the generation that had gone before.

But there still remain some Sons of God. Not all of those belonging to the Abel line were eradicated. And now we see what took place when to the question 'Where is Abel, thy brother?' Cain answered: 'Am I my brother's keeper?' No man would have said that previously. That can only be said by an understanding which reacts as though acoustically [?] to the spiritual. Now the principle of struggle, of opposition, is added to the principle of love. Now egoism is born: 'Am I my brother's keeper?'

Those who still remained of the Abel line were Sons of God, they remained akin to the divine. But they now had to guard themselves against entering the earthly sphere. And from this resulted what was to become the principle of asceticism among those who dedicated their lives to the service of God. It became a sin for such a dedicated one to have anything to do with those who had committed themselves to the affairs of earth. It was a sin when 'The Sons of God[7] saw the daughters of men that they were fair' and took them wives; they took them wives from the daughters of Cain.

From this union resulted a race of men[8] that is hardly even mentioned in the published books of the Old Testament, but is only hinted at; it is a race that is not perceptible to physical eyes. It is called 'Rakshasas' in occult language[9] and is similar to the 'Asuras' of the Indians. It consists of demonic beings who really did exist at one time and who acted seductively upon the human race and caused its downfall. This flirtation of the Sons of God with the daughters of men produced a race that worked particularly seductively upon the Turanians, the members of the fourth Sub-Race of the Atlanteans, and led to the destruction of humanity. Some things were preserved and carried over into the new world. The Deluge is the flood that destroyed Atlantis. Men who were seduced by the Rakshasas disappeared by degrees.

And now I have to tell you something which will in any case appear extraordinary to you, which is particularly important. It has been an occult mystery for the outside world for many centuries and will seem incredible to most people, but is nevertheless true. I can assure you that every occultist has often convinced himself of its truth through what is called the Akashic Record. But so it is.

These Rakshasas were real beings, they really existed—actively and effectively—as seducers of mankind. They continued to influence human desires until the time when Christ incarnated in Jesus of Nazareth and the Buddhi principle itself became present on the earth in a human body. Now you may believe it or not; this is something of cosmic significance, of significance which reaches beyond the earthly plane. It is not for nothing that the Bible expresses it thus:[10] 'Christ descended into the forecourts of Hell.' It was not human beings He met there, He was confronted by spiritual beings. The Rakshasa beings were brought thereby into a state of paralysis and lethargy.[11] They were at the same time kept in check so that they became unable to move. They could only be lamed in this manner because they were being opposed from two sides. That would not have been possible if there had not been two natures combined together in Jesus of Nazareth: on the one hand the old Chela nature, deeply connected with the physical plane, which could also work effectively on the physical plane and through its power could hold it in balance; on the other hand there was Christ Himself who was a purely spiritual being. That is the cosmic problem which is fundamental to Christianity. Something occurred at that time in occult spheres; it was the banishment of the enemies of mankind which has its echo in the saga of the Antichrist, who was put in chains but will make his appearance again, if not opposed once more by the Christian principle in its primal force.

The whole occult striving of the Middle Ages was directed towards nullifying the effect of the Rakshasas. Those whose vision extends to the higher planes have long foreseen that the moment when this could happen might be at the end of the nineteenth century, at the transition from the nineteenth to the twentieth century. Nostradamus,[12] who worked from a tower that was open to the heavens, who brought succour during the Great Plague, was able to foretell the future. He wrote a number of prophetic verses in which you can read about the war of 1870 and several prophecies about Marie-Antoinette[13] which have already been fulfilled. In these 'Centuries' by Nostradamus (Century 10, 75) the following prophecy can be found. At the close of the nineteenth century a Hermes Brother will come from Asia and bring unity to mankind. The Theosophical Society is nothing less than a fulfilment of this prophecy of Nostradamus. The annulment of the Rakshasas and the re-establishment of the primal Mysteries is an aim of the Theosophical Society.

You know that Jesus Christ remained on the earth for ten years after His death.[14] The *Pistis Sophia*[15] contains the profoundest theosophical teachings; it is much more profound than Sinnett's *Esoteric Buddhism*.[16] Jesus incarnated again and again. His task was to renew the Mystery wisdom. This is no mere fact of cultural or historical interest, but it is the fact I have described to you, which is well known to all occultists, namely, the struggle against the Rakshasas. You see there is a deep and important occult secret lying hidden therein.

You might ask: Why is that said in allegorical form and not stated openly? I must here remind you that the great teachers of humanity such as Moses, the Indian Rishis, Hermes, Christ, the first Christian teachers, all adhered to reincarnation. And this allegorical way of communicating wisdom had a good reason. When, for instance, the Druid priest spoke of 'Nifelheim' or 'Ymir the Giant'[17] and so on, that was, of course, no mere piece of poetic folklore. Rather, it was because he knew that what he was then conveying to his pupil in the form of a fairy story would, when that spirit reincarnated, have prepared it to understand the truth in a more complete form. It is not faith, but knowledge, which inspired these fairy stories, that is, the experience of reincarnation. Even the denial of the reality of reincarnation—from the third century AD onwards—was made on the premises of reincarnation, because it was the intention to involve man thoroughly in kama-manas[18] so that practically all his spiritual life was taken up into incarnation. For that reason Christianity had no knowledge of reincarnation for 1,500 years. If we were to deny man a knowledge of reincarnation any longer we would be denying him this knowledge for a second time. That, however, would be a great sin, a sin against mankind. But to deny him this knowledge on the first occasion was necessary, for the value of the *single* life between birth and death had to be acknowledged.

The Mysteries of the Druids and the 'Drottes'

Berlin, 30 September 1904

All of our medieval stories—Parzival, the Round Table, Hartmann von Aue—reveal mystical truths in esoteric form, even though they are usually only understood in their outward aspect. Where do we search for their origin? We must look to a time before the spread of Christianity. Into Christianity was blended what had lived in Ireland, Scotland ... [Gap in the notes.] We are led to a particular centre whence this spiritual life was disseminated. The spiritual life [of Europe] emanated from a mother lodge in Scandinavia, 'Drottes' Lodge. Druids = Oak. For this reason the Germanic peoples were said to receive their instructions beneath oak trees.

'Drottes', or Druids, were ancient Germanic initiates. They still existed in England till Elizabethan times. All that we read in the Edda or can find in the ancient German sagas refers back to the temples of the 'Drottes' or Druids. The author of these tales was always an initiate. The sagas not only have a symbolical or allegorical meaning, but something else as well.

Example: we know the saga of Baldur. We know that he is the hope of the gods, that he is killed by the god Loki with a branch of mistletoe. The God of Light is killed. This whole story has a deep Mystery content which all who underwent initiation not only had to learn but had to experience.

The Mysteries. Initiation: the first deed was called the search for the body of Baldur. It was supposed that Baldur was always alive. The search consisted of a complete enlightenment about the nature of man. For Baldur was the human being since going astray. Once upon a time the human being was not as he is today, he was undifferentiated, not bowed down by passionate experiences, but composed of finer ephemeral substance. Baldur, the radiant human being. When truly understood, all things that appear to us in the form of symbols must be understood in a higher sense. This human being who has not descended into what today we call matter is Baldur. He lives in each one of us. The Druid priest had to search for the higher self within him. He had to become clear about where this differentiation took place, between the higher and the lower ... [Gap]

The secret of all initiation is to give birth to the higher human being within oneself. What the priest accomplishes more quickly, the rest of mankind must undergo in long stages of development. To become leaders of the rest of mankind, the Druids had to receive this initiation.

Man who had descended deeper now had to overcome matter and regain his former higher level. This birth of the higher human being takes place in all the Mysteries in a similar sort of way. The man who had become submerged in matter had to be reawakened. One had to make a series of experiences—real experiences—which were unlike any sense experiences one can have on the physical plane.

The stages. The first step was that one was led before the 'Throne of Necessity'. One stood in front of the abyss: really experienced through one's own body what lived in the lower kingdoms of nature. Man is both mineral and plant, but the man of today is unable to experience what is undergone by the elementary substances. And yet the enduring, the constraining things in the world are due to the fact that we are also mineral and plant in our nature.

The next step led the human being to all that lived in the animal kingdom. Everything that existed in the form of passions and desires was beheld in swirling and interweaving movement. All this had to be observed by the candidate for initiation so that his eyes would be opened to what lay behind the veil of the senses. Man is not aware that what swirls around in astral space is hidden behind the physical sheath. The veil of maya is really a sheath which must be penetrated by him who is to be initiated—the sheaths drop away, the human being sees clearly. That is a very special moment; the priest becomes aware that the sheaths had dammed back the impulses which would have been frightful if they had been let loose.

The third step led to a vision of the elemental nature forces. That is a step which man finds difficult to comprehend without previous preparation. That powerful occult forces are residing in these nature forces, and through them express elemental passions, is something which makes man aware that there are powers quite outside the scope of anything he can experience as his own suffering.

The next trial is called the 'Handing over of the Serpent by the Hierophant'. One can only explain it by means of the effects that it brings about. It is elucidated in the Tantalus saga. The privilege of being allowed to sit in the Council of the Gods can be abused. It signifies a reality which certainly raises man above himself, but dangers accompany it which are not exaggerated in the story of the Tantalus curse. As a rule man says he is powerless in face of the laws of nature. These are thoughts. With that kind of thinking, which is only a shadowy brain-thinking, nothing can be achieved. In creative thinking, which builds and constructs things of the world, which is productive and fruitful, the passive kind of thinking is replaced by a thinking permeated by spiritual force. The blown skin of a caterpillar is the empty sheath of the caterpillar; when filled with [productive] thinking it is the living caterpillar. Into the sheath-thoughts, living active power is poured so that the priest is enabled not only to see the world in vision but to work in it through magic. The danger is that this power can be abused. He can ... [Gap]

At this stage the occultist acquires a certain power, whereby he is enabled to deceive even the higher beings. He must not only repeat truths but experience them and decide whether a thing is true or false. That is what is called 'The Handing over of the Serpent by the Hierophant'. [It denotes the same thing on a spiritual level that the rudimentary stages in the formation of the spinal cord signify on the physical level. In the animal kingdom we pass through the fishes, amphibians and so on till we reach the brain of the vertebrates and man. See notes.] We have a spiritual backbone, too, which determines whether we are to develop a spiritual brain. Man goes through this process at this stage of his development. He is lifted out of Kama (feelings, passions, desires) and endowed with a spiritual backbone so that he can be raised up into the spiralling of the spiritual brain. On a spiritual level, the windings of the labyrinth are the same as the convolutions of the brain on the physical level. Man gains access to the labyrinth, to the windings within the spiritual realm.

Then he had to take the oath of silence. A naked sword was presented to him and he was obliged to swear the most binding oath. This was that he would henceforth keep silence about his experiences where it concerned people who had not been initiated as he had. It is quite impossible to reveal the true content of these secrets without preparation. He [the initiate], however, could create these sagas so that they became the expression of the eternal. One who could give utterance to things in this way of course had great power over his fellow men. The creator of a saga of this kind imprinted something into the human spirit. What is thus spoken is then forgotten and only the merest vestige of it survives death. Eternal truths remain longest after death. Of less elevated scientific thought hardly anything remains. The eternal does so and appears again in a new incarnation.

The Druid priest spoke out of the higher plane. His words, though simple, being the expression of higher truths, sank into the souls of his hearers. He spoke to simple folk, but the truth sank into their souls and something was incorporated into them which would be reborn in a new incarnation. At that time men experienced the truth through fairy stories; thus today our spirit bodies have been prepared and if we are able to grasp higher truths today it is because we have been prepared.

Thus this time, which came to an end in AD 60, had prepared the spiritual life of Europe, had provided the soil on which Christianity could build. These teachings have been preserved, and whoever searches will be able to find access to what was taught in these Lodges.

After he [the Druid] had given his oath on the sword he had to drink a certain draught—and this he did from a human skull. The meaning of this was that he had transcended what was human. That was the feeling which the Druid priest had to develop concerning his lower bodily nature. He had to look upon all that lived within his body with the same objective, cool attitude as he felt towards a containing vessel. Then he was initiated into the higher secrets and shown the path to higher worlds. Baldur ... [Gap] He was led into an immense palace which was roofed by flashing shields. He encountered a man who cast forth seven flowers. Cosmic Space, Cherubim, Demiurge [Maker of the World]. Thus he became truly a Priest of the Sun.

Many people read the *Edda* and are unaware that it is an account of what really took place in the ancient 'Drottes' Mysteries. An immense power lay at the disposal of the ancient 'Drottes' priests, a power over life and death. It is true that everything becomes corrupt in time. It was once the highest, the holiest of things. At the time when Christianity was spreading much had degenerated and there were many black magicians, so that Christianity came as a redemption.

The study of these old truths alone is able to give an almost complete survey of the whole of occultism.

Unlike our present practice, not one stone was laid upon another in the building of a Druid temple without the use of exact astronomical measurement. Doorways were built according to astronomical measurement. The Druid priests were the builders of humanity. A faint reflection of this is preserved today in the views that the Freemasons hold.

*   *   *

Learning to penetrate astral substance, viewing the Sun at Midnight: First Initiation.

Handing over of the Serpent by the Hierophant: Second Initiation.

The journey into the Labyrinth: Third Initiation.

The Prometheus Saga

Berlin, 7 October 1904

I tried to show you last time how initiation took place in the ancient Druid lodges. Today I should like to speak about a related subject, but one which may appear a little remote. But we shall see how our understanding of human development will grow ever more profound.

You have certainly gathered from the Friday lectures[1] that the sagas of the different nations have a very deep content, and that myths are an expression of profound esoteric truths. I should like to speak today about one of the most interesting sagas, which has to do with the whole development of our fifth great epoch. At the same time you will see how a pupil of spiritual science passes through three stages in the understanding of sagas.

To begin with, sagas live in a particular nation, and are understood exoterically in an outer literal meaning. Next, disbelief sets in with regard to their interpretation, and an attempt is made by scholars to arrive at a symbolic meaning. Behind these two interpretations, however, five others can be found, for every saga can be interpreted in seven ways. The third is the one that can be taken literally again up to a point. But certainly one must learn to understand the language of sagas first. Today I wish to speak about a saga which is not easy to understand; it is the Prometheus saga.

You will find something about it in a chapter in the second volume of H.P. Blavatsky's *The Secret Doctrine*, and from this conclude what a profound meaning lies hidden in it. Nevertheless, it is not always possible to write about ultimate truths in something that is to be published. Today we are able to take the subject a little further than did H.P. Blavatsky in *The Secret Doctrine*.

Prometheus belongs to the world of the Greek sagas. He and his brother, Epimetheus, are the sons of one of the Titans, called Iapetus. And the Titans themselves are the sons of the oldest of the Greek gods, of Uranus and his wife, Gaia. A translation of the word Uranus would be the 'heavens', and of Gaia the 'earth'. I would emphasize especially that the Uranus of the Greeks is the same as Varuna of India. Prometheus, therefore, is one of the Titans and a descendant of the sons of Uranus and Gaia, likewise his brother, Epimetheus. The youngest of the Titans, Chronos or 'Time', usurped the throne from his father Uranus, and was himself dethroned by his son Zeus and, along with the other Titans, was cast into Tartarus or Hades. Only the two brothers, Prometheus and Epimetheus, remained loyal to Zeus. They rallied round Zeus and fought against the other Titans.

Zeus, however, wished to destroy the race of man, which had become insolent. Prometheus became the protagonist of man. He pondered how he could give man something that would enable him to save himself and make himself independent of the help of Zeus. So, we are told, Prometheus gave man writing and the other arts and, more especially, he instructed him in the use of fire. Through this, however, he drew down the wrath of Zeus upon himself, and because of the wrath of Zeus he was chained to the Caucasus and made to languish there for a long time in great torment.

It is further recounted how the gods, with Zeus at their head, caused a female statue to be made by Hephaestus, the heavenly smith. This female statue was endowed with all the outward attributes of the man of the fifth great epoch. This female statue was Pandora. She was required to bring gifts to mankind, but in the first place to Epimetheus, the brother of

Prometheus. Indeed, Prometheus warned his brother about accepting the gifts, but Epimetheus let himself be persuaded and took the proffered presents. All the gifts were showered upon mankind. Only one thing was retained—hope. The gifts consisted mostly of plagues and suffering for humanity; only hope was retained in Pandora's box.

Prometheus, therefore, was chained to the Caucasus and a vulture gnawed incessantly at his liver. Here he languished. He was aware, however, of something which was a pledge for his deliverance. He knew a secret which was unknown even to Zeus himself and which Zeus was anxious to learn. He would not disclose it, however, even though Zeus sent the messenger of the gods, Hermes, to him.

In the course of the tale his strange deliverance is recounted. We are told that Prometheus can only be set free through the intervention of an initiate. And such an initiate was the Greek Heracles, Heracles who performed the twelve labours. The enactment of these labours is the achievement of an initiate. They are the symbolic representation of the twelve tests that have to be performed by someone undergoing initiation. In addition, it is said that Heracles underwent initiation in the Eleusinian Mysteries. He was able to rescue Prometheus. Someone else had to sacrifice himself, however, and the Centaur Chiron did this for Prometheus. He was suffering from an incurable illness. He was half beast and half man. He suffered death and thereby released Prometheus. That is the outer form of the Prometheus saga.

In this saga lies the whole history of the fifth great epoch and true Mystery wisdom is revealed in it. This was actually recounted as a saga in Greece. But also in the Mysteries it was so portrayed that the candidate for initiation was actually confronted by the destiny of Prometheus. And in this destiny he was enabled to visualize the whole of the past and the future of the fifth great epoch. An understanding of this is only possible when you take one thing into account.

It was only during the middle of the Lemurian epoch that what is described as human incarnation came about—incarnation in the sense in which people are born on earth today. Humanity of that time was under the leadership of great teachers and guides, whom we call the 'Sons of Fire-Mist'. At present, humanity of the fifth great epoch is also led by great initiates, but our initiates today are of a different kind from the leaders of that time.

You must now become quite clear about what constitutes this difference. There is an enormous difference between the leaders of the two previous Root Races and the leaders of our present fifth Root Race. The leaders of those former Root Races were also united in a White Brotherhood. Its members, however, had not undergone their previous development on our earth, but on other planets. They descended to earth already in the state of more highly developed, mature human beings in order to instruct the rest of humanity, still in its infant stage, into the primal arts of which it had need. This time of instruction lasted throughout the third, fourth and even into the fifth epoch.

This fifth great epoch took its start from a handful of men, who had been sifted out from the previous great epoch. They were collected together and prepared in the Gobi Desert and from there radiated out over the whole of the world. The first of these leaders, who was the founder of this impulse in the development of mankind, was one of the so-called Manus— the Manu[2] of the fifth Root Race. This Manu was still one of that company of leaders who descended to earth at the time of the third Root Race. He was one of the leaders who underwent development not on the earth only, but who came to earth with fully developed maturity.

It is only during the fifth Root Race that the development is beginning to take place of such Manus as are akin to ourselves who have risen as it were from the ranks of humanity. We have men, therefore, who are already great Masters and advanced leaders of humanity, and we have those who are striving to become such. In the fifth Root Race we have Chelas and Masters who have experienced all that can be undergone by human beings only since the middle of the Lemurian epoch. One of these great Masters who are leaders of the fifth Root Race is predestined to take over the leadership of the sixth Root Race. The sixth Root Race will be the first great epoch to have as its Manu one who is a brother to earthly man. The earlier Masters, the Manus from other worlds, are handing over their leadership to a fellow human being.

The development in the realm of the arts coincides with the dawn of the fifth Root Race. The man of Atlantean times had a quite different mode of life. He did not make inventions or discoveries as we do. He worked in quite a different way. It is only during the fifth Root Race that everything connected with technical science and the arts, in our sense of the term, has taken place. The most important discovery was the use of fire. Be clear on that point. Just call to mind all the things in technology, industry and art which depend for their existence on the use of fire. I think that an engineer would be inclined to agree with me when I say that without the use of fire nothing of all our modern technology would be possible; so that we may say that the discovery of the use of fire was the main discovery which gave the impulse for all later discoveries.

To that you must add that at the time when the Prometheus saga arose fire was comprehended as including everything that had to do with warmth. The causes of lightning and all other natural phenomena connected with heat were also included under that heading. The consciousness of the fact that man of the fifth Root Race himself stood under the Fire Sign[3] came to expression in the saga of Prometheus. Prometheus himself is nothing else than a representative of the whole of the fifth great epoch.

The brother of Prometheus is Epimetheus. First let us translate these two words. Prometheus can be interpreted as being the one who thinks in advance, Epimetheus as the one who thinks about things after they have happened. Here you have expressed quite clearly the two activities of human thinking in the foresight and hindsight of these two human beings. The one with hindsight is the one who lets the things of this world work upon him and then thinks about them afterwards. A kind of thinking such as this is 'kama-manasic' thinking (earthly consciousness, or intellectual-soul activity). Considered from a certain point of view, this is what this kind of thinking is: letting the world work upon one and thinking about it afterwards. The man of the fifth Root Race thinks chiefly in the manner of Epimetheus.

But in so far as a man does not merely let the things of his surroundings work upon him, but creates something for the future, is an inventor and discoverer, just so far is he a Prometheus, one who thinks ahead. There would never be any inventions made if men were all like Epimetheus. An invention comes about because man is able to create something which was not there previously. First of all the thought is there and then the thought is transformed into reality. This is Promethean thinking. Promethean thinking is the 'manas' thinking of the fifth Root Race (the thinking of spiritual thoughts). Earthly thinking and spiritual thinking flow side by side in the fifth Root Race. Gradually the spiritual thinking will become more and more widespread.

This 'manas' thinking of the fifth Root Race has one particular feature which we shall understand if we look back to the Atlantean epoch. At that time thinking was more instinctive and was still connected with the life forces. The people of Atlantean times were still able to transform the power inherent in seeds into a driving force. Just as man today has a kind of reservoir of power stored up in the coal seams, which can produce steam to drive locomotives and move loads, so Atlantean man had great storehouses of plant seeds containing a force which could be used to drive vehicles, as described by Scott-Elliot[4] in his booklet about Atlantis. This art has been lost to mankind. The spiritual power of the Atlanteans could control living nature and make use of the latent power in seeds. The spiritual powers of the fifth Root Race are only sufficient to control the forces of the inorganic world of minerals. Thus the manas of the fifth great epoch is bound up with the mineral forces in the same way as the man of Atlantean times was bound up with the life forces. All Promethean powers are chained to the rock, to the solid earth. For that reason, the apostle Peter is the 'rock' upon which Christ founded His Church. It is the same as the rock of the Caucasus. Man belonging to the fifth epoch has to seek his destiny on the physical plane alone. He is bound up with inorganic mineral forces.

Just try to imagine what is meant when one speaks about the technology of the fifth epoch. What is it there for? If you are able to form a comprehensive view of it you will see that, however great and impressive the result may be, when the forces of the intellect and manas are applied to the inorganic mineral world it is nevertheless, in the main, only self-interest and egoism which is the motive behind the application of all these forces of discovery and invention.

Start with the first discoveries and inventions and carry your thoughts through to the most modern inventions of the telephone and so on. You will see how great and mighty are the forces that have been put at our disposal, certainly—but to what end? What is it that is being conveyed to us from distant lands by means of railways and steamships? We transport foodstuffs; we order foodstuffs by telephone. Basically it is human greed and the substance of our wishes and desires which creates a demand for all these inventions and discoveries during the fifth epoch. It is this which must become clear to us in objective considerations. Then we will understand how it is that the higher human being, which has been placed into physical existence, is actually chained to matter during the fifth epoch, through the fact that man's astral body seeks its satisfaction within the realm of matter.

If you consider the principles of man's nature from an esoteric point of view, you will see that they stand in definite relationship to certain bodily organs. I shall elaborate on this theme still further, but today I will only indicate those specific organs with which our seven principles[5] are connected.

First of all we have the so-called physical principle. This stands in occult relationship to the upper part of the human face, to the root of the nose. Man's physical frame (man was only astral at first and then incorporated into the physical) took its start from this point. The physical organization spread out and formed the base of the nose first of all, so that the occultist ascribes the mineral-physical to this part of the anatomy.

The second principle is prana, the etheric parallel body. This is ascribed to the liver, with which it stands in occult relationship. Next comes the astral body, kama, which has developed its activity in building up the digestive organs, having their seat in the stomach. If the astral body had not borne this particular character that it has in man, then the human digestive organs and stomach would not have had the special form that they have today.

If you behold the human being, first with regard to his physical body, next with regard to his etheric parallel body, and thirdly with regard to his astral body, you there have the basis for what, as you see, is chained by the mineral fetters in the fifth great epoch.

Through his higher bodies, man frees himself again from these fetters and rises to higher worlds. Kama-manas, in which the ego is active, works its way upwards again. Man frees himself again from the purely physical basis given by nature. For this reason there is an occult connection between this principle and that which raises man up again out of the physical, by which man is severed, so to speak, from the physical basis given by nature. This occult connection is what exists between that principle in man and his umbilical cord. If this principle in man were not developed the embryo would never be severed from the body of its mother in the way it is.

If we then proceed to higher manas, or spirit-self, this is connected in a similar way with heart and blood circulation. Buddhi, or life-spirit, has an occult connection with the larynx, with the larynx and the gullet. And atma, or spirit-man, has an occult connection with something which extends through man's whole being, namely, the akasha, or immortal part of man's being.

Those are the seven occult relationships. If you pay attention to these, then you will discover that the most important ones for our epoch are the relationships with the etheric parallel body and the astrality. And if you add to that what I said before about the Atlantean's control over the life forces—the life forces are those forces which weave in the etheric parallel body—then you will be able to understand that, in a certain way, Atlantean man was at a stage lower than we are. His etheric parallel body still retained its original connection with the etheric forces around him and he controlled with his own etheric body the prana, or etheric forces, of the outside world. Through the fact that man has progressed one stage higher, the field of his activities lies one stage lower. That is an occult law—that when, on the one hand, progress takes place, on the other hand, a retrograde step accompanies it. Whereas man previously worked upon the astral plane out of his etheric forces, he now has the task of working upon the physical plane out of his astral forces.

Now you will understand how profoundly these occult connections are symbolized in the Prometheus saga. A vulture is gnawing at the liver of Prometheus. Astrality is symbolized by the vulture, which truly devours the forces of the fifth epoch. The vulture gnaws at man's liver, at the foundation of his existence, and thus this energy belonging to the fifth Root

Race really gnaws at the life forces of mankind because man is chained to mineral nature, to the Petrine rock, the Caucasus. Through that, man has to pay for his affinity with Prometheus. And thereby man is obliged to become master over his own nature, so that he need no longer remain chained to the mineral world, to the Caucasus.

Only those who are initiated as human beings of the fifth epoch can bring release to fettered mankind. Heracles, who was a human initiate of this kind, had himself to press through to the Caucasus in order to free Prometheus. But this is how initiates raise up man from his fetters, and all that is predestined to perish must sacrifice itself.

Man who still has an affinity with his animal nature, the Centaur Chiron, has to sacrifice himself. The man of previous epochs must be sacrificed. The sacrifice of the Centaur Chiron is just as important for the progress of the fifth epoch as is the freeing through initiates of the fifth epoch.

It is said that in the Greek Mystery Schools the future was foretold to the people. It was no vague, abstract account of what was to happen to man in the future, but instructions that would lead him along the pathway to the future; and he was shown what he had to do for his future development. And what still remained to be unfolded as human strength was portrayed in the mighty Mystery drama of Prometheus.

One has to imagine the three races of the gods, Uranus, Chronos and Zeus, as three successive great leaders of humanity. Uranus denotes heaven, Gaia the earth. If we go back in time beyond the middle of the Lemurian epoch, we do not find man in the form we know him today, but one called Adam Cadmon[6] by occult science, who is still asexual, and who had never belonged to the earth previously, who had not developed organs of sight for physical observation, but was still a part of Uranus, of the heavens. Through the union of Uranus with Gaia, man was born, man who descended to the earth and at the same time became involved in time. Chronos

(Time) was the leader of the second divine race from the middle of Lemurian times until the beginning of Atlantis. These leading figures were symbolized by the Greeks, first under the name Uranus, then Chronos, and later Zeus. Zeus, however, is one of those leaders who underwent his training elsewhere than on the earth. He is one of the great immortals, as are all the rest of the Greek gods.

Mortal man has to learn to stand on his own feet during the fifth great epoch. He is represented by Prometheus. Man was the inaugurator of the arts and, above all, of the primal art of the use of fire. Zeus is jealous of him because he is predestined to produce his own initiates, who will take over the leadership in the sixth epoch. Mankind has first to pay for that, however. That is why the first great initiate of humanity must take upon himself the whole of life's suffering.

Prometheus is the archetypal initiate of the fifth epoch, who has undergone initiation not only in knowledge but also in deed. He it was who underwent the whole of suffering and will be released from his bondage by him who is becoming mature enough to set free the whole of humanity in gradual stages and to raise it up out of the mineral realm.

Great cosmic truths are thus portrayed to us in the sagas. That is why I said to you at the beginning: whoever reaches the third stage in their interpretation is able to take their meaning literally once more ... [Here follow a few unclear sentences][7] In the case of the Prometheus saga one is confronted by the picture of the vulture gnawing at the liver. That is to be taken quite literally. The vulture really is gnawing at the liver of the people of the fifth epoch. It portrays the fight which is going on between the stomach and the liver. In every single human being of the fifth epoch, this Promethean struggle is being repeated. We can take what is here said in a completely literal sense. If this struggle were not present in the man of the fifth epoch, our destiny would be entirely different at the present day.

There are thus three ways of interpreting the sagas: firstly, the exoteric literal rendering; secondly, the allegorical one, the struggle within human nature; thirdly, the occult understanding, in which again the literal meaning can be taken. From this you can judge that all sagas—at least those which bear a significance of this kind—are derived from the Mystery Schools, and are no less than a representation of what was enacted therein as the great drama of human destiny. As I was able to show you in connection with the Druidic Mysteries that [the saga of] Baldur was no less than a portrayal of what took place in the Mysteries, so, in the saga of Prometheus, you have a portrayal of what was experienced by the pupil for initiation in the inner sanctuaries of the Mystery Schools of Greece to provide energy and new strength for life in the future.

LECTURE 5

The Mystery Known to Rosicrucians

Berlin, 4 November 1904

We have spoken about various legends that contain esoteric truths in the pictures which they present. These were given to man in this form at a time when he was not mature enough to receive the truths directly. These pictures took hold of man's 'causal' body—that part of man which bore the germ of his future higher manas—and thus made him ready to understand the truths directly in a future incarnation.

I would like now to show one such legend as this which dates back only a few centuries and is still extant today in many versions. It is the following.

At the beginning of the fifteenth century[1] a personality appeared in Europe who had been initiated into certain secrets in the East. This was Christian Rosenkreutz.[2] By the time this incarnation of Christian Rosenkreutz had come to an end, he had initiated about ten other people into such matters as he himself had learned through initiation—in so far as this was possible among Europeans at that time. This small brotherhood called itself 'Fraternitae Rosae Crucis', the Brotherhood of the Rose Cross. This small group of people then gave a certain legend to a larger, more exoteric fraternity, through whom it then became generally known to the world.

Christian Rosenkreutz himself had revealed certain deep secrets of the Mysteries to those people who were sufficiently prepared to receive them. But, as I said, there were not more than ten in this small circle, consisting of initiated Rosicrucians. What was taught by Christian Rosenkreutz could not be imparted to many people, but it was embodied in a kind of myth.[3] Since it was first given out in the fifteenth century, it has often been repeated and explained in the various brotherhoods. It was told in larger brotherhoods, but was interpreted only in intimate circles.

This is the approximate content:

There was a time when one of the Elohim created a human being whom he called Eve. That Elohim united himself with Eve and she gave birth to Cain. After this, another Elohim, named Yahveh, created Adam. Adam also united himself with Eve and from this union came Abel.

Thus we see that Cain is a direct descendant of the gods, but Abel is a descendant of Adam and Eve who are human. Now the myth proceeds.

The sacrifices that Abel made to Yahveh were pleasing to him, but the sacrifices brought by Cain did not please him because the birth of Cain was not ordained by him. The result was that Cain committed fratricide. He killed Abel and for this he was excluded from communion with Yahveh. He went away into distant lands and founded his own race there.

Adam again united himself with Eve and from this union came Seth, also mentioned in the Bible, who took over the role of Abel. Thus we have two generations of mankind: the race of Cain, who was a descendant of Eve and one of the Elohim, and the other race which had human parentage and was brought into existence at the command of Yahveh.

Among the descendants of Cain are all those who have been creators of art and science, as, for instance, Methuselah, the inventor of the Tau script, and Tubal-Cain, who taught the use and working of metal ores and iron. In this line of descent, stemming from the Elohim, were all those who trained themselves in the arts and sciences.

Hiram also descended from the race of Cain, and he was the inheritor of all that had been learned by the others of his line in technology and art. He was the most significant architect we can imagine.

Out of Seth's line came Solomon, who excelled in everything which came from Yahveh. He was endowed with the wisdom of the world and all the attributes of calm, clear, objective wisdom. This wisdom can be expressed in words which go straight to the human heart and can uplift a person, but it is unable to produce anything tangible of a technical nature, in art or science. It is a wisdom which is a directly inspired gift of God and not attained from below through human passions welling up from the human will—that would be the wisdom pertaining to the sons of Cain, a legacy of the other Elohim, not Yahveh. They are the hardworking industrious ones who seek to accomplish everything through their own efforts.

Solomon now decides to build a temple and calls upon Hiram, the descendant of Cain, to be his master builder. It was at the time when Balkis, the Queen of Sheba, was visiting Jerusalem because she had heard of the wisdom of Solomon. And she was certainly impressed and charmed by the exalted and clear wisdom and beauty of the King when she first arrived, and when he made love to her she consented to be his bride. Now she heard about the temple which was being built and she desired to make the acquaintance of the master builder, Hiram. When she first met him she was captivated merely by his glance. As a result, a certain mood of jealousy arose between Hiram and Solomon and the latter wished to do something or other against Hiram, but he was dependent upon him for the completion of the temple.

Now came the following. The temple was almost complete. Only one thing was still lacking, which was to have been Hiram's masterpiece; that was the Molten Sea, which was to represent the ocean cast in bronze and was to have adorned the temple. All the necessary mixtures of ores had been prepared by Hiram in a most wonderful manner, ready to be cast. Now, however, three apprentices got to work, whom Hiram

had found so lacking in skill that he had been unable to promote them to become masters. They had therefore sworn to be
revenged on him and desired to prevent the casting of the
Molten Sea. A friend of Hiram, who got to know about these
plans, confided them to Solomon, so that he should prevent
their realization. But Solomon, through jealousy, did nothing
to stop them, because he wished to destroy Hiram. The result
was that Hiram had to look on while the whole casting dis-
integrated due to the addition of a wrong ingredient in the
mixture by the three apprentices. He tried to quench the
bursting flames by pouring water over them, but this only
made matters worse. Just as he was on the point of despairing
about the work ever being completed, Tubal-Cain, his ancestor, appeared to him and told him that he should not hesitate
to cast himself into the fire, as he was invulnerable to the
flames. Hiram did as he was advised and came to the centre of
the earth. He was led by Tubal-Cain to Cain, who there resided in a condition of pristine divinity. Hiram was thus
initiated into the Mystery of Fire and into the secret of bronze
casting, receiving from Tubal-Cain a hammer and a golden
triangle which he was able to carry with him as a pendant
round his neck. Then he returned and was able to complete the
casting of the Molten Sea and to put everything in order again.

Hereupon the Queen of Sheba consented to become
Hiram's bride. He, however, was set upon by the three
apprentices and murdered. But before he died, Hiram managed to throw the golden triangle into a well. As no one knew
where he had disappeared, a search was made. Even Solomon
was afraid and was anxious to find out what had happened. It
was thought that the ancient Master Word could be betrayed
by the apprentices, and therefore another one was devised.
The first word to be spoken when Hiram was discovered
should be the new Master Word. At last Hiram was found and
was able to utter a few last words. He said: 'Tubal-Cain had
promised me that I shall have a son who will be the father of

many descendants who will people the earth and bring my work—the building of the Temple—to completion.' Then he pointed to the place where the golden triangle was to be found. This was then collected and brought to the Molten Sea and both were preserved together in the Holy of Holies. They are only to be discovered by those who can understand the meaning of the legend of the Temple of Solomon and its master builder Hiram.

Now we shall proceed from the recounting of the legend itself to its interpretation.

This legend portrays the destiny of the third, fourth and fifth Post-Atlantean cultural epochs. The Temple is the Temple of the Occult Societies, that is to say, what is being built up by the whole of mankind belonging to the fourth and fifth cultural epochs. And the Holy of Holies is the place where these Occult Societies have their abode. The latter are aware of what is meant by the Molten Sea and the golden triangle.

We are dealing, therefore, with two races of mankind: with those who, like Solomon, are in possession of divine wisdom; and with those of the Race of Cain, who are conversant with fire and know how to make use of it. This fire is not physical fire, but the fire of wishes, desires and instincts which burns in the astral world.

Who, then, are the Sons of Cain? In the sense of this legend, the Sons of Cain are the sons of those Elohim who, during the Moon epoch, were a little retarded in their role of Elohim. We are dealing with kama, astrality, during the Moon epoch. This kama, or fire, was penetrated with wisdom at that time. But there were two kinds of Elohim. The one kind of Elohim did not remain static with the union of wisdom and fire; they went further. And during the creation of man they were no longer filled with desires and so they were able to endow their creation with calm and clear wisdom. That is the essential Yahveh—or Jehovah—religion, the wisdom of which is quite without personal desire. The other Elohim, those in whom wisdom was combined with the fire of the Moon epoch, created the Sons of Cain.

Therefore, in the case of the Sons of Seth, we find representatives of the religious type of human being with detached wisdom, and in the case of the Sons of Cain, we find those who possess an impulsive nature, who are capable of flaring up and showing enthusiasm for wisdom. These two types are creative within all races of mankind and in all periods of history. Out of the desire life of the Sons of Cain all arts and the sciences originate; out of the Seth-Abel current all detached piety and wisdom, lacking enthusiasm, has its origin.

These two types were always present and continued thus until the fourth post-Atlantean cultural epoch.

Then came the founding of Christianity. Through it, the earlier piety, which had been bestowed on mankind from above, became passionless and detached, and was merged with the element that came to the earth through Christ— Christ, who is not only the incarnation of wisdom but who is also love itself, a supreme being who has so purified His astral body or kama that it has been changed into buddhi. A pure flowing kama that seeks nothing for itself but turns every passion into unending devotion towards the things outside itself is inverted kama. Buddhi is kama that has been changed into its opposite.

A higher kind of piety is thereby being prepared among those who are of the pious type, the Sons of Wisdom. This new kind of piety can also develop enthusiasm. It is Christian piety, which was prepared during the fourth post-Atlantean cultural epoch. This whole stream is not yet in a position to unite with the Sons of Cain, however; they remain adversaries. Were Christianity to take hold of human beings too quickly they would certainly become filled with love, but the individual human heart would not become involved. It would not be a piety springing from freedom. Christ would not be born within man as His brother, but only as the *ruler*. It is therefore necessary that the Sons of Cain are active throughout the whole of the fifth post-Atlantean period. They are active in their initiates who build the temple of all mankind, constructed out of worldly art and worldly science.

This worldly element becomes more and more evident in the history of the fourth and fifth cultural epochs, thus making manifest the entire development of world history at the physical level. And alongside this worldly stream of materialism, the personal element of egoism is involved, which leads to the War of All Against All. Even though Christianity had come into the world, it was, in a sense, a secret shared by a few. But it made people of the fourth and fifth cultural epochs aware that everyone is equal in the sight of God. That is a basic principle of Christianity, but it cannot be completely understood by man on earth so long as he is enmeshed in materialism and egoism.

The French Revolution drew its conclusion from this Christian doctrine in a worldly sense. The spiritual conception that all are equal in the sight of *God* was changed into the purely earthly precept that all men are equal here on *earth*. That is couched in even more physical terms today.

Before the outbreak of the French Revolution a personality appeared to Madame d'Adhémar,[4] the lady-in-waiting of Marie-Antoinette, who prophesied all the important events of the coming strife, in order to warn against them. It was the Count of Saint-Germain,[5] the same as he who, in a former incarnation, had founded the Rosicrucian Order. He subscribed to the view that mankind at that time must be led in all tranquillity from a worldly view of life to a truly Christian culture. Worldly powers, however, desired to gain freedom for themselves by material violent means. Christian Rosenkreutz foresaw the French Revolution as a necessary consequence of this, but warned against it. He, Christian Rosenkreutz, in his incarnation in the eighteenth century, as guardian of the innermost secrets of the Molten Sea and the golden triangle, appeared with the warning that mankind should develop slowly. But he also saw what was to happen.

That is the course taken by mankind's evolution during the fourth and fifth post-Atlantean epochs when seen esoterically. The temple of mankind's earthly culture, the great Temple of Solomon, has already been built, but what is to crown it must still remain a secret. That could only be brought into being by an initiate. That initiate was misunderstood, betrayed, killed. The secret may not yet be revealed. It remains the possession of a few initiated Christians. It is sealed up in the casting of the Molten Sea and in the golden triangle. It is the same as the secret belonging to Christian Rosenkreutz, who was present in a very highly evolved reincarnation prior to the birth of Christ, and who gave utterance to a remarkable saying at that time.

Let me describe in a few words how this Christian Rosenkreutz came to repeat a certain saying at the time of the outbreak of the French Revolution. He said: 'For they have sown the wind, and they shall reap the whirlwind.'[6] This was said by him long before it was said by Hosea and written down. It stems, however, from Christian Rosenkreutz.

This saying 'For they have sown the wind, and shall reap the whirlwind' is the leading thought for the fourth and fifth cultural epochs and can be rendered in the following way: 'Mankind shall be made free. The incarnated buddhi will unite himself with this your freedom and make you equal in the sight of God, but the spirit ("wind" means spirit = Ruach) will first become a whirlwind (the War of All Against All).'

At first Christianity had to appear as the Christianity of the Cross, which had to develop through the earthly sphere, through the physical plane. But the crucifix was not the symbol of Christianity from the beginning. It was when Christianity became political that the crucified Son of God was introduced, the Son of God suffering on the Cross of the World Body.[7] It has remained thus to outward sight throughout the rest of the fourth epoch, and will continue to do so during the whole of the fifth epoch of our present Post-Atlantean cycle.

To begin with, Christianity is bound up with the purely materialistic culture of the fourth and fifth epochs, and the true Christianity of the future, which possesses the secret of the Molten Sea and the golden triangle, only exists secretly.[8] This Christianity has another symbol—no longer that of the crucified Son of God, but the Cross encircled by roses. This will become the symbol of the new Christianity of the sixth post-Atlantean epoch. Out of the Mystery of the Brotherhood of the Rose Cross will arise the Christianity of the sixth cultural epoch, which will recognize the significance of the Molten Sea and the golden triangle.

Hiram is the representative of the initiates among the Sons of Cain belonging to the fourth and fifth epochs. The Queen of Sheba is the soul of humanity—every female character denotes the soul in esoteric terminology. She has to choose between the detached piety that does not concern itself with worldly conquest and the masterful wisdom that is achieved through the overcoming of earthly passions and desires. She is the representative of the true human soul, taking her position between Hiram and Solomon and uniting herself with Hiram in the fourth and fifth epochs, because he is still engaged in building the Temple.

The Molten Sea is what is created when the appropriate amounts of water and molten metal are cast. The three apprentices do it wrongly, and the casting is destroyed, but when the mysteries of fire are revealed to Hiram by Tubal-Cain, he is thereby enabled to unite water and fire in the proper way. This brings the Molten Sea into being. This is what the secret of the Rosicrucians is. It is brought about when the water of calm wisdom is united with the fire of the astral world, with the fire of passion and desire. A union must be brought about which is 'of bronze', that is to say, is lasting and durable. It must endure into the next epoch, when the secret of the sacred golden triangle is added to it—the secret of atma, buddhi and manas. This triangle, with all that it entails, will form the content of the renewed Christianity of the sixth cultural epoch. That is being prepared by the Rosicrucians and then what is symbolized by the Molten Sea will be united with a knowledge of reincarnation and karma. That is the new occult teaching which will be united again with Christianity. The higher self of man, composed of atma, buddhi and manas, will become an open secret when the man of the sixth epoch has become ripe enough to receive it. Christian Rosenkreutz will then no longer be required to give warning, but everything that signified strife on the outer plane will be resolved in peace through the Molten Sea and the sacred golden triangle.

That is the course which world history will take in the future. What was disseminated by Christian Rosenkreutz in the Temple Legend through the Brotherhood, the Rosicrucians have made into their task: to teach not merely religious piety but also science in an external way, not merely knowledge of the outer world but knowledge of spiritual forces, too, and from both directions to go forward into the sixth Round of evolution.

LECTURE 6

Manichaeism

Berlin, 11 November 1904

We have been asked to say something about Freemasonry. This cannot be understood, however, until we have examined the original spiritual currents related to Freemasonry, which can be seen as its sources. An even more important spiritual current than Rosicrucianism was Manichaeism. So first we need to speak about this much more important movement and then, at a later time, we can shed a light on Freemasonry.

What I have to say on this subject is connected with various things that influence the spiritual life of today and will influence it in time to come. And to illustrate how one who is actively engaged in this field constantly comes across something—if only obliquely—I would point out, by way of introduction, that on many occasions I have described the problem of Faust[1] as of particular importance for modern spiritual life. And that is why the modern spiritual movement is brought into connection with the problem of Faust in the first number of *Luzifer*.[2] The allusion I made to the problem of Faust in my essay in *Luzifer* is not without a certain reason.

In order to bring the things with which we are concerned into connection with one another, we must start from a spiritual tendency which first manifested in about the third century AD. It is that spiritual movement whose great opponent was St Augustine,[3] although before he went over to the side of the Catholic Church he was himself an adherent of this faith. We have to speak about Manichaeism, which was founded by a person who called himself Mani[4] and lived about the time of the third century AD. This movement spread from a part of the world that was then ruled by the kings of the Near East—that is to say, from a region of western Asia Minor. This Mani was the founder of a spiritual movement which, although at first only a small sect, became a mighty spiritual current. The Albigenses, Waldenses and Cathars[5] of the Middle Ages are the continuation of this current, to which also belong the Knights Templar, of whom we shall speak separately,[6] and also—by a remarkable chain of circumstances—the Freemasons. Freemasonry really belongs to this stream, though it is connected with others, for instance with Rosicrucianism.[7]

What outer history has to say about Mani is very simple.[8]

It is said that there once lived a merchant in the Near East who was very learned. He compiled four important works: first, *Mysteria*, secondly, *Capitola*, thirdly, *Evangelium*, and lastly *Thesaurus*. It is further related that at his death he left these writings to his widow who was a Persian. This widow, on her part, left them to a slave whose freedom she had bought and whom she had liberated. That was the said Mani, who then drew his wisdom out of these writings, though he was also initiated into the Mithraic Mysteries.[9] Mani is called the 'Son of the Widow', and his followers are called the 'Sons of the Widow'. However, Mani described himself as the 'Paraclete',[10] the Holy Spirit promised to mankind by Christ. We should understand by this that he saw himself as *one* incarnation of the Holy Spirit; he did not mean that he was the *only* one. He explained that the Holy Spirit reincarnated, and that he was one such reincarnation.

The teaching which he proclaimed was opposed in the most vigorous fashion by Augustine after he had gone over to the Catholic Church. Augustine opposed his Catholic views to the Manichaean teaching, which he saw represented in a personality whom he called Faustus.[11] Faustus is, in Augustine's conception, the opponent of Christianity. Here lies the origin of Goethe's *Faust*, and of his conception of evil. The name 'Faust' goes back to this old Augustinian teaching.

One usually hears it said about Manichaean teaching that it is distinguished from western Christianity by its different interpretation of evil. Whereas Catholic Christianity regards evil as an aberration from its divine origin, the defection of originally good spirits from God, Manichaeism teaches that evil is just as eternal as good—that there is no resurrection of the body, and that evil, as such, will continue for ever. Evil, therefore, has no beginning, but springs from the same source as good and has no end.

If you come to know Manichaeism in this form it will seem radically un-Christian and quite incomprehensible.

Now we should like to study the matter thoroughly according to the traditions that are supposed to have originated from Mani himself, and so see what it is all about. An external clue is given us in the Manichaean legend—just such a legend as the Temple Legend, which I recounted to you recently. All such spiritual currents connected with initiation are expressed exoterically in legends, but the legend of Manichaeism is a great cosmic legend,[12] a supersensible legend.

It tells us that at one time the spirits of darkness wanted to take the kingdom of light by storm. They actually reached the borders of the kingdom of light and hoped to conquer it. But they failed to achieve anything. Now they were to be punished—and that is a very significant feature which I beg you to take account of—they were to be punished by the kingdom of light. But in this realm there was nothing that was in any way evil, there was only good. Thus the demons of darkness could only have been punished with something good. So what happened? The following: the spirits of light took a part of their own kingdom and mixed it with the materialized kingdom of darkness. Because there was now a part of the kingdom of light mingled with the kingdom of darkness, a leaven had been introduced into the kingdom of darkness, a ferment that produced a chaotic whirling dance whereby it received a new element into itself, i.e. death. Therefore, it continually consumes itself and thus carries within itself the germ of its own destruction. It is further related that just because of this, the race of mankind was brought into existence. Primeval man represents just what was sent down from the kingdom of light to mix with the kingdom of darkness and to conquer, through death, what should not have been there—to conquer it within his own being.

The profound thought which lies in this is that the kingdom of darkness has to be overcome by the kingdom of light, not by means of punishment but through mildness; not by resisting evil but by uniting with it in order to redeem evil as such. Because a part of the light enters into evil, the evil itself is overcome.

Underlying that is the interpretation of evil which I have often explained as that of theosophy. What is evil? Nothing but an ill-timed good. To cite an example which has often been quoted by me, let us assume that we have to do with a virtuoso pianist and an excellent piano technician, both perfect in their sphere. First of all the technician has to build the piano and then hand it over to the pianist. If the latter is a good player he will use it appropriately and both are equally good. But should the technician go into the concert hall instead of the pianist and start hammering away he would then be in the wrong place. Something good would have become something bad. So we see that evil is nothing else than a misplaced good.

When what is especially good at one time or another strives to be preserved, to become rigid and thus curb the progress of further development, then, without doubt, it becomes evil, because it opposes the good. Let us suppose that the leading powers of the lunar epoch, though perfect in their way and in their activity, were to continue to intermingle with evolution though they ought to have ceased their activity, then they would represent something evil in Earth evolution. Thus evil is nothing else than the divine, for, at that other time, what is evil when it comes at the wrong season was then an expression of what is perfect, what is divine.

We must interpret the Manichaean views in this profound sense, that good and evil are fundamentally the same in their origin and in their ending. If you interpret it in this way you will understand what Mani really intended to bring about. But, on the other hand, we still have to explain why it was that Mani called himself the 'Son of the Widow'[13] and why his followers were called the 'Sons of the Widow'.

When we turn back to the most ancient times, before our present Root Race, the mode in which mankind acquired knowledge was different. You will perceive from my description of Atlantis—and also, when the next issue of *Luzifer* appears, you will see from my description of Lemuria[14]—that at that time, and to a certain extent up to the present day, all knowledge was influenced by what is above mankind. I have often mentioned that *that* Manu[15] who will appear during the next Root Race will for the first time be a real brother to his fellow men, whereas all earlier Manus were superhuman, divine beings of a kind. Only now is man becoming ripe enough to have one of his brother men as his Manu, who has passed through all stages with him since the middle of Lemuria. What is really taking place then, during the evolution of the fifth Root Race? This, that the revelation from above, the guidance of the soul from above, is gradually being withdrawn, so that man is left to go his own way and become his own leader.

The soul was always known as the 'mother' in all esoteric (mystical) teachings; the instructor was the 'father'. Father and mother, Osiris and Isis, those are the two forces present in the soul. The instructor, representing the divine which flows directly into man, Osiris, he is the father; the soul itself, Isis, the one who conceives, receives the divine, the spiritual into itself, she is the mother. During the fifth Root Race, the father withdraws. The soul is widowed. Humanity is thrown back onto itself. It must find the light of truth within its own soul in order to act as its own guide. Everything of a soul nature has always been expressed in terms of the feminine. Therefore the feminine element—which exists only in a germinal state today and will later be fully developed—this self-directing feminine principle, which is no longer confronted by the divine fructifier, is called by Mani the 'Widow'. And therefore he calls himself 'Son of the Widow'.

Mani is the one who prepares that stage in man's soul development when he will seek for his own soul-spirit light. Everything that comes from Mani is an appeal to man's own spirit light of soul, and at the same time is a definite rebellion against anything that does not come out of man's own soul, out of man's own observation of his soul. Beautiful words have been handed down from Mani[16] and have been the leading theme of his followers at all later times. We hear the words: 'You must lay aside everything which you have acquired as outer revelation by means of the senses. You must lay aside all things which come to you via outer authority; then you must become ripe to gaze into your own soul.'

St Augustine, on the other hand—in a conversation which made him into an opponent of the Manichaean Faust—voiced the opinion: 'I would not accept the teachings of Christ if they were not founded on the authority of the Church.'[17] The Manichaean Faust said,[18] however: 'You should not accept any teaching on authority; we only wish to accept a doctrine in freedom.' That illustrates the rebellious self-sufficiency of the spirit light which comes to expression so beautifully in the Faust saga.[19]

We meet this confrontation also in later sagas in the Middle Ages: on the one hand the Faust saga, on the other, the Luther saga.[20] Luther carries on the principle of authority,[21] Faust, on the other hand, rebels, he puts his faith in the inner spirit light. We have the saga of Luther; he throws the inkwell at the devil's head. What appears to him to be evil he thrusts aside. And on the other hand we have Faust's pact with the devil. A spark from the kingdom of light is sent into the kingdom of darkness, so that when the darkness is penetrated it redeems itself, evil is overcome by gentleness. If you think of it in this fashion you will see that this Manichaeism fits in very well with the interpretation which we have given of evil.

How do we imagine the interworking of good and evil? We have to explain it as the harmonization of life with form.[22] How does life change over into form? Through coming up against resistance, through not manifesting all at once in one particular shape. Take note, for instance, how life in a plant— let us say a lily—speeds on from form to form. The life in the lily has fashioned, has elaborated, the form of the lily.

When this form has been created, life overcomes it and passes over into the seed to be reborn as the same life in a fresh form. And so life strides onward from form to form. Life itself is formless and could never perceptibly manifest its vital forces. The life of the lily, for instance, exists in the first lily and progresses to the second, third, fourth and so on. Everywhere there is the same life which appears in a limited form, spreading and interweaving. The fact that it appears in a limited form is a restriction imposed upon this universal flowing life. There would be no form if life were not restricted, if it were not arrested in its flowing force which radiates in all directions. It is just what remains behind, which, from a higher stage, appears like a fetter; it is just out of this that form evolves in the great cosmos.

What comprises life is always set in the framework of a form which was life in an earlier time. Example: the Catholic Church. The life which existed in the Catholic Church from St Augustine until the fifteenth century was the Christian life. The life therein is Christianity. Ever and again this pulsating life emerges anew (the mystics). Where does the form come from? It is no less than the life of the old Roman Empire. What was still alive in the old Roman Empire has frozen into form. What was at first a republic, then an empire, what lived in outward appearance as the Roman state, surrendered its life, frozen into form, to the later Christianity; even its capital city, Rome, was previously the capital city of the Roman Empire, and the Roman provincial officers have their continuation in the presbyters and bishops. What was previously life later becomes form for a higher stage of life.

Is it not the same with human beings? What is human life? The fructification from above (Manas fructification), implanted into man in mid-Lemurian times, has today become his inner life. The form is what is carried over, as seed, from the lunar epoch. At that time, in the lunar period, the life of man consisted of the development of the astral body; now this has become the sheath, the form. Always the life of a former epoch becomes the form of a later epoch. In the harmonization of form and life that other problem is expressed too: the problem of good and evil through the fact that the good of a former epoch is joined to the good of a later epoch, which is fundamentally nothing but a harmonization of progress with the things which hinder progress. That is what, at the same time, makes material existence possible, makes it possible for things to appear in outward form. It is our human existence on the solid mineral plane: soul life and what remains of the life of an earlier epoch hardened into a restrictive form. That, too, is the teaching of Manichaeism regarding evil.

If we now pose the question from this point of view, 'What are Mani's intentions, what is the meaning of his statement that he is the Paraclete, the Spirit, the Son of the Widow?' it means no less than that he intends to prepare for the time in which the men of the sixth Root Race will be guided out of their own being, by their own soul's light, to overcome outward forms and convert them to spirit.

Mani's intention is to create a spiritual current which goes beyond the Rosicrucian current,[23] which leads further than Rosicrucianism. This current of Mani's will flow over to the sixth Root Race and has been in preparation since the founding of Christianity. It is just at the time of the sixth Root Race that Christianity will be expressed in its most complete form. Its time will truly have come. The inner Christian life, as such, overcomes every form; it is propagated by external Christianity and lives in all forms of the various confessions. Whoever seeks Christian life will always find it. It creates forms and destroys forms in various religious systems. It does not depend upon a search for conformity in the outward forms in which it is expressed, but it depends upon experiencing the inner life stream which is always current under the surface. What is still waiting to be made is a form for the life of the sixth Root Race. That must be created beforehand; it has to be there so that Christian life can be poured into it. This form has to be prepared by human beings who create an organization, a form, so that the true Christian life of the sixth Root Race can find its place therein. And this external form of society must derive from the intention which Mani has fostered, from the small group whom Mani has prepared. That must be the outer form of organization, the congregation in which the spark of Christianity will first be truly kindled.

From this you will be able to conclude that Manichaeism will endeavour, first and foremost, to preserve purity in outer life; for its aim is to produce human beings who will provide an adequate vessel in the future. That is why such great stress was laid on absolute purity of mind and of life. The Cathars were a sect which rose like a meteor in the twelfth century. They called themselves Cathars because 'cathar' means 'pure one'. They strove for purity in their way of life and in their moral attitude. They had to seek catharsis (purification) both inwardly and outwardly in order to form a community that would provide a pure vessel. That is what Manichaeism was striving for. It was less a question in Manichaeism of the cultivation of the inner life—for life will flow onwards through other channels—but rather the cultivation of the external form of life.

Now let us look at what is to come about during the sixth Root Race. Good and evil will then contrast very differently from the way that they do today. What will be evident to all mankind in the fifth Round,[24] that the outer physiognomy which each one acquires will directly mirror what karma has made out of him, that will express itself spiritually in the sixth Root Race like a prelude to this event. Among those on whom karma has bestowed an excess of evil it will become particularly evident on a spiritual level. On the one hand there will be human beings possessing mighty inner forces of good, who will be gifted with great love and goodness. But, on the other hand, the opposite will also be seen. Evil will be present as a disposition without any disguise in a great many people, no longer cloaked or hidden from view. The evil ones will extol evil as something of particular worth. A glimmering of this delight in evil and the demonic pertaining to the sixth Root Race is already in evidence in certain men of genius. Nietzsche's 'blonde beast',[25] for example, is a portent of this.

The unalloyed evil must be cast out of the stream of world evolution like dross. It will be relegated to the Eighth Sphere.[26] Today we stand immediately at the threshold of a time when good must consciously come to terms with evil.

The sixth Root Race will have the task of drawing evil back into the continuing stream of evolution through kindness. Then a spiritual current will have been born which does not oppose evil, even though it manifests in the world in its demonic form. The consciousness will have been established in the successors to the 'Sons of the Widow' that evil must be included again in evolution and be overcome, not by strife but only through charitableness. It is the task of the Manichaean spiritual stream forcefully to prepare for this. This spiritual stream will not die out; it will make its appearance in many forms. It appears in forms which many can call to mind but which need not be mentioned today. If it were to function merely in the cultivation of an inner mood of soul, this current would not achieve what it should do. It must express itself in the founding of communities which, above all, will look upon peace, love and passive resistance to evil as their standard of behaviour and will seek to spread this view. For they must create a receptacle, a form, for the life which will continue to exist even without their presence.

Now you can understand how it is that Augustine, the leading spirit of the Catholic Church, who developed the form of the Church very precisely in his *City of God*, who worked out the form for contemporary life, was of necessity the most violent opponent of *that* kind of form which is preparing for the future. Two polar opposites confront one another, Faust and Augustine: Augustine, who based his work on the Church, on the form belonging to his day, and Faust, who strives to prepare in man a sense for the form of the future.

That is the contrast which developed in the third and fourth centuries AD. It is still present and finds expression in the struggle of the Catholic Church against the Knights Templars, the Rosicrucians, Albigenses, Cathars and so on. All of them are eliminated from the physical plane, but their inner spirit continues to be active. This contrast manifests again later in modified but still violent form in two currents born out of Western culture, that of Jesuitism (pertaining to Augustine) and that of Freemasonry[27] (Manichaeism). Those who lead the battle on the one side are all conscious of what they are doing—they are the Catholics and Jesuits of the higher degrees. Of those, however, who are on the other side, who lead the battle in the spirit of Mani, only very few are conscious; only those at the head of the movement are conscious of it.

Thus Jesuitism (belonging to Augustine) and Freemasonry (Manichaeism) confront one another in later centuries. They are the offspring of ancient spiritual currents. That is why you have in both these currents a continuation of the same ceremonies connected with initiation that you find in the old currents. The initiation into Jesuitism has the four degrees: *Coadjutores temporales, Scholares, Coadjutores spirituales, Professi.* The degrees of initiation in the true occult Freemasonry are similar. The two run parallel to one another but they point in quite different directions.[28]

The Essence and Task of Freemasonry from the Point of View of Spiritual Science—I

Berlin, 2 December 1904

Today I wish to make a brief survey of the rites and orders of Freemasonry, as I agreed to do. Of course I can only impart to you the main essentials, as the whole subject is so comprehensive, and so many inessential things are connected with it.

The basis for the whole of Freemasonry is to be found in the Temple Legend concerning Hiram-Abiff or Adonhiram about whom I have already spoken in connection with the Rosicrucian Order.[1] Everything to do with what is called the secret of Freemasonry and its tendency is expressed in this Temple Legend.[2] We are led to a kind of Genesis or theory of evolution of the human race. Let us therefore recall to mind the essentials of this Temple Legend.

One of the Elohim united himself with Eve, and out of this union of a divine creative spirit with Eve Cain was born. Then another of the Elohim, Jehovah or Adonai, created Adam, who is to be regarded as the primal man of the third Root Race. This Adam then united himself with Eve, and from this union Abel was born. Thus at the outset of human evolution there are two starting-points: Cain, the direct descendant of one of the Elohim with Eve, and Abel, who, with the help of a divinely created human being, Adam, is the true representative of Jehovah.

The whole conception underlying the creation story according to the Temple Legend is based upon the fact that there is a kind of enmity between Jehovah and everything that

is derived from the other Elohim and their descendants, the
'Sons of Fire'—this being the designation of the descendants
of Cain according to the Temple Legend. Jehovah creates
enmity between Cain and his race, and Abel and his race. The
outcome of this was that Cain slew Abel. That is the arch-
enmity which exists between those who receive their existence
from the divine worlds and those who work out everything for
themselves. The fact that Abel makes the sacrifice of an animal
to Jehovah while Cain brings the fruits of the earth is an
illustration, which the Bible gives too, of this contrast between
the race of Cain and the race of Abel. Cain has to wrest from
the earth with hard labour the fruits which are necessary for
the sustenance of mankind; Abel takes what is already living,
what has been prepared for his livelihood. The race of Cain
creates, as it were, the living out of the lifeless. Abel takes up
what is already alive, what is already imbued with the breath
of life. Abel's sacrifice is pleasing to God, but Cain's is not.

Thus we find two kinds of human being characterized in
Cain and Abel. The one consists of those who accept what
God has prepared for them. The others—the free humanity—
are those who till the soil and labour to win living products out
of what is lifeless. Those who regard themselves as Sons of
Cain are they who understand the Temple Legend and wish to
live by it. Out of the race of Cain spring all those who are the
creators of the arts and sciences of mankind: Tubal-Cain who
is the first true architect and the god of smithies and working
tools; and also Hiram-Abiff, or Adonhiram, who is the hero of
the Temple Legend. This Hiram is sent for by King Solomon,
famous for his wisdom, who belongs to the race of Abel, those
who receive their wisdom from God. Thus this contrast
appears once more at the court of Solomon—Solomon the
wise, and Hiram the independent worker, who has achieved
his wisdom through human striving.

Solomon called to his court Balkis, the Queen of Sheba, and
when she arrived her impression of him was as of a statue

made of gold and precious stones; it was as though she were looking at a monument bestowed on mankind by the gods. As she gazed in wonderment at the great Temple of Solomon, her desire was to meet the architect of this wonderful building, and her wish was fulfilled. Merely through a single glance which the architect cast on her, she was able to appreciate his true worth. Solomon was immediately seized by a kind of jealousy of Hiram. This grew as Balkis demanded that all the workers engaged in the building of the Temple should be presented to her. Solomon declared that this was impossible, but Hiram conceded to her wishes. He climbed onto a slight eminence; made the mystical sign of the Tau and, behold, all the workers streamed towards him. The will of the Queen had been fulfilled.

Because of this, Solomon is disinclined to oppose the enemies of Hiram and to stand out against them. A Syrian stonemason, a Phoenician carpenter and a Jewish miner were antagonistic towards Hiram. These three fellow craftsmen had been totally denied the Master Word by Hiram-Abiff. The Master Word is that which would have enabled them to work independently as master builders. The Master Word is a secret that is imparted only to those who have made the grade. Therefore they came to the decision to do Hiram some harm.

The opportunity for this came about as Hiram-Abiff was about to fulfil his masterpiece, the casting of the Molten Sea. The *movement* of the waters was to be held fast in *form*. The surging sea was to be preserved alive artistically in a rigid form. That is the point. The three apprentices conspired to make the casting in such a way that instead of flowing into the mould it would flow out over the surroundings. Hiram tried to arrest the flow of the fiery mass by throwing water over it, but this caused the metal to spray up into the air and descend again with great force in a rain of fire. Hiram was powerless to do anything. But suddenly a voice called out to him: 'Hiram! Hiram! Hiram!' He was ordered by the voice to plunge into the sea of fire. This he did and he sank down ever deeper until he reached the centre of the earth where fire has its origin. There he met two figures, his ancestor Tubal-Cain, and Cain himself. Cain was irradiated with the brightness of Lucifer, the angel of light. Then Tubal-Cain gave Hiram his hammer, which had the magical property of restoring all things to their proper order, and he said to him: 'You will beget a son who will gather about him a race of wise folk, and you will be the progenitor of those who have been born out of fire which brings wisdom and makes man thoughtful.' The Molten Sea was now restored by means of the hammer.

Hiram and Queen Balkis then met again outside the city. She became his wife, but Hiram was unable to avert the jealousy of Solomon and the revenge of the three fellow craftsmen. He was slain by them. The only thing he was able to save was the triangle with the Master Word engraved upon it, which he threw into a deep well. Then Hiram was buried and a branch of acacia was planted on his grave. The acacia branch betrayed the whereabouts of the grave to Solomon, and the triangle was also discovered. It was sealed up and buried in a place known to only a few people—27 in all. [It was agreed that] the new Master Word should be the word first uttered after the finding of the corpse—it is the Word which is used by the Freemasons. The Freemasons trace back their origin, with some justification, to the Temple Legend and to the old days in which the Temple was built by Solomon as a lasting memorial to the secret of the fifth Root Race.

And now we have to learn to understand how mankind can benefit by Freemasonry. That is not so easy. A person who gets to know something of the complicated initiation cere-monies of Freemasonry might be inclined to ask: Is what takes place in such ceremonies very trivial and petty?

I will now describe to you the initiation ceremony of an apprentice wishing to join the Order of Craft Masonry.[3] Just imagine someone has decided that he wants to become a member of the Craft Masonry. It consists of three degrees: Apprentice, Fellow Craftsman and Master Mason. After these three degrees come higher degrees which lead the candidate into occult knowledge. I will now describe what happens to a novice about to be initiated into the first degree,[4] that is the degree of Apprentice. When he is brought into the Lodge building for the first time, he is led into a remote chamber by the Brother Warden and left for some minutes to his own thoughts. Then he is deprived of all metal he has about him, such as gold, silver and other metals, his clothes are rent at the knee and the heel of his left shoe is trodden down. In this condition he is led into the midst of the brethren who are assembled in another room, a cord is passed round his neck and a sword is pointed at his naked breast. In this state he is confronted by the Worshipful Master, who asks him if he is still determined to undergo initiation. Then he is cautioned very seriously and during the further procedures the meaning of the treading down of the heel and other procedures are explained to him. There are three things which he is obliged to forego. If he is unable to forswear these three things he will never be accepted as a Freemason. He is told: If you retain the slightest curiosity about anything, then you must leave this house immediately. Secondly, he is told: If you should hesitate to acknowledge every one of your failings and mistakes, then you must leave this house immediately. Thirdly: If you are unable to rise in spirit above all things which differentiate one human being from another, then you must leave this house immediately. These three things are most strictly required from every candidate for initiation.

Then a kind of frame is held in front of the candidate, through which he is thrown, while at the same time an unpleasant noise is produced, so that he flies through the frame with the worst of feelings. In addition to this they shout to him that he is being thrown into Hell. At that same instant, a trapdoor is closed with a bang, and he is given the impression

of being in very peculiar surroundings. His skin is then
scratched slightly, so that blood is made to flow, and at the
same time a gurgling sound is made by those around him,
giving him the impression that he is losing a great deal of
blood. After that three hammer blows are struck by the
Worshipful Master. What is said thereafter in the Lodge must
be treated in the strictest secrecy. Were the candidate to reveal
it, his connection with Freemasonry would be changed, just as
the drink he is offered also changes: sweet from the one side,
bitter from the other. This drink is handed to him in an artfully
constructed vessel, so that the drink is sweet from one side, but
when turned around it changes to bitter. That is to symbolize
how it will be for the candidate if he betrays the secrets.

After these proceedings he is led to a flight of stairs in a
room which is very dimly lit. This staircase is so constructed
that it moves and thereby gives the impression that one has
descended a long way, whereas one has really only descended a
short distance. It is the same when the candidate falls. When
he thinks he has fallen into a deep well, he has in reality only
fallen a very short way. At this point it is explained to him that
he has arrived at a decisive moment. In addition to this he is
blindfolded again when he is by the staircase. Then the
Brother Warden is asked: 'Brother Senior Warden, deem you
the candidate worthy of forming part of our Society?' If the
answer is 'Yes' he is then further asked: 'What do you ask for
him?' He is obliged to answer: 'Light.' Then the bandage is
removed from the candidate's eyes and he sees himself in an
illuminated chamber. Then follows the basic question: 'Do
you recognize who is your Master?' He makes answer: 'Yes, it
is he who is wearing a yellow jacket and blue trousers.' The
blue trousers refer to the rank he possesses. Then he receives
the three attributes of apprenticeship: Sign, Grip and Word.
The Sign is a symbol of the same kind as occult symbols ...
[Gap] The Grip is a special kind of handclasp to be used when
shaking hands. These handclasps are different in the case of an

apprentice and in the case of a Master. The Word changes according to degree. It does not behove me to reveal what the Words are.

After that, the person concerned can be admitted to his apprenticeship. On admission he is asked: 'How old are you?' He makes answer: 'Not yet seven years.' He has to serve seven years as an apprentice before he can progress to become a journeyman.

When someone has progressed so far that he is eligible for his Master's degree, the initiation ceremony is somewhat more difficult. The main thing is, however, that what is contained in the Temple Legend is actually carried out in practice on the candidate himself. He who wishes to attain to the Master's degree is led into one of the rooms in the Lodge building and has to lie in a coffin and to undergo the same fate as the master builder Hiram suffered. Then the new Sign, Grip and Word are revealed to him. The Word is the same as the Master Word which was uttered at the finding of Hiram's body. The signs by which a Master is known are extremely complicated. Recognition is achieved with the help of many forms and gestures.

The Freemasonry Masters call themselves 'Children of the Widow'. Thus the Company of the Masters is directly derived from the Manichaeans. I shall still speak about the connection between Manichaeism and Freemasonry.[5]

The task of Freemasonry is connected with that belonging to the whole of the fifth Root Race. You could, of course, from the point of view of modern rationalist thinking, dismiss all I have told you about the initiation of an apprentice and the various ceremonies connected therewith as mere tomfoolery and play-acting. But that is not what it is. All the things I have mentioned are the outward symbolical enactment of ancient occult practices which once took place on the astral plane through the Mystery Schools. Such proceedings, therefore, which take place symbolically among Freemasons, are carried out on the astral plane in the Mystery temples. The initiation into the degree of a Master, the lying in the coffin and so on, is actually something which takes place on a higher level. However, in Freemasonry, it only takes place symbolically.

One could now ask: Where does all this lead? A Freemason should be conscious of the fact that one should act on the physical plane in a way that will maintain a connection with the spiritual worlds. It makes a difference whether one is a member of a community that believes in symbols that help to create a higher community, or whether . . . [Gap] A Freemason need not necessarily have different thoughts from the man in the street, but his feelings are quite different. Feelings are connected with symbolical enactments, and it is not a matter of indifference whether or no a feeling of this kind is aroused, because it corresponds with a certain rhythm on the astral plane.

The meaning behind the first part of the ceremony—the taking away of metal objects—is that the candidate should not retain about his person anything which he has not produced by his own labours. A feeling for this is necessary for anyone who has had his attention drawn to the significance of symbols. He should also retain an enduring memory of the tearing of the trousers at the knee. He should think upon the fact that he ought to present himself in life as if he were appearing completely naked in the eyes of his fellow men. In like manner, the treading down of the heel should act as a constant reminder that—even though he may be strong as far as Freemasonry is concerned—he nevertheless is made vulnerable through his heel of Achilles. All subsequent parts of the ceremony have basically a meaning of this kind—particularly in the case of the eerie feeling which is engendered when a cold, sharp-edged sword is laid against his breast. That is a feeling which persists for a long time and becomes focused in a suggestion which returns to his mind at important moments and reminds him that he should develop a kind of cold-blooded attitude. Cold-bloodedness should be the suggestion he receives. Complete responsibility for his own actions is what is symbolized by the cord laid about his neck which can be drawn tight at any moment. Presence of mind is suggested by the procedures connected with trapdoors, moving stairways, etc. Those are procedures which take place quite differently in the Mysteries because they are performed on the astral plane.

The candidate must then take the oath. Everything about him is horrible, dark, the room only lit by one or two tiny flames. I want you to consider this oath in its full portent: 'I hereby swear that by Word, Sign and Grip I shall never disclose anything which is henceforth revealed to me within this Lodge. Should I betray any of the secrets, I will allow any of the Brethren who may get to know about it to slit my throat and wrench out my tongue.' That is the oath of the apprentice. Still more dreadful is the oath of the journeyman, who consents to having his breast cut open and his heart torn out and thrown to the birds. The oath which the Master has to swear is so terrible that it cannot be repeated here.

These things are used as a means of evoking a certain kind of rhythm in the sensations of the astral body: The result of this is that the spirit is influenced intuitively. This influencing of the spirit was the main purpose of the Masonic initiation in ancient times—Freemasonry is really very ancient.

The Freemasons of old were actually stonemasons. They performed all the duties of a mason. They were the builders of temples and public buildings in ancient Greece, where they were known as Dionysiacs.[6] The building work was carried out in the service of the temple of Dionysus. In Egypt they were the builders of the pyramids, in ancient Rome, the builders of cities, and during the Middle Ages they built cathedrals and churches. After the thirteenth century they also began to build independently of the authority of the Church. At this time the expression 'Freemason' came into use. Before that they were under the authority of the religious communities and were the recognized architects.

Let us take our start from the fact that the Freemasons were the builders of the pyramids, of the Mystery temples, and of the churches. You will easily gain the conviction—especially by reading Vitruvius[7]—that the manner in which architecture was formerly studied is quite different from our present method. One did not study it at that time by making calculations, but instead definite intuitions were imparted by means of symbols.

If you read in *Luzifer*[8] how the Lemurians developed their building capacity you will get an inkling of the way in which this art was then practised. It is not possible today to build in that manner. With amazement and wonder we behold the buildings of the ancient Chinese and of the Babylonians and Assyrians, and know that they were constructed without a knowledge of our present-day mathematics. We behold the wonderful engineering feat of Lake Moeris in Egypt—a lake which was constructed to collect water which could be diverted into irrigation channels in times of need. It was not built with our modern engineering techniques. The wonderful acoustic effects produced in old buildings were achieved in a way which modern architects are not yet able to imitate. At that time men were able to build by means of intuitive faculties, not through rational understanding.

The whole of this kind of architecture stood in relationship to a knowledge of the universe. If you take the Egyptian pyramids, for instance, their measurements correspond to certain measurements in heavenly space, to the distances of the stars in space. The whole configuration of stellar space was depicted in these buildings. There was a connection between the individual building and the dome of heaven. The mysterious rhythm presented to our gaze when we behold the starry heavens (not just with our outer sense but with an intuitive gaze which penetrates to higher relationships, to rhythmical relationships), that was what the original architects included in their building—because they were building out of the universe.

This art of building was taught in a fashion as different from our own as the teaching of the art of medicine among certain primitive tribes today differs from our own. Our teaching today stems from the intellect. In primitive tribes the doctor is not trained like our doctors, but has certain occult forces developed in him. He has to undergo a bodily training that would be horrible for anybody of a nervous or weak disposition living in our modern culture. This training teaches him indifference to joy and pain and he who is indifferent to these is already in possession of occult powers. The extent to which the astral body could originally be trained was so great that it led to the development of powers which were designated as the Royal Art, which is an art derived from the mighty symbols of heavenly proportions.

Now you will have an idea of what Freemasonry used to be and you will realize that it had to outgrow its real task. It was bound to lose its significance as the world became rationalistic. It had its meaning when the fourth cultural epoch was still being developed. The fifth epoch brought about the loss of its importance. Today, Freemasons are no longer masons. Anybody can become a member. For occultists, symbols have a real meaning. A symbol that is merely a symbol, merely a copy or image, has no meaning; there is only significance in what can become a reality, in what can become a living force. If a symbol acts upon the spirit of humanity in such a way that intuitive forces are set free, then we are dealing with a true symbol. Today, Freemasons say they have symbols which mean this or that. An occult symbol, however, is one which takes hold of the will and leads over into the astral body. Inasmuch as our culture has become an intellectual culture, Freemasonry has lost its meaning.

Regarding connections with Manichaeism ... [Gap][9] And after that come the high degrees, which extend as far as the ninetieth, indeed the ninety-sixth degree, and start at the fourth degree. The importance of the first three degrees has gradually been transferred to the high degrees. There is a kind of residue still remaining in what is called the 'Royal Arch',[10] which is still extant in Freemasonry today. About these lighter sides and some of the darker sides of Freemasonry we shall have to speak again.

The Essence and Task of Freemasonry from the Point of View of Spiritual Science—II

Berlin, 9 December 1904

Last time I spoke about Freemasonry, and today I wish to add something to that. I should like you to consider that I am in a different position with regard to Freemasonry than to the other subjects we have spoken about, or which we still intend to discuss, as I usually only speak about things of which I have personal experience. In the present instance I should stress to you that I am speaking to you as a non-Mason[1] and only from a theosophical point of view, whereas to do full justice to the subject of what Freemasonry really is, it should be treated by one who is himself a Freemason. He would not do this, but this is for other reasons which it is best not to discuss. At the same time I would request that you treat what I have to say with reserve.

When I said to you that only a Freemason himself could speak about what it really represents in its innermost core, so I would beg you to take into account that, in spite of that, there is probably no such Freemason in existence in the whole of Europe. This may strike you as odd, but it is so. Since the eighteenth century Freemasonry has been in a very peculiar stage of its development, and I would ask you to regard everything I told you about it last time as being applicable to what it probably would have been like if it had remained as it was in the sixteenth or seventeenth centuries. As this is not the case, Freemasonry is, so to speak, only a kind of husk devoid of its true content. It can be compared to a petrified plant which is no longer the same as what constituted the plant, but is a crust or shell made up by something else.

The ordinary Craft Masonry does not come into consideration where the things we are going to discuss are concerned, for this Craft Masonry, with its three degrees of Apprentice, Journeyman and Master, took its start from the Charter of Cologne in 1535.[2] Today it is not really anything more than a union for mutual stimulation with regard to higher education and schooling, a union for the purpose of mutual support and stimulation among its members. It is true that these first three degrees are, as it were, only the last remaining vestiges of the original three degrees of Freemasonry, and if the ceremonies were to take place as in former times—which they do not—then Apprentice, Journeyman and Master would be initiated in the way I described last time. The regulations are certainly that they should take place in this way, but only a few people know that these regulations exist and still fewer know the meaning of these things. Everything I have told you about the effect of these ceremonies on the astral plane is something of which Craft Masonry has no clear understanding.

Now both the British and also the St John Lodges in Germany possess these three degrees which I have named. And they are actually all in the same state as I have just described. But the possibility is there, within these three degrees, through the very fact that the symbols exist, of penetrating through them to the deeper wisdom which underlies them. A proof of this is provided by the fact that a Mason whom you all know well by name has addressed his brother Masons in such a way that the germ of his theosophical awareness is thereby revealed, that he was able, in a certain sense, to speak in theosophical terms to an audience of Masons. The Freemason of whom I speak is Goethe.[3]

As theosophists you will immediately find something very familiar when I read to you two verses of his Freemasonry poem[4] which he intended for his brethren of the Lodge.

Doch rufen von drüben
Die Stimmen der Geister
Die Stimmen der Meister:
Versäumt nicht zu üben
Die Kräfte des Guten.

Hier winden sich Kronen
In ewiger Stille,
Die sollen mit Fülle,
Die Tätigen Lohnen!
Wir heissen euch hoffen.

Yet call from beyond
The voices of spirits,
The voices of masters:
Omit not to practise
The powers of the good.

Crowns here are woven
In quiet eternal
Rewarding with plenty
Those who are active!
We beg you, have hope.

Goethe speaks here of the Masters and he speaks of them within the precincts of the Lodge, in spite of the fact that he knows that those sitting around him have no inkling of the profundity of his words—because he is also aware of the fact that through the atmosphere which surrounds a Freemasonry Lodge, through the presence of symbols, vibrations are set in motion which influence the astral body and thereby bring about a certain result. That is something which scarcely enters into the consciousness of Freemasons but upon which those who know can still build today.

Those who are led beyond the first three degrees to the higher degrees possess rather more consciousness. The first of these higher degrees is the Royal Arch degree,[5] the degree of Royal Art. This degree is distinguished by the fact that its 'chapter' or 'union' has a special organization, which is filled with deeper meaning. In their gatherings—especially in those in which a new member is to be initiated into the secrets— never more than twelve fellow members are allowed to be present; so that, after the manner of occult brotherhoods, they really represent something other than themselves, something which lives among them in a mysterious fashion. They are not regarded just as persons, but as the personification of parti- cular qualities.

The first, who represents the most important in the circle of twelve, is called Zerubbabel.[6] He is a leader, the sun, from whom radiates the light which is to illuminate the others. He must needs be the cleverest and has to have a certain knowl- edge of the essence and meaning of the secret sciences. That is seldom the case with present fashions in the Royal Arch degree. I am talking about an ideal situation, in fact, which only very rarely arises when suitable people happen to be present.[7]

The next officer is Jeshua, the high priest;[8] the third, Haggai, the prophet. Together with Zerubbabel these three compose the Grand Council. The first and second Principals come next, then the two scribes, Esra and Nehemia, and the janitor or tyler without the door. After that come the so-called lesser companions. Not more than twelve people may be present at any time. These twelve represent the twelve signs of the zodiac. The whole is a portrayal of the sun's passage through the twelve signs of the zodiac. That reminds us of what I have told you about the Masons having taken their start in reproducing astronomical laws in particular buildings, in churches, cathedrals, etc.

The arrangement of the Lodge (though this is not always the case) is a large square hall with a vaulted ceiling,[9] painted blue and covered with golden stars to represent the heavens. The positions taken up by the participants is closely prescribed by ceremony. The novices, who are last to enter, take their places in the north, as they are not yet able to endure warmth. In the east stands Zerubbabel. In the west is the high priest Jeshua, and the prophet Haggai. And those who take their places in the south are roped together. Each of them has the rope wound around him three times, uniting him with his fellows at a distance of three or four decimeters.[10]

He who is initiated into this fourth degree, the first of the higher degrees, which in certain regions still provides an inkling of the significance of the Temple Legend, has to pass three veils.[11] At each passing of a veil one of the secrets is imparted to him. He is told the secret meaning of a particular verse from the Pentateuch. After this the secret of the Tau sign is explained, and the Holy Word, the Master Word, is given him, which is the word by which Masons of the Fourth Degree recognize one another. And then, before all else, it is made clear to him in his first instruction how ancient Freemasonry is. The Craft Masons do not usually get to know that, or if they do hear it, they have not the slightest understanding of these matters. The history of Freemasonry is related to them in the following way. The first true Mason was Adam,[12] the first man, who had an extraordinary knowledge of geometry at the time of his expulsion from Paradise. He was recognized as the first Mason because, being the first man, he was a direct descendant of the Light. The true, deeper origin of Freemasonry, however, pre-dates humanity entirely. It resides in Light itself which existed before mankind.

That is most profound and reveals, for those who can understand it, what theosophical wisdom has again made public through its description of the formation of the earth through the first two Root Races and into the third (the time of Lemuria). Whoever can apprehend this through Freemasonry has received into himself something of tremendous importance. But that takes place in only the rarest cases because Freemasonry is, as it were, degenerate today. This has come about because, since the sixteenth century, man has had little understanding of the true meaning of Freemasonry, namely, that a temple has to be built in such a way that its proportions are a reflection of the great cosmic proportions, that a cathedral has to be built in such a way that its acoustics reproduce something of the Harmony of the Spheres, which is the source of all acoustics in the outer world.

A knowledge of this original insight was gradually lost. Thus it came about that when Desaguliers[13] reunited Freemasonry in England during the first half of the eighteenth century no one had any proper understanding of the fact that the word Freemasonry had to be taken literally, that it really did concern the work of the practising Mason and that the Mason was one who built churches and temples and other great buildings according to cosmic laws and incorporated into them heavenly and not earthly proportions.

This original insight and its reflection in Freemasonry was lost; there was no longer any conscious appreciation of the transformation wrought by a proper use of acoustics in a building where the speaker's words are thrown back and are thereby changed in their effect. Those who built the great cathedrals of medieval times were the great Freemasons. They were aware of the importance of the fact that what was spoken by the priest should be reflected back from the individual walls and the whole congregation immersed in a sea of sound, breathing and fluctuating in significant vibration which would exercise still greater effect on the astral body than on the physical ear. That has all been lost and it was inevitable that this should be so in the new age. That is what I meant when I told you that what is left of Freemasonry is only the husk of what it was in former times.

Apart from these three degrees there are also the higher degrees. And those are possessed in a fairly complete form by the larger communities of Great Britain, America, Italy,

Egypt, and also by eastern Freemasonry—especially that known as Oriental or Memphis Masonry.[14] In Germany, where there is a branch of the Memphis-Misraim Freemasonry with world-wide Masonic connections,[15] the higher degrees are also functioning. But in Germany, within the St John Freemasonry, there is so little understanding of the real significance of the higher degrees that the St John Masons there generally look upon the higher degrees as nonsense. The Grand Orient of Germany is obliged, for this reason, merely to let the St John Masons in general pass properly as Masons.

In this respect there are great differences between the Masonry practised in Germany and that of England or Great Britain. In British Masonry a kind of reconciliation has been achieved through the Articles of Union of 1813 between Craft Masonry with its three degrees and those branches of Masonry that recognize the higher degrees.[16] Thus as an apprentice in Craft Masonry one is allowed to enter and also graduate into the fourth, fifth and sixth degrees, that is, into the higher degrees. The degrees pertaining to Craft Masonry are credited to one in England; that is not the case in Germany. The German Grand Orient of the Memphis and Misraim Order undertakes the working of the three lowest degrees itself. The Orient Freemason must therefore have passed the first three degrees at the outset. He must furthermore commit himself to rising at least to the eighteenth degree. He may not rest until he has done so. A German Mason of the St John's Order is therefore never admitted to the higher degrees of Orient Masonry [without having attained the three lesser degrees]. The Orient Masonry consists of a graded instruction in occultism. As I said last time, it gives a picture of the teaching given in the higher degrees, those which succeed the Royal Arch degree; these provide a kind of astral training which leads up to the eighteenth or twentieth degrees. Then comes that which provides a kind of mental training, a training which leads to a kind of life on the mental plane, and advances to the sixtieth or seventieth degree. Lastly comes the highest training of all, the most profound occult instruction, which can be undertaken in the Grand Orient up to the ninety-sixth degree.

There are only very few in Germany who have advanced to the ninety-sixth degree. But in spite of everything there is something in all this which will presently prove to you how little is left in present-day Masonry of what it formerly encompassed. The most interesting point is that those who have progressed to the ninety-sixth degree have not always been through a Masonic training, and that there is scarcely anyone at all who has completed the whole gamut of the training. There are indeed a few who have higher degrees. They have been invested with the third or the thirty-third or the ninety-sixth degree, but those who possess these distinctions have not gained them through Masonic training but through other occult institutions, and they have allowed their knowledge to be used to bring about the redemption of Freemasonry. If someone has attained to the ninety-sixth degree, it has not been achieved through Masonic training. Bluntly, it is considered that in this respect Freemasonry is indebted to the occult training of other schools.

In this sense we have to interpret the manifesto which has been given by the Grand Orient of the Memphis and Misraim Rite[17] as a kind of ideal document. I will read it to you with one or two explanations. What is given here must not be construed as though it could be put into practice in the present day. It must be pointed out today that no Freemason—not even one who has the ninety-sixth degree—would take responsibility for taking another Freemason through these prescriptions, since he himself has not undergone them.

Concerning the Secrets of the Higher Occult Degrees of our Order. A Manifesto of the Grand Orient.

One of the secrets belonging to the highest degree of our

Order consists in providing the appropriately conditioned Brother with the practical means of erecting the true Temple of Solomon within man; of restoring the 'Lost Word', that is, our Order provides the initiated and selected Brother with practical means enabling him to gain proof of pure immortality during his present earthly life.

That is one of the points that are of utmost importance. The next point is one that exists in all centres of occult training: no calling-up of spirits or spiritualistic activities. Anyone who practises spiritualism is strictly excluded.

This secret is one of the true Masonic secrets and rests solely in the possession of the higher occult degrees of our Order. It has been handed down by word of mouth in our Order from the ancestors of all true Freemasons, 'the Wise Men of the East', and will only be transmitted by us in like manner.

That is the practice in occult societies.

Naturally, however, the success of this practical instruction for the attainment of this secret again depends entirely on the candidate himself.

For of what use are the best and most tested and detailed instructions given to a candidate wishing to learn to swim if he is not himself prepared to move hands and feet when he comes into contact with the water? Or of what use is the most comprehensive guidance in learning to paint, or the exposition of the most vivid colours by way of example, if the candidate to whom painting is being taught will not take the paint-brush into his own hand and seek to mix the colours himself? He will never become an artist unless he does so.

Those brothers, the discoverers of this secret, guarded it as a rare, self-acquired possession and, in order not to be misjudged or even derided by the man in the street, they concealed it by means of symbols, as we do to this day.

These symbols are no longer decipherable for the Freemason of the present day. Such symbols are not arbitrarily chosen. These are not things by means of which someone can portray something, like a professor who says: I will illustrate this graphically. These symbols have been taken from the objects themselves, which have been engraved by nature. He who recognizes them for what they are, who can really read what they contain, comes into contact with their innermost being; he is led by them into their inner nature. These symbols portray the thing itself and do not have a merely symbolical meaning. Within Freemasonry there is no one who is able to give guidance that would enable a person to arrive at the object itself.

> These symbols are, however, no arbitrarily chosen pictures and they do not rest upon any chance occurrence, but are founded on the attributes of God and of man, and must be regarded as archetypal. But we will never take the form, the vessel, the ritual, the symbols for their content, but will seek the spiritual content within the form...

These words show ... [Gap] for the symbol itself portrays the object.

> ... and when we have found this [the spiritual content] and have absorbed it into ourselves, we shall recognize through this spiritual content the absolute necessity of the form, the ritual, the symbolism.
>
> Our higher degrees themselves provide the brother with certain proof of the immortality of man.

This they would do if they were worked.

> That is and has been the great longing of mankind ever since human beings who could reason existed. Mankind needs to have this assurance of a life after death in order to be truly happy in this present life. Therefore all the Mys-

teries contained in the religions and centres of hidden wisdom have occupied themselves with this question as their highest and principal task. The Church has naturally also occupied itself with this question of the 'Lost Word', the 'Lost Immortality', but it directs the candidate along the path of grace and portrays it as a gift from above and not as something to be achieved by personal effort. Our Order, however, places it within the power of each individual seeker, by practical means, to unite himself consciously and voluntarily with the World Consciousness, with the ultimate forces of Creation.

That means, therefore, to provide insight into and union with that world which otherwise is only accessible through the portal of death.

From all this you may draw the conclusion that what belongs to the world's profundities was once found in Freemasonry, but is no longer there in the empty husk which it presents today. You must ask yourselves why. Now the meaning of the Temple Legend, the meaning of operative Masonry, like all intuitive knowledge, had to be lost to humanity, because the fifth cultural epoch is actually the epoch of understanding. Intuition had for a time to lie dormant in the world and Freemasonry is intuitive in its whole attitude and manner. I would like to draw your attention to Vitruvius[18] and to the true symbolical building instructions that he gave. Only those, however, who have the right intuition for it can follow these instructions. Today these symbolical instructions have been replaced by intellectual, rational ones. Reason had to become the keynote of man's development for a while, because everything that has meanwhile come to us through great conquests of nature must be incorporated in the whole organism of human activity.

Understand what it means: the whole of the mineral kingdom will be included in the progress of the world during the present Round of evolution. It will be included in such a way that man will gradually transform the whole of nature through his own spirituality. That is the meaning of the Molten Sea, that the whole of mineral nature will effectively be transformed.

Man works in industry, so as to weave organization [his own spirituality?] into mineral nature. If you consider a machine ... [Gap]

In this way man thus works the whole mineral kingdom back and forth with his own spirit. This recasting of nature, this recasting of what is mineral, will be perfected when our present Round of evolution has come to an end. The whole of mineral nature will then have been changed. Man will have put his stamp on it, just as he imprints his stamp on a quantity of metal when, for example, he fashions a watch. Thus, when a new Round of evolution begins, the mineral kingdom can be sucked in, absorbed.

In order completely to finish the development in this sphere, the whole way of thinking that has gripped man since the sixteenth century must be carried right into the atom. Thus only when reasoned thinking can grasp the atom can Freemasonry again revive. In the first stage, the outer form will be grasped. The next step will be when man has learned to think right into the mineral atom, when he has an understanding of how to make use of what lives in the atom and place it in the service of the whole. It is true that only now—and perhaps only during the last five years—human thinking has turned to tracing natural forces as far as the atom. And indeed, he who would understand this precisely must follow the latest phase of the various developments in electricity. The speech which the English Prime Minister Balfour has made[19] on the subject of our contemporary world outlook is interesting in this connection, albeit only in its outward implications. What he said there [about new electrical theory] is something of enormous importance. He hints at the critical turning-point in the development of man's thinking. He is to a certain extent conscious of this and mentions it in one part of his speech. Thus we see how something is dawning in the consciousness of natural science which plays into the future. This has been known to occultists since 1879. I emphasize this, although I cannot prove it.[20] The occultist knows that this will come about—a new point of departure from the atom into the mineral-physical world. That will be what will enter into the world in the sixth cultural epoch, and through this Freemasonry will also be regenerated. In Freemasonry the occultist has something very remarkable, something unprecedented, for it has something primeval in its foundation. It belongs to the most ancient of traditions, which has preserved almost a hundred degrees, in a precisely specialized structure, in spite of the fact that it has lost nearly all of its content, and that none of those belonging to it in Europe are able to form an adequate conception of it. But still, the thing is there and one will only need to fill the whole outer husk with new content. The thing is there, waiting to be brought to life again.

Points from the subsequent discussion
Rites of Memphis, Oriental Rites and Grand Orient Rites. A conference of occultists discussed whether the occult doctrine could be made public or not. From that it became clear that there are two tendencies, a left and a right tendency,[21] one which is free-thinking and one which is conservative.

The Essence and Task of Freemasonry from the Point of View of Spiritual Science—III

Berlin, 16 December 1904

It is important that we should speak about the higher degrees of Freemasonry, because this manner of instruction sets itself special tasks, certain aspects of which will be discussed in the near future. We are dealing, in the main, with a special rite that is called the Combined Rite of Memphis and Misraim.[1] I have already mentioned that the Memphis and Misraim Rite possesses a great number of degrees, that 95 degrees must be undertaken, and that usually the Supreme Leaders of the Grand Orients (i.e. those of Germany, Great Britain and America) possess the ninety-sixth degree. These degrees are so arranged that up to the end of about the eightieth to eighty-ninth degree they are divided up in the way I shall presently describe to you.

From about the eighty-seventh degree onwards start the real occult degrees into which no one can be initiated who has not made a thorough study of the subject. I always make the reservation that in Europe there is nobody who has undertaken all these degrees or who has really undergone an occult Freemasonry training. But that is of no particular concern as far as Freemasonry goes, because its renewed task still awaits it in the future, and when the time comes the organization will be available; the vessel will be there which is needed to carry out what has to be achieved.

Now I must mention the various branches of Freemasonry and their tendencies, even if I am only to indicate something briefly. First of all, it is to be borne in mind that the whole of the Masonic higher degrees trace back to a personality often spoken about but equally very much misunderstood. He was particularly misunderstood by nineteenth-century historians, who have no idea of the difficult situations an occultist can meet in life. This personality is the ill-famed and little understood Cagliostro. The so-called Count Cagliostro,[2] in whom an individuality was concealed who was recognized in his true nature only by the highest initiates, attempted originally to bring Freemasonry in London to a higher stage. For during the last third of the eighteenth century Freemasonry had fairly well reached the state that I have described. He did not succeed in London at that time. He then tried in Russia, and also at the Hague. Everywhere he was unsuccessful, for very definite reasons.

Then, however, he was successful in Lyons, forming an occult Masonic lodge of the Philalethes [Searchers after Truth] out of a group of local Masons, which was called the Lodge of Triumphing Wisdom. The purpose of this Lodge was specified by Cagliostro. What you can read about it is, however, nothing but the work of ignorant people. What can be said about it is only an indication. Cagliostro was concerned with two things: firstly, with instructions enabling one to produce the so-called Philosopher's Stone; secondly, with creating an understanding of the mystic pentagram. I can only give you a hint of the meaning of these two things. They may be treated with a deal of scorn, but they are not to be taken merely symbolically; they are based on real facts.

The Philosopher's Stone has a specific purpose, which was stated by Cagliostro; it is meant to prolong human life to a span of 5,527 years.[3] To a freethinker that appears laughable. In fact, however, it is possible, by means of special training, to prolong life indefinitely by learning to live outside the physical body. Anyone, however, who imagined that no death, in the conventional sense of the word, could strike down an adept, would have quite a false view of the matter. So whoever imagined that an adept could not be hit and killed by a falling roof slate would also be wrong. To be sure, that would usually only occur if the adept allowed it. We are not dealing here with physical death, but with the following. Physical death is only an apparent occurrence for him who has understood the significance of the Philosopher's Stone for himself, and has learned to exteriorize it. For other people it is a real happening, which signifies a great division in their life. For he who understands how to use the Philosopher's Stone in the way that Cagliostro intended his pupils to do, death is only an apparent occurrence. It does not even constitute a decisive turning-point in life; it is, in fact, something which is only there for the others who can observe the adept and say that he is dying. He himself, however, does not really die. It is much more the case that the person concerned has learned to live without his physical body, that he has learned during the course of life to let all those things take place in him gradually that happen suddenly in the physical body at the moment of death. Everything has already taken place in the body of the person concerned, which otherwise takes place at death. Death is then no longer possible, for the said person has long ago learned to live without the physical body. He lays aside the physical body in the same way that one takes off a raincoat, and he puts a new body on just as one puts on a new raincoat.

Now that will give you an inkling. That is one lesson which Cagliostro taught—the Philosopher's Stone, which allows physical death to become a matter of small importance.

The second lesson was the knowledge of the Pentagram. That is the ability to distinguish the five bodies of man one from another. When someone says: physical body, etheric body, astral body, kama-manas body, causal body [higher manas or spirit-self], these are mere words, or at best abstract ideas. Nothing, however, is achieved by that. A person living today as a rule hardly knows the physical body; only one who knows the Pentagram learns to know the five bodies. One does not know a body by living in it, but by having it as an object. That is what distinguishes an average person from one who has gone through such a schooling that the five bodies have become objects. The ordinary person does indeed live in these five bodies. However, he *lives* in them, he cannot step outside [of himself] and look at them. At best he can view his physical body when he looks down at his torso, or sees it in a mirror. Those pupils of Cagliostro who had followed his methods would thereby have achieved what some Rosicrucians achieved who had basically undergone a training with the same orientation. They were in a school of the great European adepts, who taught that the five bodies were realities and not mere concepts. That is called 'Knowing the Pentagram' and 'Moral Rebirth'.

I will not say that the pupils of Cagliostro never achieved anything. In general they went as far as comprehending the astral body. Cagliostro was extremely skilful in imparting a view of the astral body. Long before the catastrophe broke over him, he had succeeded in starting schools in Paris, Belgium, St Petersburg and a few other places in Europe, in addition to the one in Lyons, out of which later emerged at least a few people who had the basis for some to proceed to the eighteenth, nineteenth and twentieth higher degrees of Freemasonry. Thus Count Cagliostro at least had an important influence on occult Masonry in Europe before ending his days in the prison in Rome. The world should not actually pronounce judgment on Cagliostro. As I have already indicated, when people speak about Cagliostro it is as though Hottentots were to speak about the erection of an overhead railway, because the relationship of apparently immoral outward acts to world happenings is not understood.

I remarked earlier that the French Revolution arose out of the secret societies[4] of the occultists, and if these currents were investigated further they would lead back to the school of the adepts.

It may be that what Mabel Collins depicted in her novel *Flita*[5] is hard to understand. In it she describes, rather grotesquely, how an adept has the World Chessboard in front of him in a secret place, and lets the pieces play, and how he, so to speak, controls the karma of a continent upon one very simple little board. It does not quite take place as it is described there, but something on a much greater scale than that does actually happen, of which what is described in *Flita* gives only a distorted picture.

Now the French Revolution certainly proceeded from such things as this. There is a well-known story contained in the writings of the Countess d'Adhémar. It related that before the outbreak of the French Revolution the Countess d'Adhémar, one of the ladies-in-waiting to Marie-Antoinette, received a visit from the Count of Saint-Germain.[6] He wanted to be presented to the Queen and to beg audience of the King. Louis XVI's minister, however, was the enemy of the Count of Saint-Germain, who therefore was not allowed into the King's presence. But he described to the Queen with great accuracy and detail the major perils that were looming ahead. Regrettably, however, his warnings were ignored. It was on that occasion that he uttered the great saying, which was based on truth, 'They who sow the wind shall reap the whirlwind,'[7] and he added that he had uttered this saying millennia previously, and it had been repeated by Christ. Those were words which were unintelligible to the ordinary person.

But the Count of Saint-Germain was right. I will only add a few more touches which are quite correct. In books about the Count of Saint-Germain you can read that he died in 1784[8] at the court of the Landgrave of Hessen,[9] who later became one of the most advanced German Freemasons. The Landgrave nursed him until the end. But the Countess d'Adhémar recounts in her memoirs[10] that he appeared to her long after the year 1784, and that she saw him six more times long after that. In reality he was at that time, in 1790, with some Rosicrucians in Vienna[11] and said, which is perfectly true, that he was obliged to retire to the Orient for the span of 85 years, and that after that time people would again become aware of his activity in Europe. The year 1875 is that of the founding of the Theosophical Society. These things are all connected together in a certain way.

In the school founded by the Landgrave of Hessen, also, there were two main concerns: the Philosopher's Stone and the Knowledge of the Pentagram. The Freemasonry founded by the Landgrave of Hessen at that time continued to exist in a rather diluted form. In fact, the whole of Freemasonry, as I have described it, is called the Egyptian Rite, the Rite of Memphis and Misraim. The latter traces its origin back to King Misraim who came from Assyria—from the Orient— and, after the conquest of Egypt, was initiated into the Egyptian Mysteries. These are indeed the Mysteries which originate from ancient Atlantis. An unbroken tradition exists from that time. Modern Freemasonry is only a continuation of what was established then in Egypt.

Before I go into details I would like to say that Freemasonry which extends to the higher degrees is something which, in its more intimate aspect, is quite different from the normal Craft Masonry. The ordinary Craft Masonry rests on a kind of democratic principle, and if the democratic principle is to be applied to matters of knowledge, it is obvious that it will lead to a state of affairs in which the brothers who have congregated together will mainly do nothing but bring forward their own views. Truth, however, is something about which one cannot hold one's own views. One either knows a truth or one is ignorant of it. No one can say that the three angles of a triangle add up to 725 degrees instead of to 180 degrees.

When people sit together and have a discussion they talk about their own views, sometimes also about the most elevated things. But all of this exists on the level of illusion, and is just as irrelevant as what a person says who is ignorant of the true sum of the angles of a triangle and only gives his own opinion about it. Just as one is unable to discuss whether the sum of the angles of a triangle have this or that many degrees, so one is also unable to have a discussion about higher truths. That is why the democratic principle is not applicable to matters of knowledge, for there is no basis of argument on which to discuss them. What distinguishes Masonry of the higher degrees from the Craft Masonry is that one learns to know the truth step by step. Whoever has recognized a thing can no longer hold more than one opinion about it. One has either recognized it or one has not done so. The 96 degrees have, therefore, a certain justification.

At the head is the so-called Sovereign Sanctuary, who is identical with what is known as the Grand Orient in Free-masonry, and is in possession of the real occult knowledge.[12] He knows the path and the speech of that which can be read in the Masonic Manifesto,[13] and which makes it possible to hear the voice of the Wise Men of the East. When he has reached this step, he is certainly in a position to hear the voice of the Wise Masters. So far, however, must one have worked one's way up that one is in possession of very definite knowledge, and also of definite inner qualities and inner capacities which are by no means purely covered by the conventional bourgeois virtues but are something more meaningful and intimate. I would note that [compared with] what we have been speaking about here, what theosophical literature reveals of a theoretical or practical nature forms only an elementary part. So that the theoretical side of the higher degrees of Freemasonry far surpasses what can be divulged in popular theosophy. What can be disclosed there is dependent upon the permission given by the adepts to allow these things to be popularized to a certain degree. But it is not possible to make all knowledge public.

It is correct to say that humanity will be astonished by some of the discoveries that will be made in the near future. But they will be rather premature discoveries and will thereby cause some havoc. The task of the Theosophical Society consists mainly in preparing people for such things. For instance, what I described at the beginning as the knowledge of the Philosopher's Stone was formerly much more universally known than it is today and, indeed, it was known already during a certain period of the Atlantean epoch. At that time the possibility of conquering death was really something which was commonly known. I only wish to remark that I was not very happy about allowing this truth to appear in print recently. Therefore where this should have come in the discussion about Atlantean times in the *Luzifer* article, a row of dots was printed in place of those things which may not yet be communicated.[14] It cannot even yet be communicated in its entirety. There is a very similar piece of information recorded by a very advanced medium, which appeared in the *Theosophical Review*,[15] dealing with exactly the same thing in a rather different form. The overcoming of death in Atlantean times is naturally preserved in the memories of the individuals concerned without their being aware of it. There are many people reincarnated today who passed through that period in their former lives and who are led to such revelations through their own memories. That will first of all lead to a kind of overrating of certain medical discoveries. People will imagine that medical science was the discoverer of such things. In reality people will have been led to them through their own memories of Atlantean times.

Certain things will mature in the near future and therefore we shall speak about them. This makes it necessary to see the need of a step-by-step advance in the gaining of knowledge. This step-by-step advance is therefore rightly emphasized by those who wish to revive the Misraim and Memphis Rite at the present time. Even if this does not succeed during the next year or two, one must not think that failure in such things is of any significance. There is a man at the head of the American Misraim movement, whose significant character constitutes a sure guarantee of constancy in the advance. This is the excellent Freemason John Yarker.[16]

It is difficult to say at the moment what form the matter will take in Great Britain and Germany. You will perceive that one must reckon with the human material concerned, and that the German movement, therefore (if it is to concern itself with such matters), will also have to reckon with what is available in this direction. If genuine occultists are to take part in such things they must needs be active in one or other direction. They will not always be able to take part in such things. Even the Masters, when they prescribe something of this kind, have to take their cue from great universal laws.

If, therefore, you hear something concerning the German Misraim-Memphis tendency, you should not imagine that this now has significance for the future. It is only the frame into which a good picture may later be put. This German Misraim Order stands under the overall guidance of a certain Reuss,[17] who holds the actual leadership in Great Britain and Germany today. Then, the well-known Carl Kellner[18] also works in this direction. The actual literary work is in the hands of Dr Franz Hartmann,[19] who serves the Misraim Rite with his pen to the very utmost. That is as much as I can impart to you in this or that fragment from here or there, concerning this movement.

Now I can only characterize what is involved here in general terms. There are four kinds of instruction given in the Misraim Rite.[20] The 96 degrees can therefore be achieved through four different kinds of instruction or disciplines. These four disciplines, by means of which one advances, are the following. First, the so-called symbolic instruction or discipline. By means of this, certain symbols can be recognized as facts. The person concerned is instructed in the occult laws of nature, through which quite definite effects are produced through cyclic movements in humanity.

The second kind of instruction or discipline is the so-called philosophic one. It is the Egyptian Hermetic discipline. It consists of a more theoretical kind of instruction. The third kind of instruction is the so-called mystical discipline, which is based more upon inner development, and which, if rightly applied, would lead above all else to the appropriate manipulation of the Philosopher's Stone, that is, to the over-coming of death. That is essentially expressed in one of the sentences which I read out to you which stated that by means of Freemasonry everyone is able to convince himself of the fact of immortality. It depends, however, as the Cabbala says, whether this is requested or not. The fourth kind of instruction is the Cabbalistic one. It consists in the recognition of the principles of world harmony in their truth and reality, the ten basic . . . [Gap]

By means of each of the four paths one can rise to a higher perception through the Misraim Rite. But there is actually no one within the ranks of Freemasonry today who would accept the responsibility of giving practical guidance to anyone, because those concerned have not undergone these things themselves. And the whole affair is a provisional arrangement and only intended to provide a framework for something which is still to come. It is possible that this framework will be filled with occult knowledge. Occult knowledge has to be cast in existing moulds. The important thing is that such moulds exist in the world. If there is molten metal and no mould into which to pour it, you are unable to do anything but let it run out in one lump. So it is also with spiritual currents. It is important that moulds exist into which can be poured the spiritual metal. That is symbolized by the Molten Sea. That will become recognized when what is now seemingly only vegetating receives form for outward manifestation.

Last time I read to you from a speech by the English Prime

Minister Balfour.[21] From that, then, it is already noticeable that certain things are physical truths today that are in primeval occult perceptions. If you read Blavatsky's *The Secret Doctrine* you will find there a passage relating to electricity, which expresses word for word what physicists are now gradually arriving at. What is written there is, however, only a hint at what is actually involved. It is the physical atom that is in question. This was misunderstood by all outward—but not occult—science until four or five years ago. It was taken to be a [body having] mass in space. Nowadays one is beginning to recognize that this physical atom bears the same relationship to the force of electricity that a lump of ice bears to the water from which it has been frozen. If you conceive of water becoming frozen to ice, so is the ice also water, and in like manner the atom of physics is nothing else but frozen electricity. If you can grasp this point completely and were to go through the statements about the atom contained in all the scientific journals until a year or two ago, and were to regard them as rubbish, you will have more or less the right idea. It is only very recently that science has been able to form a conception of what the atom is. It stands [in the same relationship to electricity] as ice does to the water out of which it has been frozen. The physical atom is condensed electricity. I regard Balfour's speech as something of extreme importance.[22]

It is ... [Gap] something which has been published since 1875 [1879?].[23] The fact has been known to occultists for millennia. Now one is beginning to realize that the physical atom is condensed electricity. But there is still a second thing to be considered: what electricity itself is. That is still unknown. They are ignorant of one thing, namely, where the real nature of electricity must be sought. This nature of electricity cannot be discovered by means of any outer experiments or through outer observation. The secret which will be discovered is that electricity—when one learns to view it from a particular level—is exactly the same as what human thought is. Human thought is the same thing as electricity, viewed one time from the inside, another time from the outside.

Whoever is now aware of what electricity is knows that there is something living within him which, in a frozen state, forms the atom. Here is the bridge from human thought to the atom. One will learn to know the building stones of the physical world; they are tiny condensed monads, condensed electricity. In that moment when human beings realize this elementary occult truth about thought, electricity and the atom, in that same moment they will have understood something that is of the utmost importance for the future and for the whole of the sixth post-Atlantean epoch. They will have learned how to build with atoms through the power of thinking.

This will be the spiritual current which will again have to be cast in the moulds that have been prepared for it by occultists over millennia. But because the human race had to pass through the era of the development of understanding and to look away from the true inner work, the moulds have become mere shells. But they still retain their function as moulds, and the right kind of knowledge will have to be poured into them.

The occult investigator obtains his truth from the one side, the physical scientist from the other. Just as Freemasonry has developed out of working masonry, out of the building of cathedrals and temples, so one will in future learn to build with the smallest of building blocks, with entities of condensed electricity. That will call for a new kind of masonry. Then industry will not be able to carry on any more as it does today. It will become so chaotic and will only be able to work purely out of the struggle for existence *per se*, as long as man does not know ... [Gap]* Then it would be possible for someone in

---

* There is a gap here in the shorthand report; however, a completion of the sentence is to be found in legible wirting: [what has to be poured into these husks in the way of thoughts].

Berlin to drive into the city in a cab, while in Moscow a disaster which he had caused was taking place. And nobody at all would have any inkling that he had been the cause of it. Wireless telegraphy is the beginning of this. What I have portrayed is in the future. There are only two possibilities available. Either things go on chaotically, as industry and technology have done until now, in which case it will lead to whoever has the possession of these things being able to cause havoc, or else it will be cast in the moral mould of Freemasonry.*

---

* This last sentence appears as follows in the notes of Marie Steiner von Sivers: 'These things will either continue chaotically, as industry and technology have done until now, or harmoniously, as is the aim of Freemasonry; then the highest development will be achieved.'

Question: Why is the Catholic Church so antagonistic towards Freemasonry?

Answer: The Catholic Church does not want what is coming in the future. Pius IX was initiated into Freemasonry. He tried, through the Chapter of Clermont, to bring about a connection between the Jesuits and the Freemasons. That did not succeed, and therefore the old enmity between these two remained. Our Jesuits know little about these things, and the clergy are also unaware of what is involved. The actual clergy ... [Large gap]

The Trappists have to keep silent, for it is known that by doing so an important faculty of inspired speech in the next life is implanted. That is indeed only to be understood through a knowledge of reincarnation.

Evolution and Involution as they are Interpreted by Occult Societies

Berlin, 23 December 1904

In my former series of lectures, I have been speaking about occult schools and secret societies, and I think it right today to bring this whole course of lectures to a close before we pass on to a different subject next time. A week from now I shall speak about the meaning of the days connected in the Church calendar with the Christmas festival—most especially about Epiphany, which follows on the less important New Year festival.[1] The lecture today, therefore, will be more in the nature of a conclusion.

The question might be asked: What is the deeper meaning of such secret societies, and what is their whole purpose in world evolution? To such a question, my answer would be that they have a real connection with the way in which beings in this world evolve and make progress. If you wish to develop yourself, you know that different kinds of exercises are necessary towards this end and that they are available. You have heard of Hatha Yoga, Rajah Yoga and other exercises of different kinds by means of which societies and brotherhoods connected with occult science have initiated their members.

Somebody might say: All this, surely, could be attained without these secret societies. But I can tell you—and in the course of the lecture you will realize it—that the world cannot do without such societies. To put it bluntly, it is quite un-justifiable to speak in public in the style of the Manifesto of the Freemasons which I read to you a fortnight ago.[2]

One cannot attain to what is usually known as immortality unless one is to some extent familiar with the occult sciences. The fruits of occult science do, of course, find their way out into the world along many different channels. A great deal of occult knowledge exists in the various religions, and all those who participate deeply and sincerely in the life of a religious community have some share in this knowledge and are preparing themselves for the attainment of immortality in the real sense. But to subsist on the knowledge of this immortality and the feeling of belonging in the spiritual world in concrete experience and with full awareness is still something different.

All of you have lived many times but not all of you are conscious that you have lived through these many lives. However, you will gradually attain this consciousness, and without it man's life is lived with incomplete consciousness. It has never been the aim of occult science to inculcate into man a dim feeling of survival, but to impart a clear, fully conscious knowledge of onflowing life in the spiritual world. And there is a certain great law which governs the progressive development of consciousness in all future stages of life. Namely, it is what man works at to help *others* attain such consciousness which contributes the most to its development. It is an apparently paradoxical proposition: everything a being works at without aiming at developing its own consciousness helps to maintain that being's consciousness.

Take as an example the building of a house. An architect builds a house; he does not build this house for himself, but undertakes the task of building it for reasons which have nothing at all to do with himself. You know well that this is very seldom the case. There are many people who, to all appearances, are not working for themselves; and yet, in reality, they *are*.

A lawyer, for example, is to all intents and purposes working for his clients. Part of his work may well be selfless, but the real question is one of earning his living. Whatever men do in business merely for the sake of their own livelihood, to the extent that their business only serves that end, just so much is lost in the way of spiritual gain. On the other hand, everything that is introduced into the work for an objective end, everything that is connected with the interests of another, helps to conserve our consciousness for future evolution. So that is quite clear.

Now, think of the Freemasons. In the original arrangement, they gave this injunction to their members: Build such buildings as make no contribution at all to, or have nothing to do with, your own subsistence. All that has survived of the good old Freemasonry are certain charitable institutions. And although the lodges have lost their living roots in the ancient wisdom and occult knowledge once in their possession, these charitable institutions are evidence of a humanitarianism which, while it is empty [of real substance], still persists and is cultivated as a tradition. Selfless activity is something that belongs to Freemasonry. Freemasonry did originally urge its members to work in the service of humanity, to build into the objective world.

We are living now in the epoch of evolution that may be called the mineral epoch; and our task is to permeate this mineral world through and through with our own spirit. Grasp exactly what this means. You are building a house. You fetch the stones from some quarry. You hew them into the shapes needed for the house, and so on. With what are you joining this raw material, obtained from the mineral kingdom? You are joining raw material with human spirit. When you make a machine, you have introduced your spirit into that machine. The actual machine does, of course, perish and become dust; it will be broken up. Not a trace of it will survive. But what it has done does not vanish without a trace, but passes into the very atoms. Every atom bears a trace of your spirit and will carry this trace with it. It is not a matter of indifference whether or not an atom has at some time been in a machine. The atom itself has undergone change as a result of having once been in a machine, and this change that you have wrought in the atom will never again be lost to it. Moreover, through your having changed the atom, through your having united your spirit with the mineral world, a permanent stamp has been made upon the general consciousness [of mankind]. Just so much will be taken from us into the other world.

It is a fact that all occult science consists of knowing how a man can act selflessly in order to attain the greatest enhancement of his own consciousness. Consider how certain men who have known this very clearly have been so selfless that they took steps to prevent their names from going down to posterity. An example of this is the *Theologia Deutsch*.[3] Nobody knows who wrote it. Outwardly, there is only 'the man from Frankfurt'. He therefore took care that his name could not even be guessed. He worked in such a way that he merely added something to the objective world without asking for honour or for the preservation of his name. By way of comparison, let it be mentioned that the Masters, as a rule, are not personages known to history;[4] they sometimes incarnate [embody] themselves, when it is necessary, in historical personalities, but this is in a certain respect a sacrifice. The level of their consciousness is no longer compatible with any work for themselves—and preservation of a name does after all involve work for oneself.

It is difficult to understand this rule. However, you will now grasp that the Freemasons' aim is this, as far as possible, to do their work in the world in such a way that it is concealed in the cathedrals, in social institutions and organizations, in charitable foundations. For selfless deeds are the real foundation of immortality—the latter is the reflected image of selfless deeds in the outer world. They need not be of great account. If someone gives a coin to someone in a selfless way, then that is an action that is to be understood in that way. But only to the extent that it was selfless does it become immortal. And very few [deeds] are selfless. A good deed may be very egotistical when, for instance, it creates a feeling of comfort. Good deeds spring extremely often from selfish motives. If a poor man living among us has no roast meat at Christmas, and I feel the need to give him some in order that I may feel justified in [eating] my own roast meat, that, after all, is egoistic.

In the Middle Ages no one could say who had built many of the cathedrals or painted many of the pictures. It is only in our epoch that people have begun to attach such value to an individual human name. In earlier epochs, more spiritual than our own, the individual name had less importance. Spirituality in those days was directed towards reality whereas our epoch adheres to the delusion that what is merely transient should be preserved.

I have said this only in order to indicate to you the principle on which these secret societies depended. It mattered to them to efface themselves altogether as personalities, and to allow what they did to live only in its effects. And this brings us to the heart of the secrets. The fact that some particular thing is kept secret is of less importance than keeping one's own share in the work secret. Everyone who keeps his own part secret thereby secures immortality for himself. The rule is therefore clear and unambiguous: as much as you yourself put into the world, that much consciousness the world will give you back. That is connected with the greatest universal laws.

You all have a soul and you all have a spirit. This soul and spirit are called upon to reach one day the highest stages of perfection. But you were already there before your first physical incarnation. You were first physically incarnated in the preceding races after the time of the Hyperborean and Polarian epochs.[5] Before that you were purely beings of soul. But as beings of soul you were a part of the world soul, and as spirit you were part of the general world spirit. The world soul and the world spirit were spread around you as nature is spread around you today. Just as the mineral world, the plant world and the animal world are around you today, so were the worlds of soul and spirit spread around you then. And what was once outside you is now your soul; you have made inward what to begin with was outside. What today is your inward part was once spread about outside. This has now become your soul. The spirit, too, was once spread around you. And what is now spread around you will become your inner life. You will take into yourself what is now the mineral kingdom, and it will become your inner part. The plant kingdom will become your inner part. What surrounds you in nature will become your inner being.

You will understand now how this is connected with the first example given: you build a church for others, not for yourself. You can take into [yourself] a world full of majesty, beauty and splendour if you make the world majestic, beautiful and splendid. To do something for the higher self is not selfish because it is not done only for the self. This higher self will be united with all other higher selves, so that it is [done] for all at the same time.

It is this that the Freemasons knew. The Freemason knew when he helped to build the spiritualized mineral world that this would one day become the content of his soul—and to build means nothing else than to spiritualize the mineral world. That is the significant thing. God once gave us the nature that surrounds us, as mineral, plant and animal nature. We take this [into ourselves]. It is not due to us that it is there; all we can do is to appropriate it for ourselves. But what we ourselves create in the world—that is what will, through ourselves, constitute our future being.

The mineral world, as such, we perceive. What we make out of it we shall, in the future, *be*. What we make of the plant world, of the animal world and of the world of men, that too we will be, in the future. If you found a charitable institution or contribute something to it, what you have contributed, you will be. If a man does nothing which he can draw back in this way into his soul from outside, he will remain empty. It must be possible for man to spiritualize as much as he can of the three kingdoms of nature—four, for mankind also belongs thereto. To bring spirit into the whole external world, that has been the task of the secret societies of every age.

You understand that that must be so. Take a child who is just learning to read and write. To begin with, all the equipment is around him. Today, the child begins to learn to read. Nothing is in him yet, but the teacher, the primers and so forth are there. So it continues until what was outside the child has been instilled into him. And the child acquires the capacity to read. And so it is with nature, too. In times to come we shall have within us what is now spread around us. We are souls, we spring from the world soul, and we drew it in when it was spread around us. The spirit was likewise drawn in, and nature, too, will be drawn in by us, in order to stay within us as an active ability.

That is the great thought at the basis of these secret societies, that all progress is the result of involution and evolution. Involution is the drawing in, evolution is the giving out. All situations in the universe alternate between these two processes. When you see, hear, smell or taste nature, you breathe it in. What you see does not pass away without leaving a trace on you. The eye itself perishes, the object perishes, but [the fact] that you have seen something remains. You will understand now that at certain times it can be necessary for an understanding of these things to be available. We are going forward to an age when, as I recently indicated, understanding will reach right into the atom. It will be realized—by the popular mind too—that the atom is nothing else than congealed electricity. Thought itself is composed of the same substance.

Before the end of our present cultural epoch one will in fact have come so far that people will be able to penetrate into the atom itself. When one is able to grasp the materiality between the thought and the atom, then one will soon be able to understand how to penetrate the atom. And then nothing will be inaccessible to certain methods of working. A man standing here, let us say, will be able, by pressing a button concealed in his pocket, to [explode] some object at a great distance, let us say in Hamburg, just as wireless telegraphy is possible, by setting up a wave movement and causing it to take a particular form at some other place. This will be within man's power when the occult truth that thought and atom consist of the same substance, is applied to practical life.

It is impossible to conceive what might happen in such circumstances if mankind has not by then reached selflessness. Only through the attainment of selflessness will it be possible to preserve mankind from the brink of destruction. The downfall of post-Atlantean culture will be caused by the lack of morality. The Lemurian race was destroyed by fire, the Atlantean by water; ours will be destroyed by the War of All Against All, [by?] evil, by the struggle of men with one another. Humanity will destroy itself in mutual strife. And the despairing thing—more desperately tragic than other catastrophes—will be that the blame will lie with human beings themselves.

A tiny handful of men will be saved and will pass over into the sixth epoch. This tiny handful will have developed complete selflessness. The others will make use of every [imaginable] skill and subtlety in the penetration and conquest of the physical forces of nature, but without attaining the essential degree of selflessness. They will start the War of All Against All, and that will be the cause of the destruction of our civilization.

In the seventh post-Atlantean cultural epoch, to be precise, this War of All Against All will break out in the most terrible way. Great and mighty forces will ensue from discoveries that will turn the entire globe into a kind of self-functioning electrical apparatus. The tiny handful will be protected in a way that cannot be discussed.

Now you will be able to picture more clearly than was possible when I spoke of these things last time why the good [and proper] form must be sought and in what sense Freemasonry becomes aware that it must construct a building [dedicated to] selfless [ends]. It is easier to survive and pass over into the future—to the tiny handful of new humanity—with the good old forms, than out of chaos.

It is easy to jeer at empty forms, but they have a deep significance. They are adapted to the structure of our [period of] evolution. After all, they are connected with necessary stages in human nature and the development of the human soul. Just think of it: we are living in the fifth period of the fifth great post-Atlantean epoch;[6] we have still to live through two more periods of this great epoch. Then the seven periods of the sixth great epoch will follow and then the seven periods of the seventh great epoch. This makes 16 stages of evolution in the future. Humanity has still to pass through these 16 stages. A man who can experience something of the conditions [of existence] that are possible there is to a certain degree initiated. There is a certain correspondence between the degrees of initiation and the secrets of the epochs still to come.

In the 'form-state' of our planet there are seven great epochs and each of these epochs has seven sub-periods (cultural epochs)—49 conditions, therefore, in all. In the next 'form-state' of our planet there are again 49 conditions. Thus there are definite stages for the investigation of the secrets of future phases of evolution. The higher degrees of Freemasonry had no other aim or purpose, originally, than to be an expression of each one of the future stages of the evolution of humanity. Thus in Freemasonry we actually have something which has been very good, namely, that a man who had attained a certain degree knew how he must work his way into the future, so that he could be a kind of pioneer. He knew, too, that one who had reached a higher degree could accomplish more. This arrangement according to degrees can very well be made, for it corresponds with the facts.

If, therefore, it were again possible to pour a new content, together with a new knowledge, into these forms, much good would accrue. Freemasonry would then be imbued with real spirit once again. But content and form belong to the Whole. The state of affairs today is, as I have said: the degrees are there, but nobody has really worked through them. In spite of this, however, they are not there for nothing. They will be brought to life again in the future.

The fifth cultural epoch is a purely intellectual one, an epoch of egoism. We are now at the high point of egoism. The intellect is egoistical in the highest degree, and it is the hall-mark of our time. And so we must make our way upwards through intellect to spirituality, which was once there . . . [Gap]

The secret of secrets is this, therefore: the human being must learn how to keep silence about the paths along which his ego unfolds, and to regard his deeds, not his ego, as the criterion. The real heart of the secret lies in his deeds and the overcoming of the ego through action. The ego must remain concealed within the deed. Elimination of the interests of the ego from the onstreaming flow of karma—this belongs to the first degree. Whatever karma the ego incurs is thereby wiped out from karma. Nation, race, sex, position, religion—all these work upon human egoism. Only when mankind has overcome all these things will it be freed from egoism.

You can identify, in the astral body, a particular colour for every nation, every race, every epoch. You will always find a base-colour there, which the person has as a member of one of these classifications or categories. This [specific colour] must be eliminated. The Theosophical Society works to level out the colours of the astral bodies of its adherents. They must be of like colour, like in respect of the base-colour. This base colour gives rise to a certain substance . . . [Gap] . . . [called Kundalini, which holds together, within the human being, the forces that lead eventually to the spirit.][7]

Bringing this levelling-out about will actually entail bloody war, and through such things as economic strife among nations, wars of exploitation, financial and industrial enterprises, conquests, etc, and through the adoption of certain measures, it will be more and more possible to set masses of people in motion and simply to compel them. The individual will acquire more and more power over certain masses of people. For the drift of this development is not that we will become democratic, but that we will become brutally oligarchic in that the individual will gain more and more power. If the ennobling of morals is not achieved, then it will lead to the most brutal events. This will happen, just as catastrophe by water happened to the Atlanteans.

PART II

LECTURE 11

Concerning the Lost Temple and How it is to be Restored—I

(In connection with the Legend of the True Cross,
or Golden Legend)

Berlin, 15 May 1905

Today we will explain a great allegory, and deal with an object
that is known to occult science as the image or teaching of the
lost temple which has to be rebuilt. I have explained in earlier
lectures[1] why in occult science one starts from such images.
Today we shall see what an enormous number of ideas are
contained in essence in this image. Thereby I will also have to
touch upon a theme which is much misunderstood by those
who know little or nothing about theosophy. There are some
people who do not understand that theosophy and practical
[everyday things] go hand in hand, that they must work
together throughout the whole of life. Therefore I shall have to
speak about the connection between theosophy and the
practical things of life. For, basically, when we take up the
theme of the lost temple which has to be rebuilt we are
speaking about everyday work.

I shall, indeed, thereby be in the position of a teacher who
prepares his pupils for building a tunnel. The building of a
tunnel is something eminently practical. Someone might well
say: 'Building a tunnel is simple; one only has to start digging
into a hill from one side and to excavate away until one
emerges at the other side.' Everyone can see that it would be
foolish to think in this way. But in other realms of life that is

not always perceived. Whoever wishes to build a tunnel must, of course, first of all have a command of higher mathematics. Then he will have to learn how it is to be made, technically. Without practical engineering knowledge, without the art of ascertaining the right level, one would not be able to keep on course in excavating the mountain. Then one must know the basic concepts of geology, of the various rock strata, the direction of the water courses and the metallic lodes in the mountain, and so on. It would be foolish to think that someone would be able to build a tunnel without all this prior knowledge, or that an ordinary stonemason could construct a whole tunnel.

It would be just as foolish if one were to believe that one could begin building human society from the point of view of ordinary life. However, this folly is perpetrated not merely by many people, but also in countless books. Everyone today supposes himself to know and be entitled to decide how best to reform social life and the state. People who have hardly learnt anything write detailed books about how society should best be shaped, and feel themselves called upon to found reform movements. Thus there are movements for reform in all spheres of life. But everything done in this way is just the same as if someone were to try to cut a tunnel with hammer and chisel. That is all a result of not knowing that great laws exist which rule the world and spring forth out of the life of the spirit. The real problem of our day consists in this ignorance [of the fact] that there are great laws for the building of the state and of the social organism, just as there are for building a tunnel, and that one must know these laws in order to carry out the most necessary and everyday tasks in the social organism. Just as in building a tunnel one has to know about the interaction of all the forces of nature, so anyone wishing to start reforming society must know the laws [which interweave between one person and the next]. One must study the effect of one soul on another, and draw near to the spirit. That is why theosophy must lie at the basis of every practical activity in life. Theosophy is the real practical principle of life; and only he who starts from theosophical principles and carries them over into practical life can feel capable of being active in social life.

That is why theosophy should penetrate all spheres of life. Statesmen, social reformers and the like are nothing without a theosophical basis, without theosophical principles. That is why, for those who study these things, all work in this field, everything done today to build up the social structure, is external patchwork and complete chaos. For one who understands the matter, what the social reformer is doing today is like somebody cutting stones and piling them one on top of another in the belief that a house will thereby come into being of its own accord. First of all a plan of the house must be drawn up. It is just the same if one asserts that, in social life, things will take shape of their own accord. One cannot reform society without knowing the laws of theosophy.

This way of thinking, which works according to a plan, is called Freemasonry. The medieval Freemasons, who dealt with and made contracts with the clergy about how they should build, wanted nothing else than to shape outer life in such a way that—along with the Gothic cathedral—it could become an image of the great spiritual structure of the universe. Take the Gothic cathedral. Though composed of thousands of individual parts, it is built according to a single idea, much more comprehensive than the cathedral itself. To become complete in itself, divine life must flow into it, just as light shines into the church through the multi-coloured windows. And when the medieval priest spoke from the pulpit, so that the divine light shone in his listener's hearts just like the light shining through the coloured panes, then the vibrations set up through the preacher's word were in harmony with the great life of God. And the life of just such a sermon, born out of the life of the spirit, spread out further in the cathedral itself. In like manner, the whole of outer life should be transformed into the temple of the earth, into an image of the whole spiritual structure of the universe.

If we go still further back in time, we find that it is just this way of thinking which was that of mankind from the very earliest times. Let me explain what I mean by way of an example. Our epoch is the time of the chaotic interaction of one human being with another. Each individual pursues his own aims. This epoch was preceded by another one, the age of the ancient priestly states. I have often spoken about the cultural epochs of our fifth great epoch. The first of these was the Ancient Indian epoch, the second, that of the Medes and the Persians, the third, that of the Babylonians, the Assyrians, the Chaldeans, the Egyptians and the Semites, and the fourth was the Graeco-Roman period. We are now in the fifth epoch.

The fourth and fifth cultural epochs were the first ones to be based on the intelligence of men, of individual men. We have a great monument to the conquest of the old priestly culture by the intelligence of men in art, in the *Laocoön*.[2] The *Laocoön* priest entwined with serpents—the symbol of subtlety—symbolizes the conquest, by the civilization of intelligence, of the old priestly culture, which held other views about truth and wisdom, and about what should happen. It is the overcoming of the third cultural epoch by the fourth. That is represented in still another symbol, in the saga of the Trojan Horse. The intelligence of Odysseus created the Trojan Horse, by means of which the Trojan priestly culture was overthrown.

The development of the old Roman state out of the ancient Trojan priestly culture is described in the saga of Aeneas. The latter was one of the outstanding defenders of Troy, who afterwards came over to Italy. There it was that his descendants laid the foundation of ancient Rome. His son Ascanius founded Alba Longa and history now enumerates 14 kings up to the time of Numitor and Amulius. Numitor was robbed of his throne by his brother Amulius, his son was killed and his daughter, Rhea Silvia, was made to become a vestal virgin so that the lineage of Numitor should die out. And when Rhea gave birth to the twins Romulus and Remus, Amulius ordered them to be thrown in the Tiber. The children were rescued, suckled by a she-wolf, and brought up by the royal shepherd Faustulus.

Now history speaks about seven Roman kings: Romulus, Numa Pompilius, Tullus Hostilius, Ancus Martius, Tarquinius Priscus, Servius Tullius and Tarquinius Superbus.

Following Livy's account[3] it used to be believed that the first seven kings of Rome were real personalities. Today, historians know that these first seven kings never existed. We are therefore dealing with a saga, but the historians have no inkling of what lies behind it. The basis of the saga is what follows.

The priestly state of Troy founded a colony, the priestly colony of Alba Longa (*alba*, an alb, or priest's vestment).[4] It was a colony of a priestly state and Amulius belonged to the last priestly dynasty. A junior priestly culture sprang from this, which was then cut off by a civilization based on cleverness. History tells us no more about this priestly culture. The veil that was spread over the priestly culture of the earliest Roman history is lifted by theosophy. The seven Roman kings represent nothing else than the seven principles as we know them from theosophy. Just as the human organism consists of seven parts—sthula-sharira [physical body], linga-sharira [etheric], kama-rupa [astral], kama-manas [ego], higher manas [spirit-self], buddhi [life-spirit] and atma [spirit-man] so the social organism was conceived, as it took shape at the time, as a sequence in seven stages. And only if it was developed according to the law of the number seven, which lies at the base of all nature, was it able to prosper. Thus the rainbow has seven colours: red, orange, yellow, green, blue, indigo, violet. Likewise there are seven [intervals in the scale]: first, second, third, fourth, fifth, and so on; likewise the atomic weights in chemistry follow the rule of the number seven. And that permeates the whole of creation. Hence it was self-evident to the Guardians of the Ancient Wisdom that the structure of human society must also be regulated by such a law. According to a precisely worked out plan, these seven kings are seven stages, seven [integral] parts. This was the usual way of inaugurating a new epoch in history at that time. A plan was devised, since this was considered a means of preventing any stupidities, and a law was written for it. This plan was actually there at the beginning. Everyone knew that world history was guided according to a fixed plan. Everyone knew: When I am in the third phase of the fourth epoch, I must be guided by this and that. And so, at first, in ancient Rome, one still had a priestly state with a plan at the basis of its culture, which was written down in books called the Sibylline Books. These are nothing else than the original plan underlying the law of the sevenfold epoch, and they were still consulted when needed in the earliest days of the Roman Empire.

The physical body was taken as a model for the foundations. That is not so unreasonable. Today people are inclined to treat the physical body as something subordinate. People look down on the physical with a kind of disdain. However, that is not justified, because our physical body is our most exalted part. Take a single bone. Take a good look at the upper part of a thigh bone and you will see how wonderfully it is constructed. The best engineer, the greatest technician, could not produce anything so perfect, if he were set the task of attaining the greatest possible strength using the least amount of material. And so the whole human body is constructed in the most perfect way. This physical body is really the most perfect thing imaginable. An anatomist will always speak with the utmost admiration of the human heart, which functions in a wonderful way, even though human beings do little else throughout life than imbibe what is poison for it. Alcohol, tea, coffee and so on attack the heart in the most incredible fashion. But so wonderfully has this organ been built that it can withstand all this into ripe old age.

The physical body, the lowest of the bodies, therefore possesses the greatest perfection. Less perfect, on the other hand, are the higher bodies, which have not yet gained such perfection in their development. The etheric body and the astral body continually offend against our physical body through the attacks of our lust, desires and wishes. Then follows, as the fourth [principle], the real baby [of them all], the human ego, which like a wandering will-o'-the-wisp must still wait for the future to offer it those rules that will act as a guide for its conduct, just as the physical body was presented with rules a long time ago.

When we develop a social structure, we must have that which will make the foundations firm. Thus the saga allows Romulus, the first Roman king, who represents the first principle, to be raised to heaven as the god Quirinus. The second king, Numa Pompilius, the second principle, embodies social order; he brought laws for ordinary living. The third king, Tullus Hostilius, represents the passions. Under him, the attacks against divine nature begin, causing discord, struggle and war, through which Rome became great. Under the fourth king, Ancus Martius, the arts develop, those things which spring out of kama-manas [the human ego].

Now the four lower principles of man are not able to give birth to the three higher principles, the fifth, sixth and seventh. This is also symbolized in Roman history. The fifth Roman king, Tarquinius Priscus, was not engendered out of the Roman organism, but was introduced into Roman culture from the Etruscan culture as something higher. The sixth king, Servius Tullus, represents the sixth member of the human cyclic law, buddhi. He is able to rule over kama [the astral body], the physical-sensual counterpart of buddhi. He represents the canon of the law. The seventh king, Tarquinius Superbus, the most exalted principle, is he who must be overthrown, since it is not possible to maintain the high level, the impulse, of the social system.

We see it demonstrated in Roman history that there must be a plan underlying the building of the state, just as for any other building in the world. That the world is a temple, that social life must be structured and organized, and must have pillars like a temple, and that the great sages must be these pillars—it is this intention which is permeated with the ancient wisdom. That is not a kind of wisdom which is merely learned, but one which has to be built into human society. The seven principles were correctly applied. The only person able to work towards the building up of society is he who has absorbed all this knowledge, all this wisdom, into himself. We would not achieve much as theosophists if we were to restrict ourselves to contemplating how the human being is built up from its different members. No, we are only able to fulfil our task if we carry the principles of theosophy into everyday life. We must learn to put them to use in such a way that every turn of the hand, every movement of a finger, every step we take, bears the impress, is an expression of the spirit. In that case we shall be engaged in building the lost temple.

Along with that, however, goes the fact, which I mentioned recently, that we should take into ourselves something of the greatness and all-embracing comprehensiveness of the universal laws. Our habits of thought must be permeated by that kind of wisdom which leads from great conceptions into the details—just in the same way as house construction starts from the finished and complete plan and not by laying one stone upon another. This demand must be made if our world is not to turn into chaos. As theosophists we should recognize the fact that law is bound to rule in the world as soon as we realize that every step we make, every action of ours, is like an impression stamped in wax by the spiritual world. Then we shall be engaged in the building of the temple. That is the meaning of the temple building: whatever we set ourselves to do must be in conformity to law.

The knowledge that man has to include himself in the construction of the great world temple has become increasingly forgotten. A person can be born and die today without having any inkling of the fact that laws are working themselves out in us, and that everything we do is governed by the laws of the universe. The whole of present-day life is wasted, because people do not know that they have to live according to laws. Therefore the priestly sages of ancient times devised means of rescuing, for the new culture, something of the great laws of the spiritual world. It was, so to speak, a stratagem of the great sages to have hidden this order and harmony in many branches of life—yes, even so far as in the games which men use for their recreation at the end of the day. In playing cards, in the figures of chess, in the sense of rule by which one plays, we find a hint, if only a faint one, of the order and harmony that I have described. When you sit down with someone to a game of cards, it will not do if you do not know the rules, the manner of playing. And this really conveys a hint of the great laws of the universe. What is known as the sephirot of the Cabbala, what we know as the seven principles in their various forms, that is recognized again in the way in which the cards are laid down, one after the other, in the course of the game. Even in the allurements of playing, the Adepts have known how to introduce the great cosmic laws, so that, even in play, people have at least a smack of wisdom. At least for those who can play cards, their present incarnation is not quite wasted. These are secrets, how the great Adepts intervene in the wheel of existence. If one told people to be guided by the great cosmic laws, they would not comply. However, if the laws are introduced unnoticed into things, it is often possible to inject a drop of this attitude into them. If you have this attitude, then you will have a notion of what is symbolized in the mighty allegory of the lost temple.

In the secret societies, among which Freemasonry belongs, something connected with the lost temple and its future reconstruction has been described in the Temple Legend. The Temple Legend is very profound, but even the present-day Freemasons usually have no notion of it. A Freemason is not even very easy to distinguish from the majority of people, and he does not carry much of importance with him into the new life. But if he lets the Temple Legend work upon him, it is a great help. For whoever absorbs the Temple Legend receives something which, in a specific way, shapes his thinking in an orderly fashion. And it [all] depends on ordered thinking. This Temple Legend is as follows.

Once one of the Elohim united with Eve, and out of that Cain was born. Another of the Elohim, Adonai or Jehovah-Yahveh, thereupon created Adam. The latter, for his part, united with Eve, and out of this marriage Abel was born. Adonai caused trouble between those belonging to Cain's family and those belonging to Abel's family, and the result of this was that Cain slew Abel. But out of the renewed union of Adam with Eve the race of Seth was founded.

Thus we have two different races of mankind. The one consists of the original descendants of the Elohim, the sons of Cain, who are called the Sons of Fire. They are those who till the earth and create from inanimate nature and transform it through the arts of man. Enoch, one of the descendants of Cain, taught mankind the art of hewing stone, of building houses, of organizing society, of founding civilized communities. Another of Cain's descendants was Tubal-Cain, who worked in metal. The architect Hiram-Abiff was descended from the same race.

Abel was a shepherd. He held firmly to what he found, he took the world as it was. There is always this antithesis between people. One sticks to things as they are, the other wants to create new life from the inanimate, through art. Other nations have portrayed the ancestor of these Sons of

Fire in the Prometheus saga.[5] It is the Sons of Fire who have to work into the world the wisdom, beauty and goodness from the all-embracing universal thought, in order to transform the world into a temple.

King Solomon was a descendant of the lineage of Abel. He could not build the temple himself; he lacked the art. Hence he appointed the architect Hiram-Abiff, the descendant of the lineage of Cain. Solomon was divinely handsome. When the Queen of Sheba met him, she thought she saw an image of gold and ivory. She came to unite herself with him.

Jehovah is also called the God of created form,[6] the God who turns what is living into a living force, in contrast with that other Elohim who creates by charming life out of what is lifeless. To which of these does the future belong? That is the great question of the Temple Legend. If mankind were to develop under the religion of Jehovah, all life would expire in form. In occult science, that is called the Transition to the Eighth Sphere.[7] But the point in time has now arrived when man himself must awaken the dead to life. That will happen through the Sons of Cain, through those who do not rely on the things around them but are themselves the creators of new forms. The Sons of Cain themselves frame the building of the world.

When the Queen of Sheba saw the temple and asked who the architect was, she was told it was Hiram. And as soon as she saw him, he seemed to her to be the one who was pre-destined for her. King Solomon now became jealous; and indeed, he entered into league with three apprentices who had failed to achieve their master's degree, and sought to under-mine Hiram's great masterpiece, the Molten Sea. This great masterpiece was to be made by casting it. Human spirit was to have been united with the metal. Of the three apprentices, one was a Syrian mason, the second was a Phoenician carpenter, and the third was a Hebrew miner. The plot succeeded; the casting was destroyed by pouring water over it. It all blew apart. In despair the architect was about to throw himself into the heat of the flames. Then he heard a voice from the centre of the earth. This came from Cain himself, who called out to him: 'Take here the hammer of the world's divine wisdom, with which you must put it all right again.' And Cain gave him the hammer. Now it is the human spirit which man builds into his astral body if he is not to let it remain in the condition in which he received it. This is the work which Hiram now had to do. But there was a plot against his life. We shall proceed from there next time.

I wanted to recount the legend up to this point, to show how, in the original occult brotherhoods, the thought lived that man has a task to fulfil—the task of restructuring the inanimate world, of not being satisfied with what is already there. Wisdom thus becomes deed through its penetration of the inanimate world, so that the world should become a reflection of the original and eternal spirituality.

Wisdom, Beauty, Strength are the three fundamental words of all Freemasonry. So to change the outer world, that it becomes a garment for the spiritual—that is its task. Today, the Freemasons themselves no longer understand this, and believe that man should work on his own ego.[8] They regard themselves as particularly clever when they say that the working masons of the Middle Ages were not Freemasons. But the working masons were precisely those who have always been Freemasons, because outward structure was to become the replica of the spiritual, of the temple of the world, which is to be constructed out of intuitive wisdom. This is the thought which formerly underlay the great works of architecture, and was carried through into every detail.

I will illustrate by an example the superiority of wisdom over mere intellect. Let us take an old Gothic cathedral, and consider the wonderful acoustics, which cannot be matched today, because this profound knowledge has been lost.

The famous Lake Moeris in Egypt is just such a wonder-work of the human spirit. It was not a natural lake, but was constructed through the intuition of the wise men, so that water could be stored in time of flood, for distribution over the whole country in time of drought. That was a great feat of irrigation.

When man learns to create with the same wisdom with which the divine powers have created nature and made physical things, then will the temple be built [on earth]. It does not depend upon how many separate things we have the power to create out of our own wisdom; we must, however, just have the attitude of mind that knows that only by means of wisdom can the temple of humanity be created.

When, today, we go about the cities, here there is a shoe shop, there a chemist, further on a cheesemonger and a shop selling walking sticks. If just now we do not want anything, why should that concern us? How little does the outward life of such a city reflect what we feel, think and perceive! How very different it was in the Middle Ages. If a person walked through the streets then, he saw the house fronts built in the resident's style, manner and character. Every doorknob expressed what the man had lovingly shaped to suit his spirit. Go, for instance, through a town such as Nuremberg; there you will still find the basis of how it used to be. And then, by contrast, take the fashionable abstraction that no longer has anything to do with people. That is the age of materialism and its chaotic productions, to which one has step by step come from an earlier spiritual epoch.

Man was born from a nature which was once so formed by the gods that everything within it fitted the great scheme of the world, the great temple. There was once a time when there was nothing on this earth upon which you could gaze without having to say to yourself: Divine beings have built this temple to the stage in which the human physical body was perfected. Then the higher principles (the psychic forces) [of man's nature] took possession of it, and through this disarray and chaos came into the world. Wishes, desires and emotions brought disarray into the temple of the world. Only when, out of man's own will, law and order once again shall speak in a loftier and more beautiful way than the gods once did in creating nature, only when man allows the god within him to arise, so that like a god he can build towards the temple—only then will the lost temple be regained.

It would not be right if we were to think that only those who are able to build should do so. No, it depends upon the attitude of mind, even if one knows a great deal. If one has the right direction to one's thinking, and then one engages in social, technical and juristic reform, then one is building the lost temple which is to be rebuilt. But should one start reforms—however well-intended they may be—lacking this attitude of mind, then one is only bringing about more chaos. For the individual stone is useless if it does not fit into the overall plan [of the building]. Reform the law, religion, or anything else—as long as you only take account of the particular item without having an understanding of the whole, it only results in a demolition.

Theosophy is thus not just theory, but practice, the most practical thing in the world. It is a fallacy to suppose that theosophists are recluses, not engaged in shaping the world. If we could bring people to engage in social reform from a theosophical basis,[9] they would achieve much of what they want swiftly and surely. For, without needing to say anything against particular movements, they only lead to fanaticism if pursued in isolation. All separate reform movements— emancipators, abstainers, vegetarians, animal protectors and so forth—are only useful if they all work together. Their ideal can only be properly realized in a great universal movement that leads in unity to the universal world temple.

That is the idea that lies behind the allegory of the lost temple which has to be rebuilt.

Notes from replies to questions
Question: What is the difference between the Sons of Cain and the Sons of Abel?
Answer: The Sons of Cain are the unripe ones; the Sons of Abel are the over-ripe ones. The Sons of Abel turn to the higher spheres when they have finished with these incarnations. The Sons of Abel are the Solar Pitris [those who underwent their human stage on the Old Sun]; the Sons of Cain are the most mature of the Lunar Pitris [those who passed their human stage on the Old Moon].

Question: Why have so many mystical and Masonic associations developed?
Answer: All higher work is only to be undertaken in an association. The Knights of the Round Table generally numbered twelve.

Question: Are you acquainted with the work of Albert Schäffle?[10]
Answer: Albert Schäffle wrote a work about sociology, and the account he gives is much more Masonic than what emanates from the lodges of Freemasonry.

LECTURE 12

Concerning the Lost Temple and How it is to be Restored—II

(In connection with the Legend of the True Cross,
or Golden Legend)

Berlin, 22 May 1905

A few more reflections on the lost temple. We must regard Solomon's temple as the greatest symbol. Now the point is to understand this symbol. You know the course of events from the Bible, how it began. In this case, we are not dealing with mere symbols, but in fact with outward realities, in which, however, a profound world-historic symbolism finds its expression at the same time. And those who built the temple were aware of what it was meant to express.

Let us consider why the temple was built. And you will see that each word in the Bible's account of it[1] is a deeply significant symbol. In this you need only consider in what period the building was erected. Let us particularly recall the biblical explanation for what the temple was to be. Yahveh addressed this explanation to David: 'A house for My Name'—that is, a house for the name Yahveh. And now let us make clear what the name Yahveh signifies.

Ancient Judaism became quite clear, at a particular time, about the holiness of the name Yahveh. What does it mean? A child learns, at a certain moment in its life, to use the word 'I'. Before that, it regards itself as a thing. Just as it gives names to other things, so it even calls itself by an objective name. Only later does it learn to use the word 'I'. The moment in the lives of great personalities when they first experience their own 'I', when they first become aware of themselves, is charged with significance. Jean Paul recounts the following incident.[2] As a small boy he was once standing in a barn in a farmyard. At that moment he first experienced his own 'I'. And so serene and solemn was this instant for him, that he said of it: 'I then looked into my innermost soul as into the Holy of Holies.'

Mankind has developed through many epochs and everyone conceived themselves in this objective way up to Atlantean times; only during the Atlantean epoch did man develop to the stage where he could say 'I' to himself. The ancient Hebrews included this in their doctrines.

Man has passed through the kingdoms of nature. Ego consciousness rose in him last of all. The astral, etheric and physical bodies and the ego together form the Pythagorean square. And Judaism added thereto the divine ego which descends from above, in contrast to the ego from below. Thus, a pentagon has been made out of the square. This was how Judaism experienced the Lord God of its people, and it was therefore a sacred thing to utter the 'Name'. Whereas other names, such as 'Elohim' or 'Adonai', came increasingly into use, only the anointed priest in the Holy of Holies was allowed to utter the name 'Yahveh'.[3] It was in the time of Solomon that ancient Judaism came to the holiness of the name Yahveh, to this 'I' which can dwell in man. We must take Jehovah's challenge to man as something that sought to have man himself made into a temple of the most holy God. Now we have gained a new conception of the Godhead, namely this: the God which is hidden in man's breast, in the deepest holiness of man's self, must be changed into a moral God. The human body is thus turned into a great symbol of the Inner Sanctuary.

And now an outward symbol had to be erected, as man is God's temple. The temple had to be a symbol, illustrating man's own body. Therefore, builders were sent for—Hiram-

Abiff—who understood the practical arts that could transform man himself into a god. Two images in the Bible relate to this, one is Noah's Ark, and the other is the Temple of Solomon.[4] In one way both are the same, yet they also have to be distinguished.

Noah's Ark was built to preserve mankind for the present stage of human existence. Before Noah, man lived in the Atlantean and Lemurian epochs. At that time he had not built the ship which was to carry him across the waters of the astral world into earthly existence. Man came by the waters of the astral world, and Noah's Ark carried him over. The Ark represents the construction built by unconscious divine forces. From the measurements given, its proportions correspond to those of the human body and also with those of Solomon's temple.[5]

Man has developed beyond Noah's Ark, and now he has to surround his higher self with a house created by his own spirit, by his own wisdom, by the wisdom of Solomon.

We enter the Temple of Solomon. The door itself is characteristic. The square used to function as an old symbol. Mankind has now progressed from the stage of fourfoldness to that of fivefoldness, as five-membered man who has become conscious of his own higher self. The inner divine temple is so formed as to enclose the fivefold human being. The square is holy. The door, the roof and the side pillars together form a pentagon.[6, 7] When man awakens from his fourfold state, that is, when he enters his inner being—the inner sanctuary is the most important part of the temple—he sees a kind of altar. We perceive two cherubim which hover, like two guardian spirits, over the Ark of the Covenant, the Holy of Holies, for the fifth principle [of man's being], which has not yet descended to earth, must be guarded by the two higher beings buddhi and manas. Thus man enters the stage of manas development.

The whole inner sanctuary is covered in gold, because gold has always been the symbol of wisdom. Now wisdom enters the manas stage. We find palm leaves as the symbol of peace. That represents a particular epoch of humanity, and is inserted here as something that only came to expression later, in Christianity. The temple leaders guarded this within themselves, in this way expressing something intended for later developments.

Later, in the Middle Ages, the idea of Solomon's temple was revived again in the Knights Templars,[8] who sought to introduce the temple thinking in the West. But the Knights Templars were misunderstood at that time (e.g. trial of Jacques Molay, their Grand Master). If we wish to understand the Templars, we must look deeply into human history. What the Templars were reproached with in their trial rests entirely on a major misunderstanding. The Knights Templars said at the time: 'Everything we have experienced so far is a preparation for what the Redeemer has wished for. For,' they continued, 'Christianity has a future, a new task. And we have the task of preparing the various sects of the Middle Ages, and humanity generally, for a future in which Christianity will emerge into a new clarity, as the Redeemer actually intended that it should. We saw Christianity rise in the fourth cultural epoch; it will develop further in the fifth, but only in the sixth is it to celebrate the glory of its resurrection. We have to prepare for that. We must guide human souls in such a way that a genuine, true and pure Christianity may come to expression, in which the Name of the Most High may find its dwelling place.'

Jerusalem was to be the centre and from there the secret concerning the relationship of man to the Christ should stream out all over the world. What was represented symbolically by the temple should become a living reality. It was said of the Templars, and this was a reproach to them, that they had instituted a kind of star-worship, or, similarly, a sun-worship. However, a great mystery lies behind this. The sacrament of the Mass was originally nothing else but a great mystery. Mass fell into two parts: the so-called Minor Mass, in which all were allowed to take part; and when that had ended and the main body [of the congregation] had gone away, there followed the High Mass, which was intended only for those who wished to undergo occult training, to embark on the 'Path'. In this High Mass the reciting of the Apostolic Creed took place first. Then was expounded the development of Christianity throughout the world, and how it was connected with the great march of world evolution.

The conditions on earth were not always the same as today. The earth was once joined to the sun and the moon. The sun separated itself, as it were, and then shone upon the earth from outside. Later, the moon split away. Thus, in earlier times, the earth was quite a different kind of dwelling place for man. Man was quite different physically, at that time. But when the sun and the moon split off from the earth, the whole of man's life underwent a change. Birth and death took place for the first time, man reincarnated for the first time, and for the first time the ego of man, the individuality, descended into the physical body, to reincarnate in continuous succession. One day that will cease again. The earth will again become joined to the sun, and then man will be able to pass through his further evolution on the sun. Thus we have a specific series of steps, according to which the sun and man move together. Such things are connected with the progress of the sun across the vault of heaven.

Now everything that happens in the world is briefly recapitulated in the following stages. Everything has been repeated, including the evolution of the global stages in the first, second and third great epochs.* It came about, then, that man descended into reincarnation. The sun split away [from the earth] during the time of transition from the second to the third great epoch, the moon became separated during the third

---

* See scheme at the end of the notes to Lecture 10.

epoch [Lemuria]. Now the earth develops from the third to the sixth epoch, when the sun will again be joined to the earth. Then a new epoch will start in which man will have attained a much higher stage and will no longer incarnate.

This teaching concerning the course of evolution came into the world through religion in the shape of the story of Noah's Ark. In this teaching, what was to happen in the future was foreshadowed. The union of the sun with the earth is fore-shadowed in the appearance of Christ on earth. It is always so with such teachings. For a time what happens is a repetition of the past, then the teaching begins to be a prefiguring of the future. Each individual cultural epoch, as it relates to the evolution of consciousness for each nation, is connected with the progression of the sun through the zodiac.

You know that the time of transition from the third to the fourth cultural epoch was represented by the sign of the Ram or Lamb. The Babylonian-Assyrian epoch gathered together in the sign of the Bull all that was important for its time. The previous Persian age was characterized by the sign of the Twins. And if we go still further into the past we would come to the sign of the Crab for the Sanskrit culture. This epoch, in which the sun was in Cancer at the time of the spring equinox, was a turning-point for humanity. Atlantis had been sub-merged and the first Sub-Race [cultural epoch] of the fifth great epoch had begun. This turning-point was denoted by the Crab. The next cultural epoch similarly begins with the tran-sition of the sun into the sign of the Twins. A further stage of history leads us over into the culture of Asia Minor and Egypt, as the sun passes into the sign of the Bull. And as the sun continues its course through the zodiac the fourth cultural epoch begins, which is connected in Greek legend with the Ram or Lamb (the saga of Jason and the search for the Golden Fleece). And Christ Himself was, later on in early Christian times, represented by the Lamb. He called Himself the Lamb.

We have traced the time from the first to the fourth cultural epoch.[9] The sun proceeds through the heavens, and now we enter the sign of the Fishes, where we are ourselves at a critical point. Then [in the future], in the time of the sixth epoch, the time will arrive when man will have become so inwardly purified that he himself becomes a temple for the divine. At that time the sun will enter the sign of the Water Carrier. Thus the sun, which is really only the external expression of our spiritual life, progresses in heavenly space. When the sun enters the sign of the Water Carrier at the spring equinox, it will then be understood completely clearly for the first time.

Thus proceeded the High Mass, from which all the uninitiated were excluded. It was made clear to those who remained that Christianity, which began as a seed, would in the future bear something quite different as fruit, and that by the name Water Carrier was meant John [the Baptist] who scatters Christianity as a seed, as if with a grain of mustard seed. Aquarius or the Water Carrier points to the same person as John who baptized with water in order to prepare mankind to receive the Christian baptism of fire. The fact of the coming of a 'John/Aquarius' who will first confirm the old John and announce a Christ who will renew the temple, once the great point of time should have arrived when Christ will again speak to humanity—this was taught in the depths of the Templar Mysteries, so that the event should be understood.

Moreover, the Templars said: Today we live at a point in time when men are not yet ripe for understanding the great teachings; we still have to prepare them for the Baptist, John, who baptizes with water. The Cross was held up before the would-be Templar and he was told: You must deny the Cross now, so as to understand it later; first become a Peter, first deny the scriptures, like Peter the Rock who denied the Lord. That was imparted to the aspirant Templar as a preliminary training.

People generally understand so little of all this that even the letters on the Cross are not interpreted aright. Plato said of it that the world soul is crucified on the world body.[10] The Cross symbolizes the four elements. The plant, animal and human kingdoms are built out of these four elements. On the Cross stands: JAM = water = *James*; NOUR = fire, which refers to *Jesus* himself; RUACH = air, the symbol for *John*; and the fourth JABESCHAH = earth or rock, for *Peter*.

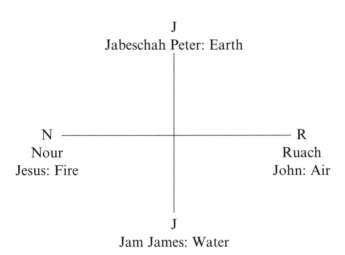

Thus there stands on the Cross what is expressed in the names of the [three] Apostles [and Jesus], while the one name J.N.R.I. denotes Christ Himself. 'Earth' is the place where Christianity itself must at first be brought, to that temple to which man himself has brought himself so as to be a sheath for what is higher. But this temple ... [Gap in text][11]

The cock, which is the symbol for both man's higher and lower selves, 'crows twice' [Mark 14:30]. The cock crows for the first time when man descends [to earth] and becomes materialized in physical substance; it crows for the second time when man rises again, when he has learnt to understand Christ, when the Water Carrier appears. That will be in the sixth cultural epoch. Then man will understand spiritually what he should become. The ego will have attained a certain stage then, when what Solomon's temple stands for will be reality in the highest sense, when man himself is a temple for Yahveh.

Before that, however, man still has to undergo three stages of purification. The ego is in a threefold sheath: firstly, in the astral body; secondly, in the etheric body; thirdly in the physical body.

When we are in the astral body, we deny the divine ego for the first time, for the second time in the etheric body, and for the third time in the physical body. The first crow of the cock is threefold denial through the threefold sheath of man. And when he has then passed through the three bodies, when the ego discovers in Christ its greatest symbolical realization, then the cock crows for the second time.

This struggle to raise oneself up to a proper understanding of Christ, first passing through the stage of Peter—none of the Templars, who were put under torture at that time, was able to convey these profound thoughts to their judges, thoughts which, first passing through the stage of Peter, raised them to an actual understanding of the Christ.

At the outset, the Templars were in a position, as if they had abjured the Cross. After all of this had been made clear to the Templar, he was shown a symbolical figure of the Divine Being in the form of a venerable man with a long beard (symbolizing the Father). When men have developed and have come to receive in the Master a leader from among themselves, when those are there who are able to lead humanity, then, as the Word of the guiding Father, there will stand before men the Master who leads men to the comprehension of Christ.

And then it was said to the Templars: When you have understood all this, you will be ripe for joining in building the great temple of the earth; you must so co-operate, so arrange everything, that this great building becomes a dwelling place for our true deeper selves, for our inner Ark of the Covenant.

If we survey all this, we find images having great significance. And he in whose soul these images come alive will become more and more fit to become a disciple of those great Masters who are preparing the building of the temple of mankind. For such great concepts work powerfully in our souls, so that we thereby undergo purification, so that we are led to abounding life in the spirit.

We find the same medieval tendency as manifested in the Knights Templars, in two Round Tables as well, that of King Arthur and that of the Holy Grail. In King Arthur's Round Table can be found the ancient universality, whereas the spirituality proper to Christian knighthood had to be prepared in those who guarded the Mystery of the Holy Grail. It is remarkable how calmly and tranquilly medieval people contemplated the developing power (fruit) and outward form of Christianity.

When you follow the teaching of the Templars, there at the heart of it is a kind of reverence for something of a feminine nature. This femininity was known as the Divine Sophia, the Heavenly Wisdom. Manas is the fifth principle, the spiritual self of man, that must be developed, for which a temple must be built. And, just as the pentagon at the entrance to Solomon's temple characterizes the fivefold human being, this female principle similarly typifies the wisdom of the Middle Ages. This wisdom is exactly what Dante sought to personify in his Beatrice. Only from this viewpoint can Dante's *Divine Comedy* be understood. Hence you find Dante, too, using the same symbols as those which find expression in the Templars, the Christian knights, the Knights of the Grail, and so on. Everything that is to happen [in the future] was indeed long since prepared for by the great initiates, who foretell future events, in the same way as in the Apocalypse, so that souls will be prepared for these events.

According to legend we have two different currents when humanity came to the earth. The Children of Cain, whom one of the Elohim begat through Eve, the Children of the Earth, in whom we find the great arts and external sciences—that is one of the currents. It was banished, but is however to be sanctified by Christianity when the fifth principle comes into the world. The other current is that of the Children of God, who have led man towards an understanding of the fifth principle. They are the ones that Adam created. Now the Sons of Cain were called upon to create an outer sheath, to contain what the Sons of God, the Abel-Seth Children, created.

In the Ark of the Covenant lies concealed the Holy Name of Yahveh. However, what is needed to transform the world, to create the sheath for the Holy of Holies, must be accomplished again through the Sons of Cain. God created man's physical body, into which man's ego works, at first destroying this temple. Man can only be rescued if he first builds the house to carry him across the waters of the emotions—if he builds Noah's Ark for himself. This house must set man on his feet again. Now those who came into the world as the Children of Cain are building the outward part, and what the Children of God have brought to it is building the inner part.

These two streams were already current when our race began ... [Gap][12]

So we shall only understand theosophy when we look upon it as a testament laying the ground for what the Temple of Solomon denotes, and for what the future holds in store. We have to prepare for the New Covenant, in place of the Old Covenant. The old one is the Covenant of the creating God, in which God is at work on the temple of mankind. The New Covenant is the one in which man himself surrounds the divine with the temple of wisdom, when he restores it, so that this 'I' will find a sanctuary on this earth when it is resurrected out of matter, set free.

So profound are the symbols, and so was the instruction,

that the Templars wanted to be allowed to confer upon mankind. The Rosicrucians are none other than the successors to the Order of the Templars, wanting nothing else than the Templars did, which is also what theosophy desires: they are all at work on the great temple of humanity.

LECTURE 13

Concerning the Lost Temple and How it is to be Restored—III

(In connection with the Legend of the True Cross, or Golden Legend)

Berlin, 29 May 1905

Since we have spoken several times about Christianity and its present and future development, we have reached the point where today we have also to consider the meaning of the Cross symbol—not so much historically as factually.

You know, of course, what an all-embracing and symbolical meaning the emblem of the Cross has had for Christianity; and today I would like just to shed light on the connection between the Cross symbol and the significance of Solomon's temple for world history.

Indeed there exists a so-called holy legend about the whole development of the Cross; in it we are dealing less with the Cross sign or its universal symbolical meaning than with that very special and particular Cross of which Christ speaks, the very Cross on which Christ Jesus was crucified. Now you know too that the Cross is a symbol for all men and it is found not only in Christianity but in the religious beliefs and symbolism of all peoples so that it must have the same common significance for all mankind. However, what particularly interests us today is how the Cross symbol acquired its basic significance for Christianity.

The Christian legend about the Cross[1] is as follows: we shall begin with it.

The wood or tree from which the Cross had been taken is not ordinary wood, but—so the legend relates—was, in the beginning, a scion of the Tree of Life, which had been cut for Adam, the first man. This scion was planted in the earth by Adam's son, Seth, and the young tree developed three trunks which grew together. The famous rod of Moses[2] was later cut from this wood. Then, in the legend, the same wood plays a role in connection with King Solomon's temple in Jerusalem. That is, it was to have been used as a main pillar, in building the temple. But then something peculiar came to light. It appeared that it would not fit in any way. It would not let itself be inserted in the temple, and so it was laid across a brook, as a bridge. Here it was little valued until the Queen of Sheba came; as she was crossing it, she saw what the wood of the bridge signified. She realized for the first time what it meant that the wood formed a bridge to cross over the stream from this side to the other. After that the Cross upon which the Redeemer hung was made of this same wood, and then it set out upon its various further travels.

Thus you see that the point of this legend is to do with the origin and evolution of the human race. Adam's son Seth is supposed to have taken this scion from the Tree of Life, and it then grew three trunks. These three trunks symbolize the three principles, the three underlying forces of nature, atma, buddhi and manas, which have grown together and form the trinity which is the foundation of all growth and all development. It is apt that Seth—the son of Adam who took the place of Abel, murdered by Cain—should have planted the scion in the earth.

You know that on the one hand we are dealing with the Cain current [of evolution] and on the other hand with the descendants of Abel and Seth. The Sons of Cain, who work upon the outer world, cultivate the sciences and arts in particular. They are the ones who bring in the stones from the outer world to build the temple. It is through their art that the temple is to be built. The descendants of the line of Abel/Seth are the so-called Sons of God, who cultivate the true spiritual part of man's nature. These two currents were always somewhat in antithesis. On the one hand we have the worldly activity of man, the development of those sciences which serve man's comfort and outward life in general; on the other hand we have the Sons of God, occupied with the development of man's higher attributes.

We must become clear about it. The viewpoint from which the legend of the True Cross springs makes a firm distinction between the mere outward building of the world temple through science and technology and what as religious element works towards the sanctification of the whole temple of humanity. Only because this temple of humanity is given a higher task—only because the outer building, so to speak, serving as it does only our convenience, makes itself into an expression of the House of God—can it become a receptacle for the spiritual inner part in which the higher tasks of humanity are nurtured. Only because strength is transformed into striving for heavenly virtue, outward form into beauty, the words of man's ordinary intercourse into the words that serve divine wisdom, and thus only because the worldly is remodelled to become divine, can it attain its perfection. When the three virtues, Wisdom, Beauty and Strength, become the receptacle of the divine, then will the temple of humanity be perfected. That is how the viewpoint underlying this legend looks at the matter.

We must therefore picture—quite in the sense of this legend—that until the appearance of Christ Jesus on earth there were two tendencies. The one was building the earthly temple, and had its impact on the doings of men, so that at a later time the Divine Word that was to come to earth through the Christ Jesus could be received. A dwelling had to be prepared for the appearance of the Divine Word on earth. Alongside that the Divine itself should for a while evolve upwards over the course of time as a kind of parallel tendency to the second current. Hence a distinction is made between the Sons of Men, the descendants of Cain, who were to prepare the worldly aspect, and the Sons of Abel/Seth, who cultivated the divine aspect, until the two streams could be united with each other. Christ Jesus united these two streams. The temple had first to be built outwardly, therefore, until, in the shape of Christ Jesus, He should arrive who was able to raise it up again in three days. On the one hand, then, we have the current of the Sons of Cain, and on the other that of the Abel/Seth line, both of which are preparing the development of mankind, so that the Son of God can then unite the two sides and make the two streams into one. This finds expression in the holy legend in a profound way.

Seth himself is the one who planted the scion that he had taken for Adam from the Tree of Life, and raised a tree with three trunks. What is the meaning of this triple-stemmed tree? Nothing else at all than the trinity atma, buddhi and manas, the threefold higher nature of man which will be implanted in his lower principles. But within man this is veiled at first. Through his three bodies—physical, etheric and astral—man is at first like an outer covering for the real divine trinity, atma, buddhi and manas. You must imagine, therefore, that the trinity of physical, etheric and astral body are like an outer representation of the higher forces of atma, buddhi and manas. And just as the artist fashions outer forms or expresses a certain idea in colours, so these three coverings also express a work of art. If you conceive these higher principles as the idea of a work of art, you will have come half-way to grasping how the life of these three bodies is made up.

Now man is indeed living in his physical, etheric and astral sheaths, together with his 'I', through which he will so transform his threefold nature that the three higher principles find their appropriate dwelling place and feel at home here on earth. That had to be provided for by the Old

Covenant. Through the arts of the race of Cain, it had to bring Sons of Men into the world, and through these Sons of Men were to be produced all the outward things that would serve the physical, etheric and astral bodies. What outward things were these?

The things which serve the physical body are firstly all that is contrived by technology to satisfy the physical body and provide for its comfort. Then, what we have in the way of the social and political institutions that [regulate] men's living together, what relates to nourishment and reproduction [of the race], all serve the development of the etheric body. And working upon the astral body we have the sphere of moral codes and ethics, bringing the instincts and emotions under control, which regulate and raise up the astral nature to a higher stage.

Thus, during the Old Covenant, the Sons of Cain were building the three-tiered temple. In all this, since it is made up of our outer institutions—in which you can include our dwellings and tools, the social and political organs, the system of morals—is the building of the Sons of Cain that serves the lower members of man's nature.

The other tendency worked alongside, presided over by the Sons of God, their pupils and followers. From this stream come the servants of the divine world order, the attendants of the Ark of the Covenant. In them we find something which, as a separate current, runs parallel to [that of] those who serve the external world. They occupied a special position. Only after Solomon's Temple had been erected was the Ark of the Covenant to be placed inside it; that is to say, everything else had to be made subservient to the Ark of the Covenant, to be arranged around it. Everything which was formerly of a worldly nature was to become an external expression, an outer covering, for what the Ark of the Covenant meant for mankind. The meaning of the Temple of Solomon will best be understood by whoever visualizes it as something that expresses outwardly in its physiognomy what the Ark of the Covenant should be in its soul nature.

What has given life to man's outward three bodies has been taken by the Sons of God from the Tree of Life. That is symbolically expressed in that building-wood later used for Christ's Cross. It was first given to the Sons of God. What did they do with it? What is the deeper meaning of the wood of the Cross? In this holy legend about the wood of the Cross lies a very deep meaning.

For what in general is the task of the human being in his earthly evolution? He has to raise the present three bodies with which he is endowed to a higher stage. Thus, he must raise his physical body to a higher realm and likewise his etheric and astral bodies. This development is incumbent upon humanity. That is the real sense of it: to transform our three bodies into the three higher members of the whole divine plan of creation.

There is another kingdom above that which man has immediately and physically around him. But to which kingdom does man in his physical nature belong? At the present stage of his evolution he belongs with his physical nature to the mineral kingdom. Physical, chemical and mineral laws hold sway over man's physical body. Yet even as far as his spiritual nature is concerned he belongs to the mineral kingdom, since he understands through his intellect only what is mineral. Life, as such, he is only gradually learning to comprehend. Precisely for this reason, official science disowns life, being still at that stage of development in which it can only grasp the dead, the mineral. It is in the process of learning to understand this in very intricate detail. Hence it understands the human body only in so far as it is a dead, mineral thing. It treats the human body basically as something dead with which one works, as if with a substance in a chemical laboratory. Other substances are introduced into [the body] in the same way that substances are poured into a retort. Even when the doctor, who nowadays is brought up entirely on mineral science, sets about working on the human body, it is as though the latter were only an artificial product.

Hence we are dealing with man's body at the stage of the mineral kingdom in two ways. Man has acquired reality in the mineral kingdom through having a physical body, and with his intellect is only able to grasp facts relating to the mineral kingdom. This is a necessary transitional stage for man. However, when man no longer relies only on the intellect but also upon intuition and spiritual powers, we will then be aware that we are moving into a future in which our dead mineral body will work towards becoming one that is alive. And our science must lead the way, must prepare for what has to happen with the bodily essence in the future. In the near future, it must itself develop into something which has life in itself, recognize the life inherent in the earth for what it is. For in a deeper sense it is true, it is the thoughts of man that prepare the future. As an old Indian aphorism rightly says: What you think today, that you will be tomorrow.

The very being of the world springs out of living thought, not from dead matter. Outward matter is a product of living thought, just as ice is a product of water. The material world is, as it were, frozen thoughts. We must dissolve it back again into its higher elements, because we grasp life in thought. If we are able to lead the mineral up into life, if we transform [it into] the thoughts of the whole of human nature, then we will have succeeded—our science will have become a science of the living and not of dead matter. We shall raise thereby the lowest principle [of man]—at first in our understanding, and later also in reality—into the next sphere. And thus we shall raise each member of man's nature, the etheric and the astral included, one stage higher.

What man formerly used to be we call, in theosophical terminology, the three elemental kingdoms [See the chart at the end of the notes to Lecture 10]. These preceded the mineral kingdom in which we live today—that is, the kingdom to which our science restricts itself, and in which our physical body lives. The three elemental kingdoms are bygone stages [of evolution]. The three higher kingdoms—the plant kingdom, the animal kingdom and the human kingdom—which will develop out of the mineral kingdom, are as yet only at a rudimentary stage.

The lowest principle in man [the physical body] must indeed still pass through these three kingdoms, just as it is at present passing through the mineral kingdom. Just as today man lives in the mineral kingdom with his physical nature, so in the future he will live in the plant kingdom, and then rise to still higher kingdoms. Today with our physical nature we are in a transitional stage between the mineral and plant kingdoms, with our etheric nature in transition from the plant kingdom to the animal kingdom, and with our astral nature in transition from the animal kingdom to the human kingdom. And finally, we extend beyond the three kingdoms into the divine kingdom with that part which we have in the Sphere of Wisdom, where we extend in our own nature beyond the astral.

Thus man is engaged in an ascent. This is not brought about by any outer contrivance or construction, but by the living self which is awakened in us. This does not use mere outward building stones, but works in a creative and growing way. This force of life must enter into evolution and must first take hold of man's innermost being; his religious life must be gripped by living forces. Therefore what the Sons of Cain did for the lower members of man's nature during the Old Covenant was a kind of preparation, and what the prophets, the guardians of the Ark of the Covenant, did was like a prophetic forecast of the future. The Divine should now descend into the Ark of the Covenant, into the soul, so that it may itself dwell in the Temple as Holy of Holies.

Adam, the first man, was already endowed, from the Tree of Life, with these living forces of metamorphosis and transformation, the creatively working forces that reshape nature. But [these forces] were entrusted to those not engaged in the work of outward building, to the Sons of God, the Sons of Abel and Seth. Through Christianity, these forces should now become common property; the two streams should unite together. And it is basically a Christian attitude today which holds that nothing external, no temple, no house, no social institution, ought to be created that is not irradiated with inner life, with the life-giving force rather than the mineral force that can only manipulate things.

The first attempt which was made to guide the lower nature of man to a higher stage was Solomon's temple, as we have seen. The pentagon was to be seen at the entrance as the great symbol, for man was to strive towards the fifth principle [of his nature]. That is to say, human nature had to raise itself up from the lower principles to the higher; each member [of man's being] was to be ennobled.

And here we come to the Cross's real meaning, which has led it to acquire such basic and real significance as a symbol of Christianity. What is the Cross? There are three kingdoms towards which mankind is striving—the plant kingdom, the animal kingdom and the human kingdom. Today man finds his reality in the mineral kingdom, to which plants, animals and man belong. You should see it as it is meant in all creeds of wisdom, that man as a being of soul and spirit is a part of the universal soul, the world soul as Giordano Bruno, for example, called it.[3] Perhaps the individual soul is like a drop in the world soul which we can imagine as a great ocean. Now Plato said about this that the world-soul has been crucified on the world-body.[4]

The world-soul, as it is expressed in man, is spread out over the mineral kingdom. It must raise itself above this, and evolve upwards to the three higher kingdoms. Hence it must become incorporated in the plant, animal and human kingdoms during the next three Rounds. The fourth Round is nothing else than the incorporation of the human soul into the mineral kingdom, the fifth Round into the plant kingdom, the sixth into the animal kingdom, and finally the seventh Round is the embodiment of man into the human kingdom proper, in which man will become wholly an image of the Godhead. Until then man has to take the world body as his sheath three times.

If we take a look at mankind's future, it presents itself to us as threefold materiality—vegetable, animal and human. This human [substance] is not the same, however, as the substantiality we have today; for the latter is mineral, since man has indeed so far only arrived at the mineral cycle [in his evolution]. Only when the lowest kingdom has [become] the human kingdom, when there are no more lower beings, when all beings have been redeemed by man through the force of his own life, then he will have arrived in the seventh Round, where God rests, because man himself creates. Then will have come the seventh Day of Creation, in which man will have taken on the likeness of God. These are the stages in the story of creation.

Now plant, animal and man, as they stand before us today, are only the germ of what they are to become. The plant of today is only a symbolical indication of something that is to appear in the next human evolutionary cycle in greater glory and clarity. And when man has overcome and stripped off animality, he will have become something of which today he is only a hint. Thus the plant, animal and human kingdoms are the three material kingdoms through which man has to pass; they are to be world body, and the soul has to be crucified on this world body.

Be clear from now on about the respective positions of plant, animal and man. The plant is the precise counterpart of man. There is a very deep and significant meaning in our conceiving the plant as the exact counterpart of man, and man as the inverse of plant nature. Outer science does not concern itself with such matters; it takes things as they present themselves to the outer senses. Science connected with theosophy, however, considers the meaning of things in their connection to all the rest of evolution. For, as Goethe says,[5] each thing must be seen only as a parable.

The plant has its roots in the earth and unfolds its leaves and blooms to the sun. At present the sun has in itself the force which was once united with the earth. The sun has of course separated itself from our earth. Thus the entire sun forces are something with which our earth was at one time permeated; the sun forces then lived in the earth. Today the plant is still searching for those times when the sun forces were still united with the earth, by exposing its flowering system to those forces. The sun forces are the [same as those which work as] etheric forces in the plants. By presenting its reproductive organs to the sun, the plant shows its deep affinity with it; its reproductive principle is occultly linked with the sun forces. The head of the plant [the root], which is embedded in the darkness of the earth, is on the other hand similarly akin to the earth. Earth and sun are the two polar opposites in evolution.

Man is the inverse of the plant; [the plant] has its generative organs turned towards the sun and its head pointing downwards. With man it is exactly the opposite; he carries his head on high, orientated towards the higher worlds in order to receive the spirit—his generative organs are directed downwards. The animal stands half-way between plant and man. It has made a half-turn, forming, so to speak, a crosspiece to the line of direction of both plant and man. The animal carries its backbone horizontally, thus cutting across the line formed by plant and man to make a cross. Imagine to yourselves the plant kingdom growing downward, the human kingdom upward, and the animal kingdom thus horizontally; then you have formed the cross from the plant, animal and human kingdoms.

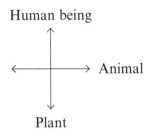

Human being

Animal

Plant

That is the symbol of the Cross.

It represents the three kingdoms of life, into which man has to enter. The plant, animal and human kingdoms are the next three material kingdoms [to be entered by man]. The whole evolves out of the mineral kingdom; this is the basis today. The animal kingdom forms a kind of dam between the plant and human kingdoms, and the plant is a kind of mirror image of man. This ties up with human life—what lives in man physically—finding its closest kinship with what lives in the plant. It would take many lectures to confirm that thoroughly; today I can only hint at it. When man wants to maintain his physical life activity he can best do so with a plant diet, since he would then be consuming what originally had an affinity with the physical life activity of the earth. The sun is the bearer of the life forces, and the plant is what grows in response to the sun forces. And man must unite what lives in the plant with his own life forces. Thus his foodstuffs are, occultly, the same as the plant. The animal kingdom acts as a dam, a drawing back, thereby interposing itself *cross*wise against the development process, in order to begin a new flow.

Man and plant, while set against each other, are mutually akin; whereas the animal—and all that comes to expression in the astral body is the animal—is a crossing of the two principles of life. The human etheric body will provide the basis, at a higher stage, for the immortal man, who will no longer be subject to death. The etheric body at present still dissolves with the death of the human being. But the more man perfects and purifies himself from within, the nearer will he get to permanence, the less will he perish. Every labour undertaken for the etheric body contributes towards man's immortality. In this sense it is true that man will gain more mastery of immortality the more the evolution that takes place naturally in him is directed towards the forces of life—which does not mean towards animal sexuality and passion.

Animality is a current that breaks across human life; it was a retardation, necessary for a turning-point in the stream of life. Man had to combine with animality for a while, because this turning-point had to take place. But he must free himself from it again and return again to the stream of life.

At the beginning of our human incarnations on earth we were endowed with the force of life. That is symbolically expressed in the legend where Adam's son Seth took the scion from the Tree of Life; this was then further cultivated by the Sons of God and is an expression of that threefold human nature, which has to be ennobled. After that, Moses cut his rod from this wood of life. This rod of Moses is nothing else than the external law. But what is external law?

External law is present when someone who has to erect an external building has a plan, that is, a systematic scheme on paper; so the outward building stones can be shaped and fitted together according to the plan. Thus, the law underlying the plan of a state is external law. Mankind is under Moses' rod. And anyone who follows a moral code out of fear or in hope of reward is only following the external law. Moreover, whoever looks at science only in an external way is only following external law, for what else can there [then] be in it but external laws! All the laws we are acquainted with in science are such external laws; through them, however, we will never find the way to higher human nature but will only follow the law of the Old Covenant, which is the rod of Moses. However, this external law should be a model for the inner law. Man must learn inwardly to follow law. This inner law must become for man the impulse of life; out of the inner law he must learn to follow external law. One does not make the inner law reality by concocting a plan; instead one has to build the temple out of inner impulse, so that the soul streams forth in the work of joining the stones together. He who lives in the inner law is not the one who merely follows the laws of the state but they are the impulse of his life because his soul is immersed in them. And it is not he who follows a moral code out of fear or because of reward who is a moral person, but he who follows it because he loves it.

As long as mankind was not ripe for following the law inwardly, as long as man was under a yoke, and the rod of Moses was present, in the law, so long would the law lie in the Ark of the Covenant—until the Pauline principle of grace came to man, giving him the possibility of becoming free from the law. The profundity of the Pauline doctrine lies in its making a distinction between law and grace. When law becomes inflamed with love, when love has united with the law, that then is grace. That is how the Pauline distinction between law and grace is to be understood.

Now we can follow the legend of the Cross still further. The wood was used as a bridge between two river banks, because it did not suit as a pillar in Solomon's temple. This was a preparation. The Ark of the Covenant was in the temple, but the Word-become-Flesh was not yet there. The wood of the Cross was laid as a bridge across a stream; only the Queen of Sheba recognized the worth of the wood for the temple, which should live in the consciousness of the soul of all humanity. Now the same wood was used for the construction of the Cross on which the Redeemer hung. He who unites the two earlier currents [of evolution], who allows the worldly and the spiritual to flow into each other, the Christ, is Himself joined to the living Cross. That is how He can carry the wood of the Cross as something [external] which He carries on His back. He is Himself united with the wood of the bridge, and can therefore take the dead wood upon Himself.

Man is today drawn into higher nature. Formerly he lived in lower nature. In the Christian sense he now lives in higher nature, and the Cross—the lower nature—he carries forward as something alien, through his inner living forces. Religion now becomes the living force in the world. Now the life in external nature ceases; the Cross becomes entirely wood. The outer body [of man] now becomes a vehicle for the inner living force. There the great mystery is consummated: the Cross is taken on [man's] back.

Our great poet Goethe presented the idea of the bridge in a beautiful and significant way in his 'Fairy Story of the Green Snake and the Beautiful Lily',[6] where he portrays a bridge being built, by the snake laying itself across the river as a living bridge. All the more advanced initiates use this same symbol for one and the same thing.

Thus we have become acquainted with the deep inner meaning of the holy legend of the Cross. We have seen how the turning-point was prepared, which Christianity brought about, and which must be fulfilled more and more as time goes on by Christianizing the world. We have seen how the Cross, inasmuch as it is the image of the three external bodies, dies; how it is only able to form an external union between the three lower and the three higher kingdoms, between the two banks divided by the stream. The wood of the Cross could not become a pillar in Solomon's temple until man recognizes it as his own particular symbol. Only then, when he sacrifices himself, makes his own body into the temple, and becomes able to carry the Cross, will the merging of the two streams be made possible.

That is why the Christian churches have the symbol of the Cross in their foundations, thereby expressing the secretion of the living Cross in the outward edifice of the temple. However, these two streams, the living divine stream on the one hand

and the worldly mineral stream on the other, have become united in the Redeemer hanging on the Cross—the higher principles are in the Redeemer Himself, and the lower ones in the Cross. And henceforth this connection must now become organic and living, as the Apostle Paul expressed particularly deeply. Without [a knowledge of] what has been discussed today, the writings of the Apostle Paul cannot be understood. It was clear to him that the Old Covenant, which creates an antithesis between man and the law, must come to an end. Only when man unites himself with the law, takes it upon his back, carries it, will there no longer be any contradiction between man's inner nature and the external law. Then that which Christianity seeks to achieve *is* achieved.

'With the law sin came into the world.'[7] That is a profound saying of Paul's. When is there sin in the world? Only when there is a law which can be broken. But when the law becomes so united with human nature that man only does good, then there can be no [more] sin. Man only contradicts the law of the Cross as long as it does not live within him, but is something external. Therefore Paul sees the Christ on the Cross as the conquest of law and the conquest of sin. To hang on the Cross means to be subjected to the law—and that is a curse. Sin and the law belong together in the Old Covenant; the law and love belong together in the New Covenant. It is a negative law which is involved in the Old Covenant but the law of the New Covenant is a living, positive law. He who united the Old Covenant with His own life is the One who has overcome it. He has at the same time sanctified it.

That is what is meant by those words of Paul which are to be found in the Epistle to the Galatians, Chapter 3:11–13:

But that no man is justified by the law in the sight of God, is evident, for the just shall live by faith and the law is not of faith, but the man that doeth them shall live in them. Christ hath redeemed us from the curse of the law, being made a curse for us, for it is written: Cursed is every one that hangeth on a tree.

With the word 'tree' [literally 'wood' in the German Bible] Paul connects the concept with which we have been dealing today. We must indeed keep penetrating deeper into what the great initiates have said. We do not come closer to Christianity by adapting it to what might be termed our demands, by adapting it to the contemporary materialistic judgements that deny anything higher—but by continually raising ourselves further into spiritual heights. For Christianity was born of initiation, and we shall only understand it and be able to believe that it contains infinite depths if we abandon the view that we have to bring Christianity nearer to contemporary ideas. Instead, we must raise our anti-spiritual materialistic way of thinking back again to Christianity. The contemporary view must raise itself from what is mineral and dead to what is living and spiritual, if it is to understand Christianity.

I have presented these views so as to arrive at a conception of the New Jerusalem.

*Answer to a question**
Question: Is the legend very old?
Answer (1): This legend existed at the time of the Mysteries, but it was not written down. The Mysteries of Antioch were Adonis Mysteries. In them was celebrated the Crucifixion, the Entombment and the Resurrection as an outer image of initiation. The mourning of the women at the Cross already appeared there; this appeared to us again in [the persons] of Mary and Mary Magdalene. This links up with a version, similar to that in [this] legend, which is also to be found in the Apis and Mithras Mysteries, and again in the Osiris Mysteries. What was still apocalyptic there is fulfilled in Christianity. The old apocalypses change into new legends, in the same way that John portrays the future in his Revelations.

*   *   *

Answer (2): The legend is historically medieval, but was previously recorded in all its completeness by the Gnostics. The further course of the Cross is given there. Moreover, the medieval version also contains indications of this. The medieval legends indicate the way to the Mysteries less clearly, but we can trace them all back. This legend is connected with the Adonis Mysteries, with the Antioch legend, in which the Crucifixion, Entombment and Resurrection become an outward image of inner initiation. The mourning women also appear there, and there is a connected version which is very similar to the Osiris legend. Everything that is apocalyptic in these legends is fulfilled in Christianity. The Queen of Sheba sees deeper and is versed in the true wisdom.

---

* Text (1) is taken from Seiler's notes, text (2) from those of Reebstein.

LECTURE 14

Concerning the Lost Temple and How it is to be Restored—IV

(In connection with the Legend of the True Cross, or Golden Legend)

Berlin, 5 June 1905, Whit Monday

The Allegory of the Lost Word and its Quest
in Connection with the Whitsuntide Festival

Among the allegories and symbols we wished to discuss in these lectures, there is also the symbol of the so-called Lost Word, which is to be found again. We have spoken about the temple which was lost and is to be restored; we can all the more appropriately add to that a brief account of the Lost Word and its quest, since this theme has some connection with the symbolic meaning of the Whitsuntide festival. I did speak about some of the things to be mentioned today, a year ago.[1] But there are some among us who may not have heard last year's lecture; so it may not be superfluous to refer to these things again. Moreover, we are in a position to consider such matters annually, and treat them fundamentally and exhaustively. We have added somewhat to our knowledge, so that several things can now perhaps be discussed that could not yet be mentioned last year.

Pentecost is connected with just that symbol which is known both in the Church and in Freemasonry as the symbol of the Lost Word which is to be found again. But with it we touch on Christian mysteries of a real and extraordinary profundity.

With it we touch again—and more thoroughly than could be the case last week—upon the purpose and mission of Solomon the Wise, and upon the whole future meaning of Christian truths.

Pentecost is connected with that perception of man's inmost being which was present in early Christianity, but which has been gradually lost in Christianity as it has survived in the various western Churches. Pentecost is the festival which every year should freshly remind man of his liberation—of what we call the freedom of the human soul.

How has man really come to what we call his freedom, that is to say, to his ability to distinguish between good and evil and in freedom to do either good or evil? You know that man has passed through a long sequence of evolution before arriving at the stage where he stands today, and that we have passed the mid-point of this evolution. The mid-point of the whole of human evolution lies roughly in the middle of the Atlantean epoch, which preceded our own epoch. Now we have already gone past this mid-point. Because of that we are the first missionaries of the second half [of evolution], the first apostles of an ascending arc; whereas man was in a descending arc until the time of Atlantis and was involved in a kind of descending evolution until he had submerged himself in the uttermost depths of material life. Now he is climbing back again towards spiritual development.

What we human beings did not possess before the mid-point of our earth evolution was freedom of choice between good and evil. Now we cannot talk about good and evil in the subordinate kingdoms of nature. It would be ridiculous to discuss whether a mineral wanted to crystallize or not; it crystallizes if the appropriate conditions are present. It would be equally ridiculous to ask whether the lily wants to blossom or not or to ask the lion to abstain voluntarily from killing and devouring other animals. Only with man, only in our phase of evolution, do we speak about what we call freedom of choice.

Only to human beings do we ascribe the capacity to distinguish between good and evil. How man got this capacity is described in the Bible, in the great symbol of the Fall, in the scene of the temptation, where the devil or Lucifer appears to Eve and persuades her to eat of the Tree of Knowledge. Through that, man obtained free will; with it he began the second part of his evolutionary path. We can no more enquire into freedom, good and evil for man prior to that evolutionary mid-point than we can for minerals, plants and animals. Something else is connected with that.

In all esoteric [teaching] our contemporary world and everything connected with it signifies the Cosmos of Love. And the Cosmos or Universe of Wisdom preceded this Universe of Love. We want to look at this in a rather deeper way.

You know that our Earth evolution was cosmologically preceded by the Moon evolution.[2] A still more distant precursor of our earth was the Sun; earlier still was Saturn. Man has passed through these three evolutionary stages: Saturn, Sun and Moon. Our earth has passed through three cycles already, in which the Saturn development was repeated in the first Round, the Sun development in the second Round, and the Moon development in the third Round. Each of these Rounds commences thus. The planet forms itself as an exceptionally fine substance, as mind-substance. The earth was present as such a substance when it began its fourth Round, that is, the contemporary cycle. Then it began to reiterate the three previous Rounds: the Saturn Cycle in Arupa, the Sun Cycle in Rupa and the Moon Cycle or Round in the astral. [See diagram at the end of the notes for Lecture 10.]

Thus our earth passed once more through earlier material conditions before arriving at its present physical density. Before our present condition it was astral. We refer to the astral Globe as a kind of Cosmos of Wisdom. Each Cosmos or Globe is again divided into seven epochs. Thus we have seven Race-cycles [or great epochs] in our present Globe: the Polarian, the Hyperborean, the Lemurian, the Atlantean and now the Aryan Race [or epoch] in which we live. The sixth and seventh Races are still to come. After that the earth will return to the astral condition. These Race-cycles constitute seven successive periods of our physical evolution on earth. The astral predecessor presents itself to us in like manner, in seven consecutive periods, corresponding to seven Races. However, it is not quite correct to speak of Races here; the forms which then lived cannot properly be called Races. It stretches the analogy too far to keep speaking of Races. There were other forms that became manifest. In esoteric language these previous astral periods are called the Kingdom of Wisdom, and their forms are called the seven Periods of Wisdom, in which the seven Kings of Wisdom, the seven Kings of the Dynasty of Solomon, were ruling. For in each of these periods lived a being of similar kind to the soul of Solomon, to the soul that incarnated in Solomon. This Cosmos of Wisdom was superseded by the earthly Cosmos proper, the Cosmos of Love.

Now let us be clear about what took place during the formation of the earth, from our standpoint. As the earth began to aquire form, it was still united with the sun and with that which we now call the moon. Together with these two bodies the earth formed a single whole. First of all the sun separated from the earth. The whole of earth life thereby became different. At this point death made its entry, somewhat in the form in which we know it in the cell-bearing plants, whereas before there could be no question of death because there was continuous material life. So long as the plant consists of a single cell, no decay sets in when the next cell is born. It is different when a whole organism is built up [out of many cells]; this [organism] decays into its parts, and the individual part is no longer the whole living [process]. This kind of death came in for the first time when the sun separated from the earth. The schism between the sexes began in the middle of the Lemurian Race, as a result of the splitting-off of the moon. The separation of the moon brought about the partition of the [being that is both] male and female into [beings that are either] only male or only female. Thus humanity took the shape that it now has in the world.

What then happened during these weighty cosmic events as first the sun and then the moon separated from the earth? If we want to become clear about that, it would be well to point out that at that time the earth was changing from a very thin but already physical matter into something continually getting more dense. The first physical substance was etheric substance, which was present in all human beings on earth, and which was a very fine substance, finer than our gas.

At present we distinguish three forms of matter on our earth—solid, liquid and gaseous bodies, the latter formerly known as air. Moreover we esoterically distinguish four forms of ether: firstly fire [or warmth] ether which makes all bodies capable of being permeated by warmth; secondly, light ether; thirdly, chemical ether, in which atoms are made to mingle according to certain laws of number (the 'elective affinity' of atoms); and fourthly the physical or life ether; in all, four kinds of ether bringing life to the earth. Next, the earth, essentially speaking, evolved into these four types of ether. Then it condensed itself out of these ethers. This densification took place for the first time during the Lemurian epoch. Before that, one has to think of an etheric earth, which was accessible to quite different forces than is our present physical earth. I wanted to clarify this for you.

When I say that this etheric earth was accessible to quite different forces, then be clear that all living beings, whether plant, animal or man, were indeed accessible to these forces, in their inmost being. The ether is accessible to what is called in esoteric language the 'Word', the 'Cosmic Word'. I can also make clear to you how the etheric relates to what we call the

'Word', through the example of a process of initiation. As you know, man consists of physical, etheric and astral bodies, and then of the 'I' proper. The etheric body becomes visible if one [can dismiss] the physical body from one's mind. But man as he is today can in no way act upon his physical body; he is unable to move the tiniest blood corpuscle. The physical body is controlled by high cosmic forces; it is higher beings who can exercise power here today—later on man will have this ability. When he is able to control the forces of his own physical body, which the materialist speaks of as nature forces, then man will have become a god. To ascribe these powers to him today would be idolatry, for in truth we have to do with high beings who can influence the physical body.

When man is able to control the substance of fire-ether, he will be able to control all that is physical. When he is able to control the physical in man, then he will also be able to control the rest of what is physical as well. This force is designated the Father force, or simply the 'Father'—everything through which a being is connected with our earth, everything by which that being can control physical matter. When a person can penetrate into the physical body with such Father forces, that is called atma; this is how atma can be assigned to the physical.

The second member of [man's] being is the etheric body, which corresponds to the Son principle, or the Logos, the 'Word'. The etheric body can be moved and inwardly shaped by buddhi, set in vibration by the Son principle, just as the physical [body can be] by atma.

The third member is the astral body. This we cannot at first control; only very few people at present have any significant control over their astral bodies. We say a man is endowed with manas, to the extent that man can control his astral body from within.

Man began to work on his astral body during the middle of Lemurian times. If you could have observed a man at the stage he had attained when the Lemurian Race began, that is, when he was bisexual, you would have found that his body was built from elsewhere. But in the middle of Lemurian times, man then began to work on his astral body himself. Everything which man weaves into himself out of his ego, which he does out of duty or by command, to overcome the unwrought appetites and passions, helps to refine the astral body. When it has become completely permeated by the work of man's own ego, then we can no longer call it astral body; it has become manas. When the whole astral body has been transformed into manas, man can then begin to work upon his etheric body to transform it into buddhi. What he weaves into it is nothing else than the individualized Word. Christian esotericism calls this the 'Son' or 'Logos', and calls the astral body, when it has become manas, the 'Holy Spirit', and the physical body that has become atma 'Father'.

What happens here on a small scale within man happens also on a large scale in the world at large. These world secrets were carried out in the Mysteries, in initiation; thereby something was done which for most human beings would only happen in a distant future. Already, in the Egyptian Mysteries one could only be initiated if one had worked one's way through one's entire astral body, so that the astral body could be completely managed by the ego. Now such a person would stand before the initiating priest. He had no influence on his physical body, nor yet on his etheric body. But his astral body was of his own making. Now it was indicated to him how he could act on his etheric body and on his physical body. The physical body was brought into a lethargic condition; it had to remain in this state for three nights and three days, and during this time the etheric body was raised out of it. And since the initiate had become powerful in respect of the astral body, he could therefore now gain the power to act on the etheric body. He could learn to let what he had in his astral body work on the etheric body. Those were the three days of the Entombment and the Resurrection in an etheric body that was completely permeated by what one calls the Holy Spirit. Such an initiate was called a man endowed with the Logos, with the 'Word'. This 'Word' is nothing else than the wisdom, manas, which has been worked into the astral body. This wisdom can never enter the etheric body unless the astral body has first been permeated by it.

It was just the same for the earth. Not until the whole earth had been brought thus far into the astral could such an event occur. The condition which the neophyte in the Egyptian Mysteries had to be in corresponds to this time of the Astral Globe which I have spoken of as the immediate precursor of our earth; that is the Globe of Wisdom. All wisdom was worked into it by the cosmic powers. And this transfer of wisdom into the Earth Globe itself made it possible that after the separation of sun and moon from the earth something could again be incorporated from above, from higher spheres [into the earth] just as this happened on a small scale in the initiation.

Seven times the Astral Globe [stage] of earth [see the chart at the end of the notes to Lecture 10] came under the rule of the Wise, after the manner of Solomon. Then the earth became clothed with an etheric body, and earthly matter was crystallized or formed. The 'Word' was laid into that; this Word is thus, as it were, entombed in earthly matter, but it must be resurrected. This is also the beautiful meaning of the myth of the God Dionysus. The Holy Wisdom of our earth's precursor is laid into all the earth beings of our earthly world. Take this as deeply as you are able. Take the human etheric body as every human being has it. If you look at it clairvoyantly it has nearly the same form as the physical body. At death man's physical body dissolves, and the etheric body too; the physical body dissolves into the physical world, and the etheric body into the general cosmic ether. But this etheric body has been very elaborately created for man by the wisdom which first implanted it from out of the Astral Globe. This etheric body disperses after death. Only *that* etheric body which has been built up from within is a living body, which stays eternally. This is the etheric body of the Chela [the candidate for initiation], and that does not dissolve after death. If you see a modern civilized man die, you may see the etheric body for a while, but then it dissolves. With the Chela it remains. The renunciation of Devachan by the Chela consists in the fact that the Chela stays on the astral plane and there makes use of his etheric body. With ordinary human beings a new etheric body has to be formed at each rebirth; the ability to create a new one is attained in Devachan. The etheric body which the Chela has built up from within will never be lost again whereas that which is made by cosmic wisdom from elsewhere indeed dissolves again. It is the same with the etheric bodies of plants and animals. What is now still etheric body came to be built up out of cosmic forces which flowed into it out of the Astral Globe [state] of our earth. This wisdom which you find in the astral earth is expressed in the legend of Dionysus.

Now in the Lemurian epoch the denser [state] had to be formed. Then the Father principle had to be worked in. That is the last [principle] to take control of our earthly matter. What has been worked in, in this way, is deeply hidden in the physical world. First the Holy Spirit worked itself into the astral material. Then the Spirit allied to the astral matter—that is the Son—worked itself into the etheric substance; and then came the Father, who controls physical density. Thus the macrocosm was built up in a threefold progression—Spirit, Son and Father—and man, as he progresses further upwards, goes from the Spirit, through the Son, to the Father. All of this takes place under guidance in the evolution of the earth.

Up to Lemurian times the only evolution was outward. Then this Trinity was drawn into our physical evolution. In the Aryan epoch, what had taken place in an earlier epoch was introduced into man's thinking as religion, making a stage by stage recapitulation.

We are in the fifth Sub-Race of the Aryan Root Race [the fifth post-Atlantean cultural epoch]. Four other Sub-Races have gone before. The first Sub-Race is that of Ancient India. This venerable ancient race was led by the ancient Rishis. We can only form a hazy conception of them. We are acquainted with their religion from the accounts that have come down to us in the Vedas. The teaching of the Rishis was far greater and mightier than our present traditions about it. Only during the third Sub-Race were records made, which are preserved for us in the Vedas. The original religion of the Rishis had great traditions from the divine predecessors of men, the astral initiates of the dynasty of Solomon. Living in the spirit of the Ancient Indian Rishis were archetypal forms; the great intuitions derive intelligence and knowledge not only from the laws of earth but also from the archetypal forms, who themselves created the said wisdoms. This was the first religion, that of the Holy Spirit.

The second religion was fostered in the Near East; in it the Second Principle [of the Trinity] was revered as a recapitulation of the first time that the Son made His influence felt on earth. The thrusting down of certain beings accompanied the [coming in of] the Son Principle; there is no higher development of the one without others being thrust down into the depths. The mineral, plant and animal kingdoms were thrust down in this way. Whoever develops upwards takes upon himself a tremendous responsibility. That is the great tragedy; the corollary of every saint is that a great number of beings are thrust down. There would be no development if this kind of thrusting down did not take place. A man must continually thrust others down as he develops himself upwards. That is why all development that takes place out of self-interest is evil and reprehensible; it is only justifiable if done for the development of other beings. Only he who would raise up those who have been thrust down is fit for development. Thus the evolution which manifested itself on earth and which had already been prepared on other cosmic bodies, the evolution aiming at endowing the etheric body with the Logos, with the Word, has been accompanied by the thrusting down of other beings connected with the earth's development. These [beings] were regarded as adversaries, as the luciferic principle. Thus we have precisely this duality, the principle of Evil accompanying the principle of Good, in the Persian religion. It is good if a man or indeed any being works manasically into himself but he is always confronted by evil. Ormuzd and Ahriman are the names for Good and Evil in the Persian religion.

We encounter the third stage with the Chaldeans, the Babylonians, the Assyrians and the Egyptians; through [all of] these a recapitulation of the third stage of the Godhead takes place. Thus from that time onwards, with all peoples, we encounter the Trinity, the Three-in-Oneness of the Godhead. The second Sub-Race had no Triune Godhead, still less the first. [But] now, in this threefoldness, the ascent is gradually prepared for the whole of humanity. The initiates tread the path in advance ... [Gap][3]

In the first three Sub-Races there was a mirroring in the religious [sphere] of what had been active in macrocosmic processes. Now a new structure is formed: first Wisdom, then Son, then Father. The first gleam of wisdom came during the fourth Sub-Race through the Semitic people, who arose during the third Sub-Race and continued into the fourth. From them Christianity derives. In the initiates of the Jewish people we find the whole course of past events on earth—all the events that had taken place in the heavenly sphere being repeated in the element of the intellect. Kama-manas, which we call lower spirit, developed there; this has to be endowed with other forces. This endowment, this element, is Christ Himself, the Word made Flesh, who points to the future Word by which all human beings will be in a position to control their etheric bodies with their astral bodies—if they so work the

Word into the etheric body that it wakens to life therein. The possibility of this development in the future is foreshadowed in the appearance of the Word made Flesh in the fourth Sub-Race. The whole of mankind must have attained control over the etheric before the Logos can be incarnated in the etheric body. This as an originating impulse has proceeded from the Christ incarnated in the flesh. When man, through the power of the Son, has endured [this], he will then come to the Father.

Now the stages arrived at by Christ through His appearance in the flesh must be achieved gradually by the whole of mankind. In the spirit which developed itself in Judaism, the higher manas had to be kindled. Therefore, the new era begins with the descent of the Holy Spirit, which will lead mankind through to the point in the sixth epoch when the Christ Principle, which is only hinted at in Christianity today, finds its fulfilment. 'No man cometh to the Father save through Me,' says the Son. He sent the Spirit to mankind so that it should be prepared for the time in the sixth epoch when Good and Evil will be separated. Man would never have developed this impulse without that other element, which we have named as the so-called Evil principle. Man had to receive free will so that his understanding could be called into play in deciding between Good and Evil. This element of the Spirit's descent is consummated at Pentecost.

Spirit, Son and Father are as though entombed in the earth: the Father in the physical body, the Son in the etheric body and the Spirit in the astral body. However, man has developed his ego and has become self-aware. Now he must learn to work right down into the physical. That will be in the future. At present man is working into his astral body. The symbol for that is the descent of the Holy Spirit into those who are to become the leaders of humanity. What has been taken up by this spirit is something within man which is akin to this spirit.

Before the Son could become effective (which was in

Hyperborean times) a part of the universal principle of Spirit had to break away, be thrust down, and wander other paths. This is expressed in the Serpent, the symbol of knowledge, the luciferic principle. It was this spark from the Spirit which made man into a free being and enabled him to desire the Good out of his own impulse. This Spirit which has come down to man through the great Whitsuntide festival is akin to that Spirit which was thrust down, which is indeed embodied in Prometheus, which has blown the spark into a flame, so that our ego can make up its mind to follow the Spirit, just as it will later follow the Son and still later the Father. Man was certainly able to become evil, but on the other hand this potentiality for evil was the price of being guided back to the world of the Gods from which he originated. That is the connection between Pentecost and the luciferic principle. Thus the Whitsuntide festival is also the festival of Prometheus and of freedom.

Now you will understand the connection between the Sons of Cain and the seven Salomonic Kings of pre-earthly times— of whom the King Solomon of the Bible appears as a descendant. Wisdom was first transmitted to man from outside. Later it had to spring up from within. Solomon built the temple but only with the help of Hiram-Abiff; in association with this Son of Cain he appropriated the arts needed for erecting the temple. Thus the streams run together again that were flowing apart [from each other] in the world.

When the sun separated from the earth, the Word became entombed in the earth. It will be resurrected when the earth has advanced as far as the sixth Root Race. Man will raise this Word from the dead out of the earth but first the spirit must live in him that will enable the Word to strike a chord in him. This was attained by the Apostles at Pentecost. In *Light on the Path*[4] we find the words: 'Acquire knowledge and you will have speech.' Speech comes with true knowledge, which descends like the tongues of fire on the Apostles at holy Pentecost.

When the inner Word which is akin to the holy divine Word comes and sinks down into everything etheric so as to make it come alive, then man will no longer speak out of himself but out of the divine Spirit. He is then the messenger of the Godhead and proclaims the inner Word of the Godhead out of his own free will.

Thus did the inner Word become alive in the Apostles; thus did it spread its influence outwards from them. They proclaimed the fiery Word and were aware of their role as the messengers of the Godhead. Therefore the Holy Spirit hovered over them in the form of fiery tongues. They prepare humanity to receive the Logos. The great initiate Christ Jesus went on in advance. The Holy Spirit followed, fertilizing the astral bodies so that they would become ripe for making their etheric bodies immortal. Once this has happened, the Christ Principle will be drawn into humanity. This is what the initiates too had in mind when they said, somewhat as Heraclitus did: If, in escaping from the earthly,[5] you ascend to the free ether with faith in immortality, you become an immortal spirit free of death and of the physical.

Every single person will reach this point in the middle of the sixth Root Race. Now, however, man is still vulnerable to death, in that his etheric body has still not attained immortality. Christianity contains the secret of how man can gradually develop himself towards the resurrection of the etheric body. This is where the third great festival is connected with the other two Christian festivals.

I wanted to come to the conclusion here that the Whitsuntide festival has infinite depths, and to show how man gradually develops a living awareness of the world around him and that he is related to all the things around him, to everything which happens around him. In the names of the days of the week you will find what has transpired around us set forth.

Man celebrates Pentecost best by making it clear to himself

what deep truths have been implanted into this festival by the wise. And to celebrate a festival really means to unite oneself in spirit with the Cosmic Spirit.

Atoms and the Logos in the Light of Occultism

Berlin, 21 October 1905

If we want to appreciate theosophy at its true value, then we need to be imbued with the fundamental perception that in the theosophical stream we receive a widening of the soul, we feel the heart broadened and uplifted for higher tasks, for participating in the affairs of the universe. No one can have an inkling of this who does not know something about occultism.

The great purpose is often discussed of leading humanity, through the theosophical movement, towards that point when, in the future, a new race of human beings will arise, when our intellectuality, as it now is, will no longer play the leading role in the world but will be made fertile by buddhi. We have to work together with this great world current, and therefore we have a great responsibility towards the theosophical movement. The task of the theosophist extends into the distant future. In this we do not withdraw into some cloud-cuckoo-land; for what we learn about so distant a future is invigorating for us, is something productive for us, that is useful also in everyday things. Anyone who allows these great world perspectives to occupy his mind for even only ten minutes a day will behave differently from someone who is immersed in everyday matters. He can bring something to contemporary life which is new, productive and original. All progress depends on bringing originality into humanity.

We want to start with something which belongs to the influence of the Devas.[1] Devas are beings who are at a higher stage than man and are able to work on higher levels of existence. Thus we find Devas when we enter the higher planes clairvoyantly. We find Devas on the astral plane, on the Rupa plane, on the Arupa plane, and higher still. What does the influence of the Devas mean for the world in which we ourselves are? We will answer this question by asking another: What is the purpose of our human existence, of this continuing reincarnation? Man would come into this world quite purposelessly if he learnt no particular lesson, fulfilled no particular task at each coming. Every time [man incarnates] the earth must have changed so much that he meets a situation that he has not encountered before in his earlier incarnations.

A male and female incarnation [together] are occultly reckoned as one incarnation. Between two such connected incarnations lie 2,600 to 3,000 years. The experiences which men undergo during this present stage of earthly evolution are so different in man and woman that it is most necessary for this to be so.

The changes which are brought about in the world between two incarnations of a person are really rather incomprehensible for people outside the theosophical world. Actually, however, people find quite different situations, not only morally but physically as well. For anyone who looks back occultly, the physical circumstances have fundamentally altered as well, in the last three thousand years. On average, we would encounter our previous incarnations in the time of the ancient Greeks, the Homeric Greeks 800 BC. At that time there were quite different geographical and climatic conditions, a basically different plant life and even a different animal world. In these kingdoms, [continual] change is taking place. An outer expression of these changes is the progress of the sun across the vault of heaven. We have twelve signs of the zodiac, and the sun continually moves on from one to another at the vernal equinox. Eight thousand years ago the sun entered the constellation of the Crab for the first time. The time during which the sun traverses a constellation lasts some two thousand six hundred years.[2] That is also the time between two human incarnations. At about the turn of the eighteenth to the nineteenth century, the sun left the constellation of the Ram for that of the Fishes, so that it now stands in the constellation of the Fishes at the spring [equinox].

Those who still had a feeling for occultism knew something about the connection in man's life with these changes in the firmament. Earlier, before the sun entered the constellation of the Ram, the cult of the Bull (Mithras, Apis) prevailed in Asia. Then began the worship of the Ram, which began when the legend of Jason and the Golden Fleece originated. Christ is called the 'Lamb of God'. Still earlier one finds the Persian symbol of the Twins. That is connected with the [Persian] culture of that time [and its view] of Good and Evil.

If the sun shines on the earth from a different aspect, then the situation there changes too. Hence the entry of the sun into a new constellation also leads each time to a new incarnation. Above, in the heavens, is the progression of the sun, below, on earth, an alteration in climatic conditions, in vegetation and so forth.

Who causes this? The theosophist has to ask this because for him there can be no miracles. There are facts on a higher level, but no miracles. Faced with the question of the connection of the human being to the manifestations of the earth, one must adopt a higher vantage point.

After death, man is in Kamaloka. We do not ask: *Do* the animals and plants have [any] consciousness? Instead we ask: *Where* is their consciousness located? We know that the animals have their consciousness in Kamaloka, on the astral plane, the plants on the Rupa plane, and the minerals on the Arupa plane. Man has his consciousness on the physical plane. Let us suppose that man now comes to Kamaloka. He will then be in the same place as the consciousness of the animals. He then ascends to Devachan, where the plants have their consciousness. At the present stage of evolution, man is not in a position to exercise any influence on the animal kingdom or plant kingdom. However, he does have such an influence in the lower regions of the Devachanic plane. His companions there are all those who possess a Devachanic consciousness; these are powers, beings, who work out of Devachan to promote the growth and welfare of the plant world. The whole life of the plants is controlled from the Devachanic plane. There, man helps create and transform the plants. Powers develop in him there, so that he can really develop an influence on the vegetation. But the Devas are still there to manage this activity. He is guided by them so that he can help in the transformation of the plant world. He makes use in Devachan of the powers he has gathered in incarnation to reshape the plant world. As man's life forces alter during his time in Devachan, so does he participate in changing the vegetation on earth. From Devachan, man actually changes the surroundings that grow about him.

By remaining a long time in Devachan, [man] also helps transform the physical forces. If one goes back a million years in Germany,[3] one finds volcanic mountains still there, and the Alps as low undulating hills. The subsequent changes were brought about by man [working] from the Arupa plane, so that he would meet with suitable physical configurations in Europe later on. The activity of man in the universe is the inner aspect of what we see outwardly in the environment.

Now we come to what will influence transformation in the world from a still higher plane and in another form.

One often reads about the Logos streaming down from above, and asks oneself how this is [to be conceived], how one can come to a conception of the Logos, to a conception that is something more than a mere word. We will now examine the connection between the Logos and the smallest [particles]. I will give you a description—not speculations—of the results of very ancient occult research, as they have been handed down and worked upon specifically in the occult schools of Germany especially from the fourteenth century onward.

If we meditate on the atom, what strikes us is that it is a very tiny thing. Everyone knows that this small thing called the atom has never been seen through any kind of microscope, no matter how sophisticated. Yet occult books give descriptions and pictures of the atom.[4] Where were these pictures obtained? How can one, as an occultist, now know anything about the atom?

Now just imagine it to be possible to make an atom grow continually bigger and bigger until it was as big as the earth; one would then discover a very complicated world. One would perceive many movements, different kinds of phenomena, within this small thing. Keep in mind this analogy of the atom being enlarged to the size of the earth. If it were actually possible to enlarge the atom to that extent, we would be able to observe every single process in it. Only the occultist is in a position to enlarge the atom so much and to contemplate its interior.

Let us next look at the range of human motives on earth, beginning with the lowest human levels of development, with the instincts and passions, rising to moral ideals and religious communities, and so on. We will then see that human beings are, as it were, spinning threads between each other, which weave from person to person, forming continually higher associations—the family, the tribe and further ethnic and political groups, and finally religious communities. In this, the activity of higher individualities comes indeed to expression. Such associations have sprung up out of the springs and wells of pure universal wisdom, through a religious founder. All religions agree [in the deeper sense], because they have founders who belong to the great Lodge [of the Masters].

There is a particular White Lodge which has twelve members, of whom seven have a special influence, and these seven indeed founded religious groupings. Such were the Buddha,

Hermes, Pythagoras, and so on. The great plan for the whole of human evolution has actually been spiritually devised in the White Lodge, which is as old as humanity itself. A co-ordinated plan for the guidance of all human progress confronts us here. All other associations are only subordinate branches; even family groupings, etc, are all linked up in the great plan which leads us up to the Lodge of the Masters. There the plan according to which all mankind develops is spun and woven.

Let us follow all that subsequently happens. Now we must first become acquainted with a particular plan, namely, the plan for our earth. Let us contemplate the fourth Round of the earth in which we now are. It is intended to humanize the mineral kingdom. Think how human understanding has already transformed the mineral world, for example, Cologne Cathedral and modern technology. Our humanity has the task of transforming the whole mineral world into a pure work of art. Electricity already points for us into the occult depths of matter.

When, out of his inner being, man has restructured the mineral world, the end of our earth will then have arrived; the earth is then at the end of its physical evolution. The particular plan by which the mineral world will be reshaped exists in the Lodge of the Masters. This plan is already finished; so that if one studies it one can see what is yet to come by way of wonderful buildings, wonderful machines, and so on. When the earth has reached the end of the physical globe [state] the whole earth will have an inner structure, an inner articulation, given to it by man himself, so that it will have become a work of art, as planned by the Masters of the White Lodge. That accomplished, then the whole earth will pass over into its astral state. That is something comparable to when a plant begins to fade; the physical vanishes, everything goes into the astral. In passing into the astral world, the physical gradually contracts, becomes a shrinking kernel encircled by the astral, going over into the Rupa state and then the Arupa state, until it vanishes in a sleeplike condition.

What then is left of the physical? When the earth has passed over into the Arupa state, there is then still a very condensed tiny imprint of the whole physical evolution that was devised in the Masters' plan—like a tiny miniature version of what the mineral earth once was. That is what is transferred [from the physical]; the physical is there only as this tiny miniature version of previous evolution, but the Arupa is large. When it passes over out of the Devachan state, it multiplies outwardly into innumerable similar things. And when the earth again passes back into the physical state it is then composed of countless tiny globules, each of which is a print of what the earth previously was. All these globules are, however, differently arranged, although sharing a common derivation. Thus the new physical earth of the fifth Round[5] will consist of innumerable tiny parts, each of which contains the purpose of the mineral world which the Masters have in the form of a plan in their Lodge. Every atom of the fifth Round [of Earth evolution] will contain the whole plan of the Masters. Today the Masters are working on the atom of the fifth Round. Everything which happens, in humanity, is compressed into a result, that is the atom of the fifth Round.

Therefore, if we examine the atom in its present form and then go back in the Akashic Record, we will then see that today's atom is undergoing a process of growth. It is growing more and more, it is becoming more and more separated [Gap in text] ... and contains the interweaving forces of mankind from the third Round of evolution. In that we can consider the plan of the Masters for the third Earth Round. What is at first entirely external becomes quite inward, and in the smallest atom we see mirrored the plans of the Masters. These tiny particular plans are nothing else than a piece of the whole plan for humanity. If one thus considers that the plan of one Round is the atom of the next Round, then one can see the pattern of the great universal plan. The great universal plan develops in continually higher stages, to beings who have continually higher plans for world development. When we contemplate this plan we arrive at the third Logos. The Logos is thus continually slipping into the atom; first it is outside and becomes the blueprint for the atom, and then the atom becomes an image of this plan. The occultist simply notes the plan from the Akashic Record for the earlier Rounds and so studies the atom.

Now from where do the higher beings obtain this plan? We find an answer to this if we consider that there are still higher stages of evolution where the plans are devised. That is where world evolution is worked out. These higher stages are indicated to us by the Ancients, for instance by Dionysius, the pupil of the Apostle Paul,[6] and also by Nicolaus Cusanus.[7] His perception was: Higher than all knowledge and perception is the lack of perception. But this Unknowing is a higher knowing, and this lack of perception is a higher perceiving.

When we stop looking at what we hold in our thinking and concepts of the world, and turn ourselves to what wells up, to our inner powers, then we find something still higher. The Masters can weave the [third] Logos because they have ascended still higher than the nature of thinking. When the higher powers are developed, then, in such beings, thought appears as something different. It then corresponds to our spoken word with us. The thought which constitutes the innermost being for the Masters can itself be the expression of a higher being, just as the word is the expression of thought [with us]. If we ourselves consider thought as the word of a still higher being, then we come near to the concept of the Logos. Knowledge taken out from thought stands on a still higher level.

When we behold the world we find the atom at the one extreme. It is an image of the plan that proceeded out of the depths of the spirit of the Masters, which is the Logos.

If we now look for the transformation of man himself during the great world epoch, then we are led back again into the world.

Just as man has descended, has plunged down to the physical plane, so is it also with the world as a whole. What contributes to the development of man's self lies around him in the world.

But then we are led down to the lower planes, which however, themselves contain the higher planes . . . the Lodge of the Masters.

The Spirit of the Earth is living with the Masters today and this Spirit of the Earth will be the physical clothing of the next planet [the future Jupiter]. The slightest thing we do will affect the smallest atom of the next planet. This feeling gives us first a full connection with the Lodge of the Masters. That should provide a central focus for the Theosophical Society, since we know what the Wise Ones know.

When Goethe speaks of the Spirit of the Earth[8] he is expressing a truth. The Spirit of the Earth is weaving the clothing of the next planet. 'In life's floods, in the storm of action' [*In Lebensfluten—im Tatensturm*] the Spirit [of the Earth] weaves the clothing for the next planetary Godhead.

COMMENTS ABOUT THE ATOMS IN CONNECTION WITH FREEMASONRY

Supplement: Two years later, on 21 October 1907, again at the time of the General Meeting, Rudolf Steiner spoke once more—in an as yet unpublished lecture—about the atom in the context of how spiritual influence passes from one planet to another, how therefore this will be 'between the [Old] Moon and the Earth and again between the Earth and its successor, the [future] Jupiter'. This lecture is to be published in German in Volume 101 of Rudolf Steiner's complete works.

The relevant extract runs as follows:

You all know that the earth is guided in a particular way by the so-called White Lodge in which highly developed human individualities and individualities of a still higher kind are combined. What do they do there? They work; they lead the evolution of the earth; while leading this evolution, they are devising a quite specific plan. It is really the case that during the evolution of each planet a specific plan is worked out by the guiding powers. While the earth is evolving, plans for the atom for the evolution of Jupiter—which succeeds the earth—are drawn up in the so-called White Lodge of the Earth. The plan is worked out in full detail. Therein lies the blessing and salvation of progress—in that it is undertaken in harmony with this plan.

Now, when a planetary evolution comes to its end, thus, when our earth has completed its [present] planetary cycle, then the Masters of Wisdom who harmonize perceptions will be ready with the plan that they have to work out for the Jupiter [cycle]. And now, at the end of such an evolution of planets, something very special occurs.

This plan will, through a procedure, be endlessly reduced in size, and endlessly multiplied in number; so that innumerable copies of the whole plan for Jupiter are to hand, albeit very much miniaturized. Thus it was on the [Old] Moon, too: the plan of Earth evolution existed there, infinitely multiplied and miniaturized. And do you know what they are, these miniaturized plans that have been spiritually developed there? They are the actual atoms which underlie the earth's structure. And the atoms which will underly the Jupiter [planet] will also be the plan, reproduced in the smallest possible unit—the plan which is now being worked out in the guiding White Lodge. Only he who is aware of this plan can indeed know what an atom is.

If you want to develop your knowledge of this atom, which underlies the earth, you will then, by exploring it, encounter precisely those mysteries which come from the great Magi of the world.

Naturally we can now only speak by way of allusion about these things, but we can at least give something that will impart a concept of what is involved.

The earth is composed of these, its atoms, in a specific way. Everything that exists, yourselves included, is composed of these atoms. Hence you exist in harmony with the whole earth evolution, since you carry in you an infinite number of miniaturized [copies] of the plan for the earth which was worked out in the past. This plan for the earth could only be evolved in the previous planetary condition of our earth, the [Old] Moon; the guiding beings worked it out in harmony with the whole planetary development through [Old] Saturn, [Old] Sun and [Old] Moon. Now the point in question was to introduce something into this infinite number of atoms which would bring them into the right relationship [with one another], which would arrange them in the right way. To introduce this was only possible for the guiding spirits of the Moon, if, as I have often already said, they managed the evolution of the earth according to a very specific plan.

The way the Earth appeared again after the Moon evolution was not at first really 'Earth' but 'Earth plus Sun plus

Moon'—a body such as you would have if you mixed the earth and the sun and the moon together to make one single [heavenly] body. That was how the Earth was to begin with. Then first the Sun separated itself, taking with it all those forces which were too thin, too spiritual for man, under whose influence he would have spiritualized himself far too quickly. If man had merely stayed under the influence of the forces which were contained in the joint Sun-Moon-Earth body, then he would not have evolved downwards towards physical materiality, and he would not have been able to attain to that consciousness of self, of ego, to which he had to attain...

PART III

LECTURE 16

The Relationship of Occultism to the Theosophical Movement

(Given at the conclusion of the General Meeting of the German Section of the Theosophical Society)

Berlin, 22 October 1905 (afternoon)

May I once more make it known[1] that I intend to hold a lecture tomorrow morning about certain contemporary occult questions connected with Freemasonry. And that will take place, following an ancient occult practice, separately for men and for women. The lecture for men will take place at ten o'clock, for women at half past eleven. Perhaps you may ask why this custom is retained, since—only through the theosophical view of things—it will become superseded. That will become clear through the content of the lecture. I would also like to say that the Besant Branch[2] will have its regular meeting tomorrow evening at eight o'clock.

Now I would like to speak about the relationship of occultism to the theosophical movement and about a few other connected questions. On that topic, it is very often debated whether the theosophical movement, and the Theosophical Society in particular, should be an occult movement, or whether it should be kept distinct from all occultism.

The theosophical movement as such, in so far as it is expressed in the Theosophical Society, cannot be an occult movement. An occult movement is based on different assumptions from those which can find expression in the Theosophical Society. There have been occult societies in all periods. One thing above all else has been necessary for them, namely, that on account of the whole manner of their endeavours they have some kind of hierarchy in their organization. That means that the members of such a society, of such a brotherhood, were ranked by degree. Every degree, from the first up to the ninetieth, had its quite specific task. In each degree there were quite specific tasks. Nobody could be promoted to a higher degree until he had fulfilled the tasks of the lower one.

I can only indicate very broadly why that is so. We must then speak only generally about the tasks of such occult brotherhoods. The honoured friends who have so often heard me speak about such things will understand me all the better today. Occult brotherhoods are the guiding brotherhoods of mankind. They have the task of preparing the things of the future. Everything that is to happen in the future is indeed preparing itself now, is finding its expression now, as an idea, as a plan, and will then be realized in the future. Even when you consider the development of the human race on the outward physical plane, you would then find that things which later find fulfilment were much earlier in the bud as ideas, bursting to find expression in the minds and souls of leading personalities and individualities. Take the steam engine for example. You will find, if you trace the matter back, how the steam engine was developed from the simplest facts; how the pan filled with boiling water already contained the idea of the steam engine, which was then developed from this simplest form to the most complicated mechanism.

These are, however, trifles compared with the great structure of humanity that we confront. The most important matters are based on much greater and more significant perspectives. They presuppose that what is to happen in the far distant future is already, in a specific way, being prepared today. How can anything happen in this way? Through it being in one's grasp today already to introduce forces into the world that will take effect in the future. Whatever is going to take place here on the physical plane in the future has been prepared on the astral and Devachanic plane, long before its physical manifestation; so that the forces bringing about really distant future events can be identified in the higher planes and worlds. However, one cannot satisfactorily influence the future unless one prepares the effect in the light of a knowledge of the influencing forces. Man is a self-aware creature, and has to take his destiny into his own hands. Therefore, there have always been advanced Brothers of our human race, who can see not only on the physical plane but also on higher planes.

Let us seek to conceive what it means to have foresight on higher planes. Let us suppose you have water in a pond. You can foresee that the pond will become frozen if the temperature falls, so that skating and so on will be possible. In a similar way do we have [foresight] with regard to the relationship of the so-called astral plane to the physical plane, that is, to the world in which we are involved. If therefore one follows events on the astral plane one can then in fact see what will be, in a later period, with the help of astral happenings, as if it were a densification of them. And so one can watch those astral events which subsequently appear, solidified, on the physical plane. Physical events are nothing else than such densified occurrences which have already taken place in the higher worlds.

An example. Throughout antiquity there were Mysteries. These had the task of receiving individual men and initiating them into the secrets of existence, or—as John of the Apocalypse says—showing what must 'shortly', that is to say in the future, come to pass. In the precincts of such temples, the pupils who were to be received into the first degree were instructed. Now there was a further instruction for each successively higher level of development attained by the pupils. The first stage was for the candidates to purify their astral bodies. This meant that they did not merely embrace the ordinary bourgeois ethic; the bourgeois ethic was the pre-liminary requirement. What was then involved had to be fol-lowed by the strictest performance of duty. For, as the pupil progressively advanced to higher ideals, passing beyond the passions and instincts of ordinary life to yearnings above human pettiness, so purifying his sympathies and antipathies that the great world-embracing affairs of the human race became his own—as he reached out beyond himself in his feelings and perceptions, then he was on the way to completing what one calls the purification of the astral body. Then he was allowed to work upon the denser bodies. He was allowed to work upon his etheric body, and was no longer restricted to reshaping the soft, flexible and compliant astral substance of his soul and spirit bodies but was allowed to work on his etheric body. He was then what is called a Chela. Such a Chela is one who acknowledges not only higher duties, who has undertaken not only enough purification to make humanity's duties his own, but is so advanced that he has outgrown the lower and higher affairs of individual nations and even of individual creeds. His gaze is now addressed to the life of the whole of humanity. And through his by now thoroughly structured etheric body he becomes a participant in the great affairs of the building of the earth. To do all this, the following must happen.

The Chela has to immobilize all the forces which hinder his work on his etheric body. If you have a human being before you, he has indeed a physical body, an etheric body and an astral body. The Chela has refined his astral body, and is allowed to work upon his etheric body. What happens when the astral body has been purified? What then penetrates the etheric body?—that which is organized in the astral body. The things which live in the astral body stamp themselves on the etheric body. The more you work on your astral body, the more you can redress its defects; the astral substance is thin and soft, you can always bring it back into balance again.

However, if a person has begun to develop his etheric body as a Chela, then these qualities stamp themselves on the etheric body, and that is much more permanent. The man who made his earthly defects permanent would thereby become dangerous as a member of humanity. Hence the constant stress on necessary purification. The etheric body is stamped by the forces that work on it. Think of it separated from the physical body; it would then have quite a different elasticity. If it is fixed in [the physical body] this is held in by the form. But so long as it remains there, it is at first too weak to stamp into itself what has undergone catharsis as astrality.

Therefore throughout ancient times the following had to be done. One had to set aside those forces which impeded the elasticity of the etheric body. That was achieved by bringing the whole physical body into a lethargic condition. The human being lay down, and the etheric body was drawn out of the physical body. While the physical body lay as if dead, the astral body came to be formed by its autonomous forces. That is the entombment, the [body] concerned being kept in a lethargic state for three to three and a half days. And then he could work on the etheric body. And then, after he had formed his etheric body in conformity with his astral body, he returned into his physical body. He had thus awakened an inner life in himself; he was one of the resurrected and was given a new name.

This was a transaction on the astral plane. Everything which I have described took place on the astral plane; the physical body had nothing to do with it. This event was repeated in all the ancient Mysteries. Every initiate knew it. Now imagine it densified, translated down into the physical plane, so that something [physical] has happened, through this event, which had previously only happened astrally (analogous to, for example, your having a piece of ice where you had water before). Many such astral events must combine, must flow together, for the physical thickening eventually to become possible. Through this means the Mystery of Golgotha became historically possible; it could be translated down on to the physical plane, in that, through the appearance of Christ, things happened on the physical plane which previously had happened over and over again on the astral plane. We learn to conceive, through this example, how the future is actually prepared in the occult brotherhoods.

If we were now to ask ourselves, 'What then is really happening here?'—then we should answer, 'One can certainly comprehend a great deal in thought, in ideas. But ideas have no real existence. An idea is nothing more than what has been brought down from higher planes to the physical plane.' What man thinks about [something] is, however, the most ineffectual aspect, since this is only extant on the physical plane. It is different when such an idea is brought face to face with something which also originates from the higher spheres. Take as an example Pythagoras's teaching about the Music of the Spheres[3] as he imparted it to his pupils. Philosophers try to make the occult music of Pythagoras out to be quite a simple notion. Reason could easily grasp it. But what was important [for Pythagoras] was that the pupil only approached this [subject] when his soul, his disposition had been prepared for it. Thus it is impossible to explain the deeper meaning of Raphael's *Sistine Madonna* to anyone who has no feeling for pictures which originate in the astral. One has to raise heart and soul up to it. What leaves one cold as an idea appears in the picture as artistically full of life, as divine universal thinking, as something the divine forces followed in creating the world—and a simple line becomes something holy! Thought, by twining itself around a divine element, is brought face to face with divine influence. Thus what matters in this sort of training is to prepare man step by step to approach the great world thoughts, and to receive them. Then he will gradually unite his penetration into these great cosmic thoughts with that operative, but otherwise occult, power which has been prepared in the astral world for the future life on the physical plane. If the leading brother of mankind perhaps has pupils who follow such spirit-filled ideas, then these will be a force which also helps him forward in his work for the outward world; great centres of spiritual activity will spring up. You see, therefore, that what I have called occultism really has very much to do with the progress of humanity. And in our times we have a quite particularly important task. Let us seek just to indicate, in a few words, how we have come to this our task.

We are within the great Root Race of humanity that has peopled the earth since the land on which we now live rose up out of the inundations of the ocean. Ever since the Atlantean Race began slowly to disappear, the great Aryan Race has been the dominant one on earth. If we contemplate ourselves, we here in Europe are thus the fifth Sub-Race of the great Aryan Root Race. The first Sub-Race lived in the distant past in Ancient India. And the present-day Indians are descendants of that first Sub-Race, whose spiritual life is still extant in the ancient Indian Vedas.[4] The Vedas are indeed only echoes of the ancient culture of the Rishis. At that time there was of course no writing yet—there was only tradition. Then came the second, third and fourth Sub-Races. The fourth Sub-Race adopted Christianity. Then, half-way through the Middle Ages, we see that the fifth Sub-Race was formed, to which we and the neighbouring nations belong.

The Ancient Indians of the first Sub-Race lived under conditions different from ours, and were also basically organized differently. Even the modern descendants, the Indians of today, are essentially differently organized from our European races. He who, as an occultist, investigates the difference, finds that, in the ancient Indian people, the etheric body was much less closely fettered to the physical body, had not so totally submerged itself into the physical body, and that it was much easier to influence it from the astral body. The corollary of that is that the Indian race can easily transfer something from the astral to the etheric body, can easily work on the etheric body. That signifies no less than that the Indian can more easily attain to certain higher perceptions through occult training. The easier it is for the etheric body to be influenced through the astral body, the easier it is to work into the etheric body with pictures, without abstract concepts. And the easier it will be for someone who undergoes yoga training in the astral to come into contact with higher realms through pictorial concepts. These work into the etheric body, which is still pliable. One does not have to work with harsh concepts, since one can work upon the soul of an Indian person with very straightforward pictorial images; and he will [thereby] be able to arrive at very high stages of development.

The human race has undergone change through the various Sub-Races. Our etheric body is today much more strongly under the influence of the physical body than was the case with the Ancient Indians. And thus it comes about that we have to work much harder and more inwardly in order to influence the etheric body. We cannot remain content with half-dreamlike concepts. We must subject everything to rigorous concentration; we must work upon our inner being by strongly concentrating our soul in the purely supersensible, not merely by means of imaginative concepts. Such a concept, which brings about a strong concentration of our inner being, can then influence the etheric body fettered to the physical body much more strongly. For the astral body to be able to work upon the etheric body, it had in earlier times to be outside of the etheric [physical?] body. Nowadays, however, the etheric body can be influenced by the astral body from inside the physical body. Were we to make the same experiment that was customary in the ancient Mysteries, and induce a state of lethargy, we would then be in a position to influence the etheric body. But when the earthly consciousness, the mobility of thought, returned, what the astral body had imprinted onto the etheric body would immediately be erased again. We have to influence the etheric body very strongly if we want it to retain what we have impressed upon it. The occult task has become different today and is now more inward.

Thus you see also how great differences arise in the course of time in the successive occult schools. The yoga system of the Indians is something different from the instruction of the Rosicrucians. The Rosicrucian teaching takes into account what I have just explained. But something else still crops up. For such a step forward to be able to occur at all, the reasoning power had to be influenced. The reasoning was exerted much more than hitherto, and could then be led towards comprehending the supersensible through inner concentration. In more recent times, therefore, much more was taught through concepts; more importance was ascribed to the development of reason and to the ability to conceptualize abstractly.

Just compare the difference in culture between the Ancient Indian age and our own. In Ancient India you have high intuition and very little outward expression of civilization; nowadays, in our time, it is the other way round. The consequence is that even the position of occultism has become something quite different; the consequence is that much of what was formerly kept secret has today become a matter of common knowledge. Many, many such perceptions and concepts were formerly guarded within the occult brotherhoods, and people only came near to these things if their whole hearts had been transformed. Today this no longer lies in the hands of the occultist. Much of what was formerly reserved for the later stages of instruction must now be acknowledged as having been revealed in the culture of the outward world. The initiate in the Mysteries must reckon with that. And so many of the truths which had been taught in the occult schools were perforce gradually disseminated on the physical plane.

Even what is taught in present-day elementary schools

would deflect us from the spiritual, if occult backgrounds did not come into play from another side. In earlier times the pupil knew that behind what he received in school and in the academic world as precepts there was something still higher, and that he himself might perhaps one day attain this higher knowledge. He knew that he was a cell in a spiritual organism. Today, in the democratic world, one receives many concepts which do not lead to such an insight. Therefore to the structure of outer democratic knowledge the apex of the pyramid has, as it were, to be added. The elementary knowledge of the powers hidden in the world had now been imparted; the apex was missing still, which would lead to a spiritual view of the world. To provide this, a world-embracing movement had to be founded. The theosophical movement was conceived as such. Hence, in certain brotherhoods, it was resolved, as the popularization of the hitherto secret knowledge went still further and further, to share with the world as much as was necessary of the underlying secrets, in order to bring the knowledge of the outer world into harmony with the all-embracing occult knowledge of the brotherhoods.

We have here arrived at the point where we can see the connection of the theosophical movement and the Theosophical Society with occultism. The theosophical movement is no occult movement, no occult brotherhood, for it is formed on a democratic basis by which each member is as worthy as the next. Nevertheless, it is another matter if one is to understand the Theosophical Society's task. The Society's task is on the physical plane. If one wishes to grasp it fully one must be able to see into the higher worlds. But the point is not that the theosophist is already able to see into higher worlds, but that, within the movement, occult forces are indeed being developed, so that the Theosophical Society can be a place from which occultism can emanate and come to be discussed. It is a different question, whether a society is an occult brotherhood or whether it says to itself: We are, indeed, no occult brotherhood, but, in our society, occultism comes to be discussed.

Today, when basically the whole of mankind longingly gazes towards the higher worlds without finding the way there, yet another instalment of occult knowledge must be popularized in a form appropriate for it. And the occultism within the Theosophical Society has this task. Spiritual movements have always had a fruitful influence on cultural development, even on the physical plane. Its outward expression is nothing else than the realization on earth of what has been spiritually prepared. What difference is there, if we contemplate, for example, the works of Michaelangelo and Leonardo da Vinci? In these works you have something spiritual conjured up onto the wall in colour and form; the picture is permeated with what first lived in the soul of the artist as something spiritual. The spiritual preceded its subsequent expression as a manifestation in the material world.

And the materialistic external culture is only the copy of the materialistic tendency in mankind's inner convictions. The purely materialistic urban culture has spread throughout civilized countries since 1850. We can see the great things that it has achieved on the physical plane, but we also see what it has been unable to achieve. In the realm of art, for instance, no really new style has been evolved, with one exception, and that is the style of the department store. This is something which, in relation to our outward civilization, is inwardly real. All else, which has been inherited from the past, has no relation to the present. Only if we have formed a society whose members are seized by a spiritual power such as that which used to live in Christianity, and as it still lives as a longing in the best Christian souls and can be won back again, will we again have a spiritual culture. And such a culture will again produce artists in all spheres of life. Only let theosophy live in the souls of men and it will flow out of those souls again as style, as art, it will be visibly and audibly there. The world can again be an outward expression of the spiritual, if this can already be brought to life in such a society today.

In this sense the Theosophical Society could help to shape the culture of the distant [future]. When we are together, we must be clear that we are the cells that have to combine to create a future culture. In our souls, those powers will be prepared which will so transform the future world that it will be a physical copy of our present state of mind and outlook on life. Everything which is now revealed and manifest was once occult. Just as electricity is a revealed force today, so it once used to be an occult force. And what is still occult today is destined to become a motive force for the future. Exactly as our human body has been prepared in advance millions of years ago by forces which are all around us, so a higher body is being prepared in us today—a body of the future. However, this body of the future will only become ours in a far-off time.

Let us briefly trace the path of our evolution. What used to be there?—a dim dreamlike human consciousness, mirroring a world very different from our own. Men had a dreaming awareness. And even when their communal existence developed, they had no parliament for the exchange of opinions; they had nothing of that kind. Everything was merely mirrored in the consciousness that was developing in man. As for present-day bodily organs, how did they originate? Through those forces having worked upon man. Just as the animals in the dark caves of Kentucky lost their ability to see[5] because they did not use it, so too, what we possess in the way of eyes and ears was organized by outward forces. These were formed by the forces of sound and of light, and evolved out of our organism. Our spiritual organism of the future will be evolved out of what lives in us today. Those things which stand before us as the expression of our spiritual culture, the churches and so on, the works of culture which bring beauty and truth to us, these will impress themselves in the higher members of our being. And when one day these develop an independent life of their own, then what lives in the outward civilization as beauty and truth will rise up in our inner being. What eyes and ears perceive now, these will be the stones for building and organizing a higher future. If we contemplate the world from this point of view, then man's inner being takes on a totally different meaning.

Here we are confronted with a fact that can explain in a simple way what is called yoga, or inner training. From the words I have spoken, you will be able to gather that the forces which have created the world, that are working and creating in the world, were formerly taken from our inner being. What is in me today was formerly outside me—that is the fundamental thought in occult training. Before our physical body existed, our etheric body was already there. Again, our etheric body is a structure which has been formed by our astral body. And that is the starting-point of the yoga training. Whoever engages in yoga training descends into his etheric body, and knows that he will find forces in it which formed it once, millions of years ago. The physical body slowly developed from the basis of the etheric body.

I can only describe broadly how the descent into the etheric body takes place. Certain currents exist in the etheric body which are the precursors of the physical bodily organs. The nervous system, the nerves themselves, the sympathetic [nervous] system which extends into the back, the ganglia of the sympathetic nervous system, these are parts which were developed etherically in primeval times. That is a process which took place in the remote past. Then, after man had progressed further and further, there came a time when, within his body (which already contained within it the potentiality to develop the physical nervous system) a structure developed which gave man the ability to develop his inner bodily warmth, which prepared him for warm blood. That, again, is a later structure from the etheric body, which then was already strongly influenced by the forces of the astral body. And out of what we subsequently find to be the basic structure of the brain the spinal column developed, again out of the etheric body, as the other pole of the etheric body, which on the one hand developed towards the brain, and on the other hand towards the inner warmth of the blood. That happened in the past. It was not only natural forces that worked on this development of man, but also higher spiritual beings.

When the yogi descends step by step into his etheric body he penetrates into the times gone by in which his spiritual archetypal form was influenced by these forces and beings, times when what lives in us today was produced. When a person thus descends into life, he can then reach that point once again in his descent. He descends from the head down into the lower parts of the body, which were formed in the most ancient times, and then goes back into the head. That is a description, if only a sketchy one, of the path of occult perception. More can be imparted in the occult schools. The pupil of Mystery wisdom thus developed the ability to look back into past epochs; then the time comes when he is able to undertake his occult pilgrimage. He attains to this by means of a special exercise through which he overcomes his own personal self and thereby ceases to be a small fettered ego. Only then can he accomplish his ascent into the universe. Once again he descends into the ocean of the past, taking the world forces with him. Then, taking the ascending curve, he can slowly retrace point by point the way that he has thus travelled. Slowly, gradually, the person learns to descend into the ocean of his formative forces, and at length he arrives at a point near to [his] origin. Thus must it have been for the person in whom an eye first evolved, with which to direct his gaze into the universe. Then, for the pupil, the flowing together of his ego with the great universal ego opens up. And now he must learn to say to the little ego: I am not thou.

It is an important moment when he realizes what this means: I am not thou. That is a moment when a person begins to understand that in nature there are higher forces than thought, that there is something outside of him which cannot be expressed in contemporary thought but which brings it about that two people, both able to speak about the same thing, can in the case of one of them talk clearly but be dull whereas the other's speech is vibrant with the warm light that will create the future.

When the pupil is thus far, he can learn now in another way than was hitherto possible for him. He thereby experiences something very special. A spiritual being confronts him in the supersensible world; he meets that individuality with whom he was formerly very close. It is a great and significant mystery, when particular stages of our existence are recapitulated. We rise consciously from manas to the higher forces. We once descended from spiritual worlds, and at that time this same being implanted something in us, whom we now meet again at the level corresponding to that point in the past at which he was with us. It is the teacher, the so-called guru. Long ago we met him for the first time; we now meet him again, when we can grasp consciously what he implanted into us at that time, and was received by us unconsciously. And if we descend still further we meet with the spirits who shared in our creation aeons ago. We meet with the Twelve Spirits: the Spirits of Will, the Spirits of Wisdom, the Spirits of Form, the Spirits of Movement, the Spirits of Personality or of Egoism, the Spirits of Warmth or Fire, the Spirits of Dusk or Twilight, and so on. All of this is offered to our spiritual sense through this descent into the universe, through this pilgrimage. And this alone makes it possible for us to gaze into the future, makes it possible to anticipate what 'shortly'—as the writer of the Apocalypse puts it—will happen.

That is the task of occultism. It is to be discharged, because that discharge is necessary. There are movements in plenty which are idealistic, which are ethical. But the movement called theosophy is distinguished from the others in that occultism consciously comes to expression in this move-ment.

With that, the connection between occultism and theosophy is made clear. The Theosophical Society can never want to be an occult brotherhood. What must give it the strength to fulfil its task, what must give it life, can only be the things that emanate from occultism. Therefore the Theosophical Society will thrive if the cultivation of occult teaching and occult life is understood. That is still not a demand that the members themselves should be occultists. But if the Theosophical Society were to forget that this blood pulses in it, then it might remain an interesting society, but what was intended for it by the sublime powers who assisted at its birth would not be achieved.

Whoever understands this will never want to take away the Theosophical Society's occult character. All the same, who-ever thus belongs to the Theosophical Society will be brought into a two-sided situation. He must necessarily give an ear to the side whence flow the occult truths, on the other hand he must turn his attention to the exoteric life of the Society. These aspects must be kept strictly apart; they must never be mixed together. When one talks about the outward Theosophical Society, one must never, however, even mention the occult personalities who stood over its inception. The powers who live on the higher planes and who live for the sake of man-kind's evolution, outside of the physical body, never interfere in these affairs. They never impart anything other than impulses. Whenever we are engaged, in a practical way, in extending the Theosophical Society, the great individualities whom we call the Masters are standing at our side; we may turn to them and allow them to speak through us. When it concerns the propagation of occult life, it is the Masters who speak. When it only concerns the organization of the Society then they leave it to those who are living on the physical plane. That is the distinction between the occult current and the framework of the theosophical organization. Allow me to express the difference between what flows as inward spiritual stream and what manifests through individual personalities, as it can perhaps best be expressed: When it concerns spiritual life, then the Masters speak; when it only concerns organization, since error is possible, the Masters are then silent.

Freemasonry and Human Evolution—I

(Lecture for men only)

Berlin, 23 October 1905 (10.00 a.m.)

I have asked you to attend a short discussion on occult questions, because one must acknowledge that anyone participating in the theosophical movement should be clear not only about the outward things that are dealt with in the programme but also about the direction in which this theosophical movement can lead. Now those occult streams that are living in the theosophical movement are in fact akin, in a particular respect, to earlier occult currents. The topic we mean to broach today concerns precisely one of these, which still persists to the present day: Freemasonry.

You know that, at least until the late seventeenth century, any kind of female member was, for Freemasonry, strictly taboo.[1] At that time, there was a good reason for this. When the reason for the Freemasons having no female members ceases to exist at some point in world evolution, then the time will have come for the work of Freemasonry on the physical plane to be taken over by the work of theosophy. *Pro tem*, the work of theosophy is preparatory work. Men and women will participate in the theosophical work on the same basis.

If I were now to be permitted to say briefly why women had to be excluded from the activities of Freemasonry, I could only say that one does not exactly give away one's secrets to the opponent; one hardly sends him one's plan of campaign. That is not done in the conduct of any war. And we will see that

Freemasonry is in a particular respect in opposition to the female world.

Freemasonry is the continuation of very ancient secret societies and brotherhoods. Such secret societies—at least in the form in which they survive in Freemasonry—originated just at the very beginning of our fourth post-Atlantean epoch, that is to say in the same epoch in which Christianity later began.

You know that the outward compilation of the Bible is rightly ascribed to only a few hundred years before the birth of Christ.[2] But the biblical revelation was a [living] tradition for thousands of years before that. It was not the custom in antiquity to write such things down; they were instead passed on from mouth to mouth. Therefore it can be assumed that the secrets which Moses entrusted to the priesthood were only later written down.

Now in the same period as that when the Bible first made its appearance in world history as a document, what is known as the Freemasonry legend also came to be compiled and to be circulated.

In world evolution it is always to be regarded as a law that what happened earlier is later briefly recapitulated. Every human being recapitulates, in the maternal womb, the stages through which the [human] race has already passed. Every planetary stage of the Earth repeats, in its initial stages, the previously completed steps of its evolution. What has already gone before is always briefly recapitulated. So is it with the races, too. Hence, the first, second and third post-Atlantean races [epochs] are the recapitulation of earlier earthly conditions, only in a specific higher realm. What began with Lemuria developed throughout Atlantis, and was recapitulated in our three cultural epochs in a specific higher realm. So that we thus have a recapitulation of what occurred earlier, in Lemurian times, in a less-developed realm. Before the system of two sexes originated, there was a kind of bisexuality, a single [combined] sex, in so far as in each individual both sexes were represented. For the separation into two sexes only came later; only then did male-female become male *and* female. On a spiritual level something similar is recapitulated in our epoch. Actually, that kind of knowledge and wisdom which pertained to pre-Vedic Ancient India had a male-female quality, and thereby, at the same time, something quite unconnected with any kind of duality or with any kind of outward principle. Then came the civilization of the second cultural epoch; this was pre-eminently a spiritual culture having two sexes. Dualism then appeared—Ormuzd and Ahriman, Good and Evil. All this now merged with man's cognition.

Now we want to clarify how that came about. It came about thus. In the beginning, before there was a separate male and female sex, there was a twofold sexuality within each single individual. We must now ask: What was it that could become fertilized, and what was it that did the fertilizing, in the one single individual? In ancient Greek mythology Zeus is por-trayed with ample female breasts.[3] A truth is expressed therein, which was known in the old Mysteries and which we also learn from the records, that the sex (if I may call it that) that immediately preceded our own outwardly and physically resembled not the male but the female gender. So that before the outward separation we have thus both sexes in one indi-vidual that outwardly—in physical expression and in all per-ceptions and being—was female. Therefore, at the beginning of the human race, we have to do with a bi-sexual individual tending towards the female. Only later did the male sex follow. Now we must be clear that in this individual, which had both sexes in it, a fertilizing agent, or male seed, was also present. Woman contained man within her. When we have grasped the fact that the woman had the male principle within her, then we can conceive, with our ordinary scientific concepts, that reproduction was ensured. We want to bear in mind that at that time this happened *via* the woman.

Now came the time when things had to go their separate ways. What character did the fertilizing principle in the woman then have, which on the physical plane would fertilize the female nature? What worked in the female [body] as a seed was the male, and that was what was spiritual, the wisdom. Woman contributed the substance; the spirit gave [it] form. Any structuring on the physical plane is a realization of wisdom. Wisdom worked in the female. Now the two differentiated themselves, in that the two things which had previously worked as one now appeared as two separated poles. What was previously united in a single human organ became separated, whereby a duality in human development originated. This duality came about thus. First, the fertility—the ability of the female egg to fertilize itself—within the one individual ceased [to function]. The female egg lost the possibility of becoming fertilized from its own body. So we are now dealing with a female which has become infertile and, above everything, the spiritual. The division of the two sexes came about through the separation of the physical organs, and the other sex was now endowed with the possibility of fertilization. Two individuals appeared, one with physical femininity and the other with physical masculinity. With the man, wisdom has a female character; with the woman, it has a male character.

The separation is a very definite event that one can follow; we will now have to be satisfied, however, with [mere] indications. We are dealing, then, with male-tinged wisdom in the woman and female-tinged wisdom in the man. This female-tinged wisdom is passive, suited to receiving, listening, watching—to taking in from the surroundings. The male-tinged wisdom, the active wisdom, is productive. Thus we have a twofold wisdom. There is the female wisdom that is active and *that* naturally will also be transferred to the men. Thus there may indeed be plenty of men to take over the female wisdom. The race [is propagated] below [on the physical plane]; and above, we are dealing with an active intuition stemming from women, and with a passive cognition, decidedly male in character.

This figures in the old Mystery teaching as the antithesis between the Sons of Abel, or Sons of God, and the Sons of Cain, or Sons of Man. Abel represents the female, active intuition. Therefore he is unable to take hold of anything from the outside world which needs to be worked upon. He takes up the divine, which streams through him, which flows into his intuitiveness. The 'Herdsman' symbolizes that. He tends and nurtures life, while intuition nurtures the divine life of wisdom. Cain has the male wisdom that receives the outward. This [wisdom] espouses the earth in order to till it; the material is outside [himself]. He is the 'Field-builder' [Literal meaning of German *der Ackerbauer*, = 'agriculturalist']. What does the wisdom of Cain now achieve? This science of Cain that, being a passive science, only receives—what does it accomplish?

Now there is a very interesting and important legend in which these truths are symbolically expressed for the Freemasons. That is the Temple Legend. And the reason for it is as follows.

The Bible itself, the Old Testament, derives from the female, the intuitive wisdom, and bears its stamp. The Old Testament is female wisdom. Male wisdom was not able to attain to intuition. It confined itself to building and work. It took stones and constructed buildings. It took metals and made implements. The Temple Legend puts it thus.

One of the Elohim impregnated Eve and Cain was born. Afterwards, another of the Elohim, Jehovah, also known as Adonai, created Adam. And Adam begat Abel by Eve. This legend counterposed the wisdom of Cain and the biblical wisdom, so that by the beginning of the fourth post-Atlantean epoch we have two opposing currents: the Bible, representing womanly wisdom, and the Temple wisdom as its opposing male counterpart. Already, in pre-Christian times, what the man [male wisdom?] wanted stood in opposition to the female wisdom. Moreover, Cain slew his brother Abel. That too comes into the Temple Legend. Jehovah caused strife between the race of Cain and the race of Abel, and Cain killed Abel. That means nothing else ... [Some very obscure sentences follow here in the (German) transcript.]

What was the consequence of the appearance of this Cain wisdom? The outcome of it all was that the fruitfulness that was propagated through its own wisdom was killed. By killing Abel the male knowledge in Cain killed the possibility of self-propagation that had been brought into being by the gods. That means it is because knowledge has been transferred to the man that the Abel in man has been killed.

That is a process in man himself.[4] Through male knowledge the creative force, the Abel [within], has been killed. There now stand in hostile opposition to one another the descendants of Cain and the race of those who were put in the place of Abel, the descendants of Seth. The descendants of Cain are those who use their masculine wisdom to build up the external world; the passive wisdom is applied to external construction. The divine wisdom does not stream down into it. It must build in the world out of what is free. It has no divine intuition. Through trial, through experience, results the harmonizing of the purely mineral products of the earth. Thus Tubal-Cain is born out of the race of Cain and thus, later on, will Hiram-Abiff or Adon-Hiram be born from the same lineage.

I have reserved for myself ... [See note].[5]

Among the Abelites, you find the strongest representative in Solomon. During the third cultural epoch all the representatives of the Abel line were priests. The ancient priestly wisdom was the intuitive wisdom that formerly worked in woman as the power of fertilization but was then transformed, at a higher level, to spiritual wisdom. Out of this priestly wisdom came the Bible; in this way the Bible came to be a feminine wisdom. This feminine wisdom is able to make great revelations about the Divine and to say how this relates to the angels and spirits. The business of the Sons of Cain is to shape the earth. Thus the original father of all smiths is indeed Tubal-Cain. Therefore Solomon had to send for Hiram-Abiff, who could build the temple for him. He built it for King Solomon, the inheritor of the ancient priestly wisdom; for him, for Solomon, who transformed this priestly wisdom into external power. Kingship, as an outward institution, derives from the rule of the priests.

Thus Solomon sent for Hiram-Abiff. And thus Solomon's temple was built. But now the Queen of Sheba came to Solomon's court and a kind of betrothal was celebrated there between the two. Now the temple was shown to the Queen, and she desired to be introduced to the builder of this marvellous temple. When she was introduced to Hiram-Abiff, something quite special happened in her. A glance from Hiram-Abiff fell on her, and that worked in her like fire. And then a second thing happened, as follows. She wanted to see the workers and to be shown how all this was accomplished on the physical plane, so Hiram-Abiff took the Tau symbol, held it aloft and the workers all came streaming together like ants. Through this she [was so impressed that she] deserted Solomon [for Hiram]. Some of Hiram's apprentices, whom he had refused to make into masters, came to Solomon's aid. Now they sought to spoil Hiram's masterpiece, the casting of the Molten Sea. Instead of it coming out as a work of art, streams of fire spurted out in every direction. Hiram-Abiff tried to quench it all with water, but all he achieved by this was a complete wreck. A rain of fire sprayed down on everything, including Hiram-Abiff. A voice called to him, however, not to be afraid, for out of this would come his greatest success. Then he was led by a figure to the centre of the earth. There he met Cain himself, to whom he had been led by Tubal-Cain, who founded the art of metal-working. Here an important wisdom was revealed to him. He was told: 'Now know the true Jehovah, who is the cause of your being here. Jehovah hates the Sons of Fire, and wants to destroy them; he wants to destroy his own creation. But you need have nothing to fear. To you will be born a son, whom you will not yourself see, but from whom shall spring a race out of which a new fire worship will develop on the earth.' With the hammer which Tubal-Cain gave him, he was able to complete the projected Molten Sea, thereby rising still further in the Queen of Sheba's affections. During a walk, a bird appeared in the air, showing her the mystical Tau sign. From this the Queen's nurse realized that the wisdom of the future was hidden under this sign of the Tau. During a feast, at which Solomon became intoxicated, the Queen of Sheba took the betrothal ring back from his hand. Hiram-Abiff was, however, set upon by the apprentices and killed. He was only just able to write the secret word on a golden triangle and hide it. It was later retrieved and enclosed in a stone shaped in the form of a cube. The Ten Commandments are inscribed on this stone that conceals the hidden word.

That is the temple wisdom, which male science has counterposed to the female wisdom. These are things that need only to be clarified, to be examined as to their occult meaning, for their deep significance to be recognized.

Consider that Hiram-Abiff was brought before the original father of his race. He was told that Jehovah was the enemy of the Sons of Fire. Who are the Sons of Fire? They are those who could only come into existence after the separation of the sexes, through the penetration of a physical female by a physical male. Fire is the active principle in the male semen. In male semen lives fire, in the occult sense. Jehovah had to create this basic force, so that the race could propagate itself. Jehovah created the Sons of Fire, which was only possible on the basis of this [occult] fire. Hence he is the opponent of change. He it was who continued the old kind of propagation. For it was an expedient which had been created, and therefore he turned again to the priests and made them into his prophets. He caused the power and the glory of his own wisdom to be proclaimed through the priestly wisdom; through the priestly wisdom, Jehovah's wisdom came to be made known.

Hiram-Abiff is thus appointed to undertake the creation of the Molten Sea, which means the transformation of the mineral kingdom through art. He was also told that a son would be born to him, who—even though he would not himself be able to see him—would bring forth a new race. This son is nothing else than the new race which will one day take the place of the old, the present one—the new race for whom it will no longer be necessary for two sexes to unite with one another, but will again be able to bring about propagation through the one human individual. This refers to a far distant future. The old female culture will be relieved by a male culture. The female, as a physical form, will die out. The male must then have the power in itself to produce another individual out of itself. And where is this power located?

Male and female used to be in one individual. And when these two separated an unfolding of today's individuality took place. The upper part [of the human being] was formed. What [today] is the upper part was at that time combined with the sexual organs. The sexual organs of today are only half of the then [procreative] force. The power in the larynx is indeed the other half. Speech is not as yet creative today. It has to be penetrated by the wisdom of Cain first, and then it must produce. When man has attained the power for his larynx so to develop that his word will be creative, so that he will produce his own kind through the Word, then the whole of the productive force will be transferred to the male. Then [the work of creation] which was once done by the Gods, will be given over to man. When did the Word come to be lost? When the system of two sexes originated. It was buried, hidden. The Sons of Cain had it only through the original father of their race.

Hiram-Abiff should at least have the prophecy about it. However, he was killed immediately afterwards.

The Word lies buried, but it is still there. If it were not buried, man would be self-creative, just as the Elohim are self-creative. Therefore the 'Word' of present-day Freemasonry is not the true Word but the false one. The true Word is concealed. The Ten Commandments are inscribed on the stone which contains the hidden Word. What are the Ten Commandments? They are the laws of the moral world order. They maintain the outer intercourse [of mankind], as it now is, subject to the influence of a race having two sexes. Such laws will not be needed when there are no longer two sexes. They are that human code which originated out of the context of two sexes.

Thus we have, preserved in Freemasonry, the remembrance of the Lost Word, which those who work in Freemasonry must strive for, and which can only be gained when the passive male wisdom awakens activity in itself. The Freemasons therefore say: Everything which does not stem from one's personal knowledge about the world must be a remnant of the female priestly rule of ancient times. Rather than contenting ourselves with merely inheriting this [conquering it?], we actually want to start on a new spiral of existence; we ourselves must bring intuition to the male wisdom of Cain. That would be impossible if one took the female into the secret, which would take man's power from him. It would all be useless the instant it was discussed in front of women.

It thus became necessary for the whole female sex to be excluded from Freemasonry. This hangs together with the link between the organ of speech and gender or sexuality. Therefore the man's voice changes when he reaches puberty. The change [of voice] is nothing else than the expression of the former connection between the organs of speech and of sexuality. Now you too can grasp what the Freemason is saying: It is only the man who is appointed to utter the Lost

Word at all and to re-establish it; only the male form of the larynx is in a position to say, to know, what can be regained through the Lost Word. When we grasp it in this way, one will understand why woman was not permitted to let what was new pass her lips. It is comic to see scholars give as the reason for this that women were not admitted because they blabbered out everything. The female larynx has remained as a rudiment. It is the male larynx which will, however, form the organ of the future.

You see that deep and meaningful relationships are involved, and that the expression 'Mason' has to be taken as literally as possible. That is why the masons of Greek and Roman times were the builders of things made to express beauty. Cathedrals, temples and other significant buildings were built by these master builders.

The matter rests thus, that a part of what came to be accomplished by the Order of Freemasons had naturally to be taken over again from the old priestly wisdom. So, once again, we have an intermingling of womanly wisdom and male striving. In essence, the secret of Freemasonry is something which has not yet been revealed, which is not even there yet, so that it cannot be revealed, precisely because it does not yet exist. It is something which will be uttered when the word is once more imbued with productive force.

Those are a few words which will clarify the thinking of Freemasonry for the occultist. Up to the eighteenth century it was known that things were so. Only when the connection with higher worlds was lost did the consciousness of what was lost fade from Freemasonry too. And yet again, not so. Freemasonry was watered down; it was said that people no longer knew its meaning. One must be clear, however, that everything which existed as symbols was derived from the old priestly wisdom and that what is implanted therein, in the symbols, must still first come into the open. The true female wisdom is gradually becoming quite lost. Because of that, the so-called higher degrees of Freemasonry, which preserved the female wisdom, have been allowed to vanish. All that is still left is what is called Craft Masonry, which only concerns itself with worldly things, and only understands a little about them, in any case.

But that is, after all, quite natural; as materialism developed, then the priestly wisdom did indeed have to fade away. What can happen now? The old wisdom has gone away. We have to live in the externalities. What follows from that? This—that something better can come along again only when a wisdom arrives which is again asexual, which is connected neither with the male nor with the female wisdom, neither with the female Bible, nor with the male Temple Legend. We find this wisdom in theosophy. In this wisdom both sexes understand each other. In it, the man that is in woman is at work on woman, and what is once more asexual is working on man. Male and female meet each other there in the knowledge of higher planes. It is therefore quite natural that the proper occult basis has come about in Freemasonry, and that a new start has been made. Something such as this is called a 'vortex':

old
new

In our time, these things are thus intertwining in their influence. We must therefore think of them as interacting. Thus, theosophy has relied neither on the biblical legend nor on the Temple Legend, but asexually seeks the kernel of wisdom that has to be restored again in everything. Now you see how theosophy is the bringer of peace, the harmonizer.

How does this work together in our Root Race? Our Root Race recapitulates what already was there before. It brings the antithesis of what was already there in Lemurian times to meaningful expression in the spiritual realm. An opposition had therefore to come about, because the female sex was there originally, and follows a falling curve, whereas the male sex is in a rising curve, and is seeking in itself the procreative force which the female already has. When we remain in lower spheres, we have to make an exact distinction, through occultism: whoever is racially an Atlantean man need not also be Atlantean in his soul [qualities]. Hence, the soul is not tied to [a particular] sex either. The souls of female gender work through [this] until they can live equally with men in the bodies the latter have made for themselves, and there will [then] be *one* sex on earth.

As long as men still stood in opposition to the female, they had to hold their tongues. The founding of the Adoption Lodges in the eighteenth century paved the way for the sexes to come together.[6] The first of these was founded in 1775. A Freemasonry was practised in them that had different symbols from the male Freemasonry. However, the induction of women in such Adoption Lodges of the male Freemasons did pave the way for the sexes to come together. The founder of our Society was indeed a [female] member of such an Adoption Lodge.[7] What must be pointed to as the beginning of theosophy did indeed thus play a part in the matter. So, theosophy is a world task, connected with occult currents, and must take over where Freemasonry left off. Freemasonry could indeed still be reawakened, and could help us.

But the more profound thought is this: these one-sided male endeavours must be vanquished in theosophical circles. Throughout the Middle Ages there was a sublime preparation for spiritually engendering the opposite sex in man. Man developed in himself by concentrating, at first as a thought, what had to become a reality in him later on. Therefore, as a preparation for this, the cult of Mary resulted during the Middle Ages. This is nothing else than concentrating to engender the female in the male, while for the female the cult of Jesus served the parallel purpose. The cult of Mary had its origin in this foundation.

You will now see what confusion must result when an Order arose which broke with all this and sought to regain the female wisdom. It is world dominion which is at stake in this; if anyone wants to leave the old wisdom as it is, he will have to conquer the world for the old powers. There is such an Order. It is the Jesuit Order. It has consciously set itself this task. That is why the Jesuits and the Freemasons confront each other so sourly.

Freemasonry and Human Evolution—II

(Lecture for women only)

Berlin 23 October 1905 (11.30 a.m.)

The things which we wish to discuss today have not hitherto been discussed in front of women. Therefore, it is a rather bold step I am taking to speak about these things to you. However, particular occult currents make it necessary.

Within these currents there are some things of an intimate nature which, up to a short while ago, could not be mentioned in the presence of women because the occult brotherhood, whose task it was to nurture these intimate things, had a strict rule to admit no women members. What they had to do in the world might not be done in co-operation with the female element. Until just recently, this rule has been strictly adhered to. Nowadays, the sole possibility of creating a balance between the two sexes exists only in the Theosophical Society. Here is indeed the only place where these things are discussed in front of women.

Now we ask: Why has this separation of the sexes come about, which has taken such a grotesque form in the Lodges of Freemasonry? If one wants to understand why this segregation really became habitual, one has to use a rather grotesque metaphor. When two powers are at war with each other, it would be very foolish if the general of one side were to reveal his plan of campaign to the enemy general before the battle started. It would be the same as handing over one's weapons to the enemy, if one were to enlist women in the Freemasons.

For it is a matter of war for the Freemasons, a war indeed against the female spirit, a matter of sharp opposition to the female spirit as such. This war was necessary, yes, occult Freemasonry was founded precisely for this purpose. Therefore it was the custom to speak about occult matters to the two sexes separately. First, a form must be found in which these things can be spoken of to women.

The founding of Freemasonry lies far back in the past. It took place at the beginning of the fourth cultural epoch of our present fifth [post-Atlantean] Root Race. The Old Testament, which gives us an explanation of these things, was written down at that same time. We are told that higher spirits made revelations to Moses, which he then wrote down. The knowledge of higher things was already there, however, much earlier and was handed on from generation to generation, from priestly mouth to priestly mouth, until it was put into documentary form by Ezra,[1] to whom the writing of these things is ascribed. When the Old Testament began to gain power through the priests, a tremendous opposition to this priestly book arose in the Freemasonry brotherhoods, for a particular reason. To be sure, this opposition has always been there—and it was necessary. We must be clear about why.

Let us agree that everything which happens on the physical plane has to recapitulate earlier stages in a particular way. On earth there is always a recapitulation of the events of earlier times. [In his life] before birth man has to go through the stages which he once experienced with his dull animal consciousness [in earlier times]. So, for instance, the Renaissance period of the Middle Ages was a recapitulation of ancient Greek times. We also find such recapitulation in planetary events. Before the present earth became what it is today, it had to recapitulate earlier conditions before it could become an independent planet, our earth in fact, in the Fourth Round [or recapitulation]. Thus, whenever anything new has to appear on earth, the earlier stages must always be recapitulated in a new form. So the human spirit in the fifth Root Race [our present Race] has worked through a recapitulation of the [happenings of] the Lemurian Root Race [the third Race] when humanity was still of one sex only, and then became two-sexed. That had a great influence on its spiritual development. In the third Sub-Race of the fifth Root Race, the Egypto-Babylonian period, there was a progressive recapitulation in the realm of spiritual life of what had happened physically to man of Lemurian times.

Before there was [separate] male and female, the two were combined; then the two sexes separated from each other. As regards spiritual development, we have this happening in the fifth Root Race:

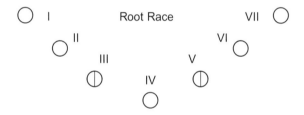

Third Root Race: Lemuria: division of physical evolution into two sexes, male and female.
Fifth Root Race: Division of spiritual evolution into male and female spirit, into Jehovah worship, or priesthood, and Freemasonry.

In the first post-Atlantean epoch, in the [Ancient] Indian culture, everything was still at a higher level than the physical plane. The original Indian wisdom, which stems from the first post-Atlantean civilization, is spiritually speaking primarily connected not with the present physical plane but with the conditions of that earlier time when humanity was still [combined] male-female. Therefore, at that time, little regard was paid to the existence of [separate] sexes. There was no question of a dualistic principle in this; that comes only in the following

Sub-Race. The Vedas belong to a much later time. Already, in the second Sub-Race, there was a great schism. The outward expression of this schism is depicted for us in the Old Testament, quite wonderfully. Genesis has expressed it very beautifully and clearly. Before Yahveh created man, he made fruits and animals and so on, on earth, and only then did he create man, Adam, whom he then divided into two sexes.

This account rests on occult perceptions of the physical facts. Now, of course, all occult wisdom presents a relationship between physical events and later spiritual wisdom; for physical events arise out of Divine Wisdom and wisdom later re-emerges out of physical life, out of man. There is a connection there between wisdom, perception and physical life.

The whole fertilizing and fructifying force by which a new person is created used to be combined in one sex. Then the human being was separated into male and female. Which sex can best lay claim to the generative power? It is the female. Therefore Zeus, who was worshipped as the progenitor of the human race, was portrayed in the oldest [versions of] Greek mythology as having female breasts.[2] Zeus, as a superhuman being, was nearer to the female sex. The female sex was thus the first, the earlier one, and at that time had the power in itself of producing the complete human individual. This generative power lay within a human being of undivided sex, who approximated, in its outward physical form, more towards the female. In this single-sexed human being, the fertilizing [principle] was wisdom—the spirit itself. And the fertilizing of the female spirit by inspired wisdom is a later recapitulation of this. This human being of the single-sex era was the result of the fertilization by the Divine Spirit of the substance produced in the woman.

Now you understand what it was by which a woman could give birth to a human being. Physically, there is first of all a woman, who is fertilized from above. It was the Divine Spirit in woman which was the fertilizing principle. When the separation of the sexes happened, the differentiation started in the transformation of the female's spiritual organs of fertilization into organs of wisdom. The masculine power that the woman had in herself turned the creative force into organs of wisdom. So half the generative force stayed with the woman; the creative physical forces stayed with the man. As a result of this separation, the spinal cord and the brain with the nerve branches appeared, as portrayed in the Tree of Life and the Tree of Knowledge. The organ of wisdom is formed in the vertrebrae by the spinal cord and its extension into the brain. From that time on, there is a duality in man, namely, the two Trees of the biblical record, the Tree of Knowledge and the Tree of Life.

And now the new beings adapt themselves to the change. The individuals who had previously been female did not all subsequently take on the female form. The female side—the capacity to produce human beings—withdrew from one section and left behind, in substitution, the power to fertilize in a quite different way. Physical nature had separated into what fertilized and what needed to be fertilized. Spiritual nature, too, had been similarly divided. In female individuals the spirit acquired male character and colouring; in the male the spirit had a female character. That is still the female within man.

The biblical legend shows this very clearly. As is known, the man having two sexes was forbidden to eat from the Tree of Knowledge. The power with which Jehovah had invested mankind was: to make his wisdom become active in the woman. 'Thou shalt not eat of the Tree of Knowledge' means the same as 'Thou shalt not separate off the force of fertilization and make it independent.' For Jehovah's power, the fertilizing power, would thereby be lost to the woman. When woman ate from the Tree of Knowledge, she thereby laid the basis for becoming independent in respect of wisdom, thereby ceasing to remain a mere tool of Jehovah as he had planned. But thus she lost, along with Jehovah's power, the power to fertilize herself through wisdom as well. By eating [from the Tree of Knowledge] and giving the apple to man, she wiped this power out. Thus woman became dependent on man. It was Lucifer who led mankind along this path in order to make him independent. Jehovah was against this, and forbade man to eat from the Tree of Knowledge for that reason. However the woman did eat and gave to the man. The man ate too, so that the punishment decreed by Jehovah ensued. New bodies have to come into existence, which will work out the karma of previous existence; death and [re-] birth come into the world. Woman is now no longer fertile through herself, but has become barren. And with fertilization coming from outside, the possibility of this kind of death enters the world.

The biblical story of Paradise reveals this deep connection in images; ancient priestly traditions became the content in these images, and ancient priestly wisdom was vividly incorporated in them. Woman has, then, become infertile in respect of spiritual wisdom, because she has demanded physical perception. She gave to man and he ate as well; they were guilty, and were driven out of Paradise, to the formation of which they had made no contribution. That is the old priestly tradition about the origin of the sexes; this contains a profound insight into the connection between actual events.

What now happened as the result of the female separating herself from the male? Which of the sexes still possessed a shadow of that power of productive spiritual wisdom, the male or the female? We have seen that the wisdom of the female actually had a male character; this is the creative, the productive, the intuitive, what is original, what is fertile. The same divine power which formerly worked within woman to fertilize, to produce the physical human being, now worked as fertilizing principle in the perception of the divine centre in man's being. The religions work through words and images to further this process.

The female being becomes physically infertile, in the sense

that she cannot produce offspring out of herself as she did before. The masculine, passive spirit is the one which is spiritually infertile, but the man is the one who can fertilize physically. Spiritually, he now lets himself be fertilized by everything in the world; he now becomes spiritually fertilized so that he himself can fertilize physically. The whole world penetrates him first; he becomes fertilized spiritually, the woman physically. Woman, by contrast, is spiritually self-fertilizing, whereas man is fertilized by the spirit. The male wisdom is fertilized by everything external being gathered and combined. Male wisdom thus resulted, which was orientated towards assembling worldly wisdom. This [kind of wisdom] was not actually there at first, as [against] that which flowed down from above; it had first to be put together by perceiving the physical world. Female wisdom, by contrast, was actually transferred to the priesthood. The wisdom of the priests became the substance derived originally from the ancient feminine wisdom. Indeed, only if he separated it into two sexes could Jehovah preserve the human race. Two opposing factions resulted, Freemasonry and priestly rule, which were symbolized by Cain and Abel.

Now, there is a difference between the female priestly wisdom and the male aspiration. This is described to us in the legend of Cain and Abel. Abel was a shepherd and occupied himself with the life that was already there. He is the symbol of the inborn divine force which works in man as the wisdom which he does not acquire for himself, which flows into him. Cain creates something new out of what the world offers. He represents the passive masculine wisdom, which must at first be fertilized from outside, which goes out into the world to gather wisdom and to create from what has been gathered. Cain killed Abel which means that male wisdom offers resistance against the female wisdom since it feels that it must subdue and remodel physical wisdom.

The old Freemasons set themselves the ideal, therefore, of

taking up this challenge. They wanted to use male wisdom to work against the female wisdom that had been taken over by the priesthood. The great images of the Bible were to be considered as intuitive female wisdom transferred to the priests to which they wished to counterpose the wisdom self-acquired by the male. This battle against the wisdom of the priests expressed the opposition of the Freemasons. Those who took part in it had to be kept free of every influence of the female wisdom. This battle was concerned with physical evolution, and it was therefore necessary for the Freemasons to avoid any contact with the female sex as far as their work was concerned. They knew that their opposition to the female spirit could only be carried through if they were undisturbed by female thinking. One had to affirm something positive and generally prevent any disturbing element interfering.

Freemasonry thus created the Temple Legend as an answer to the Bible Legend. This was to be the sword of battle against the priesthood. We therefore want to bring this Temple Legend before your soul. It has the following content.

In the beginning one of the Elohim created Cain by uniting himself with Eve. Another Elohim, Yahveh, countered by creating Adam, who united with Eve, as a result of which Abel was born. Cain killed Abel and Jehovah therefore made the race of Cain subject to the race of Abel.

That means that originally the worldly wisdom rebelled against the priestly wisdom and was defeated; for the Abel line was continued in Seth and all worldly wisdom was made subservient to the priestly wisdom.

Next, it is related how the descendants of Cain conquered the world, how they developed the arts. Music, arts and sciences were cultivated by them. Tubal-Cain (Genesis 4:21–22), the master of brass and ironwork, Jubal, from whom the pipers and violinists are descended, and Hiram, the builder of Solomon's temple (I Kings 7:13) are numbered among the descendants of Cain.

So, with Hiram, we have arrived at the transition from the third to the fourth post-Atlantean epoch,[3] when priestly rule turned into rule by kings. Kingship results from God's grace, as represented by King Solomon. Solomon's power was not sustained by work done on the physical plane, but was the manifestation of God's grace. Priestly wisdom was turned into rule by kings. This was thus regarded as the successor to priestly rule, which was [now] unable to do—from its own resources—what was necessary for the progress of mankind on earth. The one who was to build the temple had to be enlisted from among the descendants of Cain, because he would possess the autonomously worked out thinking.

The legend goes on to relate that Balkis, the Queen of Sheba, was betrothed to King Solomon. She visited him and was [astounded] at the temple building—as he was at her wisdom. She wanted to see the master builder himself, for she could not conceive how [such a] wonderful building could result from human wisdom. Hiram came and made a forceful impression on her, simply by his glance alone. Next she asked to see those who worked on the temple as well. When Solomon said this was impossible, Hiram made the mystical Tau sign in the air and all the workers streamed together immediately. In the mystical Tau sign lie the forces which the Sons of Cain use to work on the physical plane.

Three of Hiram's apprentices are discontented because he did not promote them to the master's degree. They conspire to hurt him. They want to spoil his masterpiece. Now he intends to make the Molten Sea; this is a major work of art, to be cast out of a fluid element, out of molten brass. This is a symbol of the Great Work of Art for which the entire mineral kingdom must be re-cast [which is] the task of our Manvantara.[4] The three apprentices do the following: they wreck the casting of the Molten Sea. Hiram tries to put this right by pouring water on the casting; everything then flies apart in a shower of fiery rain. As Hiram, in despair, gives himself up for lost he is led to the centre of the earth by a figure whom he recognizes as Tubal-Cain. There he is told that Jehovah, or Adonai, is nothing else than an enemy of the Sons of Fire; he wants to destroy the Sons of Fire. Hiram, however, would have a son, whom he would indeed never see, but who would found a new race on earth. Tubal-Cain then gave him a hammer with which he can complete the casting of the Molten Sea. However, the three apprentices murder him. Before his death, he breathes out a word, which he inscribes on a golden triangle, and buries. No one understands the word; it is the Lost Word of the Freemasons. Hiram is buried and an acacia twig is planted on his grave. The triangle is dug up again, but no one knows its worth. It is buried again and a cube set up, on which the Ten Commandments are inscribed.

Now what is meant by 'Jehovah hates the Sons of Fire?' These are the people who were born by means of the single sex (Cain). In them wisdom is mingled with kama, the earthly kamic fire [= the astral body]. Those who have devoted themselves to the female priesthood are the sons of Abel. Hiram was promised: 'You will have a son who will found a new race. However, you will not know him.' This new race must come when the Lost Word regains its power, and is installed in a new way. The occult tradition which is embodied in Freemasonry works to bring about the re-establishment of the Lost Word. It works to enable the introduction of the active into the passive male element so that it can regain the procreative [force] in the spirit, to turn what is passive into something active, so that the Sons of Cain can produce out of themselves.

The following tradition developed. The female was the primeval force. This gave the world everything that was in the world as wisdom. However, [the female element] lost part of the physical power of reproduction, which was transferred to the male. Now everything becomes spiritualized again, in which process the male power attempts to grab control for itself. The male element in thinking seeks to outlast the female. There will come a time, however, when sexlessness will again be re-established and the struggle is about which of the two sexes will first attain this state of sexlessness. Hence Freemasonry endeavours to make the male sex—or, to express it better, the male spirit—outlast the female and attain to the state of sexlessness.

Now there is an occult connection between the power of speech and the power of sexual production. The Word has made everything. Originally it lived in man. Then man lost it. He can no longer create independently because he no longer has the Word. Only someone who was present at the Creation can know it. Tubal-Cain knew it and gave it to Hiram. Whoever wants to regain the power of procreation must gain possession of the Word. The truly creative power must unite itself with the Word. The Word will bring forth the man of the future. Then the son of Hiram really will be seen. Fire, the divine power, will then establish itself in a new way. A new race will replace the old. In the ancient Hebrew language there is a Word, a mantra, which, it is said, will create the world if uttered sufficiently strongly.[5] Man will thus beget spiritual man by means of speech itself once the Word has been developed sufficiently. Now we grasp what is represented by the Tree of Knowledge. The serpent is what winds itself upwards in the backbone as spinal marrow. Perception in the physical is that [kind of knowledge] which originates in the nervous system. 'I will put enmity between thee and the woman and between thy seed and her seed;'[6] by that is meant enmity between the seed of the physical, physical perception, and the seed of the spirit, spiritual perception. The spiritual, the woman, indeed bruises the head of the serpent, but only after it has wounded her in the heel. This is that [power] which presses against the foot [of man] from the centre of the earth.

The power of speech changes at man's puberty. This was regarded as a portent of the new Son of Hiram (II Chronicles

2:13). The ideal which the Freemasons had set themselves was therefore to bring about the procreation of this son from the male sex, which is to result from the power of the larynx. Everything which subsequently appeared on the earth in physical form had its origin in the spirit. In the very beginning, the only things active on earth were those which originated from the Divine Spirit. There then appeared, on the one hand, the female image-wisdom of the priests, and on the other, the imageless wisdom of Cain. Now it is interesting that when an image-content was sought for the wisdom of Cain, the male wisdom then borrowed from the female wisdom; the Temple Legend and the entire content of Freemasonry derives from the old priestly wisdom, from the revelation from above. That was concealed in symbols. However, the symbols gradually ceased to be understood. Gradually, everything occult vanished from Freemasonry. The three Craft Masonry degrees are orientated wholly towards the physical plane.

Because we have seen why these spiritual currents run parallel to each other, we will now also understand the significance of the theosophical movement. It is preparing, in the spiritual realm, what will later happen on the physical plane—the reunion of the sexes. The divided wisdom must likewise flow together again in the *one* divine wisdom. Through theosophical wisdom, a balance must be found in man, between the religious priestly wisdom and the wisdom of Freemasonry. The wisdom of the future must evolve out of the higher human, which lives equally in both male and female. To develop what is needed, and what is completely uninfluenced by things of the physical plane, is the purpose of the theosophical movement.

Theosophy is truly male-female wisdom, wisdom which is equally valid for both sexes. Through the teaching of reincarnation one recognizes that what comes to expression in every new earth life is not the personality of that particular earth life, but that the causal body, the entelechy, creates itself asexually. When we become aware of this we are spiritually quickened with what is higher than the sexual, with what is independent of the causes of conflict between the two currents. Thus theosophy is the balancing movement; and it alone can bring about the balance. Only in theosophy can one speak about an occultism that applies equally to both sexes; only from this source can one think of a real balance between the two sexes. Everything else is an after-effect of the previous dual sexuality.

Freemasonry sets itself the task of preparing for the future. So the wholly exclusive principle of former times was abandoned as early as the eighteenth century. And in 1775 the first of the so-called Adoption Lodges was founded—a Lodge for women, since the law of the balance of the sexes was recognized. And so the connection was established between men and women through the founding of a Lodge for women. But every member of a women's Lodge had to be adopted by a man from a men's Lodge. Indeed, H.P. Blavatsky belonged to such an Adoption Lodge.[7] And so this theosophical experiment was made by Freemasonry itself. This shows you that whatever is correct is always preceded by an experiment; only the reason why such an experiment is made may not be understood immediately. However, man can equally not expect that fundamental forces in the world will always be understood right away. It may be that one prefers one or the other current; therefore the two currents will run parallel to each other for a long time yet. In order to achieve a harmonious balance it may be necessary to pour into Freemasonry what will lead it over towards the theosophical movement.

Now you will also grasp why, in the Middle Ages, the Church had to evolve a quite specific ideal. Freemasonry created its ideal for the future, the Church created its ideal for the future. It had nothing to do with Freemasonry. Christ lived in the Church as ideal—a male ideal, indeed. This male ideal could not suffice for the occult current within the

Church. Man needed the active as well as the passive [principle]; he had to think out what he lacked. He needed something that would complete him, as a means of concentration. He was already a man; he had to add the woman to himself in thought. The occultist who understood something about this, who was not a Freemason, must conceive the woman. Thus did the cult of Mary spring out of monasticism. This came to the Church—to the priesthood, and to Freemasonry, that is—as a third current.

All three currents had basically the same aim—to make mankind independent of the sexes. But the way of achieving this aim varied. The Christian occultist sought the male principle in woman, to embody it in himself.

One has to be clear about the fact that the true inner man is independent of the sexes, which are divisive; that is why one passes through both sexes during different incarnations. And now you must consider that, for Freemasonry, the battle on the outer physical plane is waged so that all individualities which incarnate in female bodies are gradually led towards the male, so that the male lasts longer than the female. It should outlast the female, because the female was the earlier one. This was in the back of the Masonic mind as an ideal, but it was one-sided.

What ideal does theosophy have in the back of its mind? The ideal of theosophy is to use the wisdom that comes from higher planes to bring about, on the physical plane itself, a human race that is above sexuality. Therefore theosophy is indeed a wisdom that is not broken up into [various] religions, that does not rely on any particular religion but falls back on the primal wisdom that made the world, that replaces that wisdom which, as priestly wisdom, was differentiated in the various wisdoms. It must do this because, in the course of time, the priestly wisdom has completed its task. Theosophy, however, wants to conquer the future, to conquer what still has to come rather than what has already been; it is in a particular sense a continuation of the ancient priestly wisdom, of the Mysteries, and nevertheless, in another sense, is in contrast with them.

Opponents of the theosophical movement would be those who want to stick rigidly to the ancient priestly wisdom, who seek to retain it and, so to speak, mummify it in its old form. The plan of the higher [worlds] for world development is to guide evolution towards a modern spiritual life which will forge the future. The very first blush of the dawn of a new wisdom—which has to come—showed at the time when the Rosicrucians brought a new spiritual life to human development, in the fifteenth century. This was a matter of a new impulse coming into the world. The theme of this was that the old priestly wisdom should be transformed into a new [wisdom].

Forces also existed that wanted to reconquer the world for the ancient priestly wisdom. An Order was thus founded with the aim of winning the earth back for the old priestly wisdom. This Order [the Jesuit Order] chose the ideal male in contrast to the cult of Mary. It used occult powers to erect something like a dam to hold back the whole stream of independent life, and to conserve what seeks to cling to the Cross. It championed the male principle, the Cross by itself, without the roses. However, another Order added roses to the Cross and new life sprang out of them.

So we have two modern currents. The one has brought the old into the present and seeks to check progress with all its might. The other has surrounded the old Cross with roses. It has grafted a new shoot—the Cross entwined with roses. These two currents run parallel with each other—the one order having a Cross without roses and the other which reveres the roses on a new Cross, which must come. These are the Rosicrucians. The theosophical movement grew out of this current; it springs from the newly flourishing scion of the rose, which must mature in the future.

Thus we have seen how this battle started, in which women were not allowed to play a part. Our task is to bridge the gulf between the Freemasons and the Rosicrucians. The work is difficult, but it must be done. It involves reaching towards the awareness of the higher humanity beyond sexuality. It is difficult to win through to that, but it is possible and this will succeed—this will become reality.

The Relationship Between Occult Knowledge and Everyday Life

Berlin, 23 October 1905 (evening)

Today, may I say a few things relevant to some of the questions that have been coming before your souls recently. Today, may I amplify something that may have been provoked [in your minds] by remarks made in the last few days. Much has been said about the relationship of occultism to theosophy, of esotericism to theosophy, and so on. But nothing has been said yet about the relationship of theosophy to everyday life. I already indicated a week ago that I wished to say a few words precisely on this subject[1] and that I might direct your attention rather less to higher vantage points, but rather speak about how occult perception directly influences everyday living. Not only is our perspective directed into distant time and space by the theosophical world outlook, but in addition we can gain a quite different explanation of everyday questions through occult concepts which would not be possible through other concepts. We shall then see how erroneous is the opinion which we so often encounter, namely, that occultism is something impractical, uncommonly far removed from ordinary everyday life.

And we will mention another question as well. This question is: How can anyone who has not yet developed the faculty (which, however, every human being is destined to have in the future) of seeing into supersensible worlds—how can such a person, given the standpoint that everyone absorbs in their ordinary education, gain a conviction that theosophical teachings are true and that the endeavours of theosophy are valid in practice? The evidence need not be obtained only by occult observations. Indeed, they cannot be so obtained until they have first been drawn out of another realm, that of everyday life, which [in fact] prepares us to acquire conviction about the higher realms of existence. Whatever may have happened in the past is still happening today in our daily life.

If we trace humanity back to the earliest periods of its development, we find that man originated from a much finer, more spiritual substance than that of which he is composed today. Present-day man displays a form consisting of three main bodies—the physical body, the etheric body and the astral body. The etheric body is a kind of archetypal image of the physical body. The astral body, the auric sheath that envelopes and permeates the human being, is the structure in which the soul life, the life of the instincts and passions, and every thought as well, all find expression. Basically it was from the still undifferentiated astral body that the whole human being evolved in the course of time. If we go back far enough, to the early primeval epochs of humanity, we find that the physical and etheric substance that distinguishes modern man used to be dissolved in the original astral body, like a seed [buried] in the earth.

Present-day man is so to speak condensed out of the astral basic substance. This process is still taking place every day. When two people confront each other, then it is above all the astral bodies which confront each other in love or hate, in kindness or displeasure, anger or good nature, antipathy or attraction. These are all phenomena which are manifest between astral bodies. Interaction between people consists of continual exchange of astral body conditions and relationships. When I confront another person, my physical body experiences no great change, nor does my etheric body, but my astral body certainly does. If a person says something filled with hate to me, then the waves of hatred enter my astral body and change it. I have to accept what streams out of him into my own astral body, which is then imbued with very different attributes, depending on whether it is love and patience or anger and impatience which stream towards me from the other person.

Something very similar takes place between teacher and pupil. It makes a great difference whether a teacher has a loving disposition or is a narrow-minded egoist. In the astral body of a child we have something that differs in appearance from the astral body of an adult. The astral body of a child is bright and clear, and reveals itself to us as something virginal compared with an astral body that has developed during the course of life. What is the astral body of a child? It seems like an undifferentiated cloud of light which only gradually acquires form. Whatever [will] gradually make the astral body fixed has as yet scarcely begun to be engraved in it, so that everything possible can still be born to it. It will be formed by the concepts which the child acquires from its surroundings. These enter it, colour it, and make it different.

Different structures flow into the child's astral body and form it, according to whether what the child absorbs by way of concepts derives from a materialist or an idealist standpoint. For a process of progressively filling the soul with concepts begins. If a child is treated lovelessly, the echo of this love-lessness manifests itself in the child's astral body. It then seals itself in, as if with a hide, against the outer world. All this shows us that a continual remodelling of the astral body is actually taking place, and that interaction with people has a major influence on this reshaping.

The child thus has an astral body which is still undiffer-entiated in form, but which contains a limitless abundance of possibilities. Take the astral body of a child that has met with an idealistic teacher who has a harmonious soul, who views the world with devotion and is susceptible to its beauty and sublimity, a teacher who is in a position to create within himself an image of the beauty of the world. Such a teacher will also develop the ability to enter into the disposition of the child's soul. He will thus encourage tender and sensitive structures in the child, into which he can direct currents which become absorbed in the child's own astral substance. A teacher who is so harmoniously formed within himself continually directs harmonious currents towards the child. The characteristics of the teacher flow quite naturally into the child, and together with them all that world harmony which the teacher has gleaned from his surroundings in the form of beauty. As teacher he directs into the child's nature all the greatness he as a fine person and good observer has received, thereby bringing about harmonious development in the child.

Let us take by contrast a teacher who confronts the child as an egoistical and pedantic person with narrow and opinionated concepts and ideas. These qualities conjure up structures in his own astral body which give it the appearance of being covered with a hard crust, which make it thoroughly rigid and ponderous in structure. It then emits darts which are rigidly enclosed within themselves, so that it is impossible for the child's astral body to absorb them. At the most they wound the child's astral body like a dart, but they cannot be absorbed [by it] and they simply go right through.

Or take something still more everyday. Two people are talking to each other. One can very well observe in two such people the interaction of their astral bodies which results from reciprocal communication with each other.

Something new is always coming into being in the astral, in the astral substance. I will make this intelligible to you in the following way. Through his concepts, a person is continually creating structures in his astral body. These show themselves in the most varied forms. The astral substance that lies unused between the individual structures is called 'intermediary' astral substance, to distinguish it from that which has been shaped into structures. This intermediary astral substance is continually being added to out of the astral substance in our surroundings, is continually flowing in and out, is continually renewing itself. But the structures that man has cultivated by the way he feels and thinks and decides remain fixed.

Let us then assume we have two people engaging in an ordinary conversation with each other. One of them has cultivated rigid, fixed concepts, which have correspondingly engendered very fixed structures in the astral substance. The other talks to him and tries to explain something to him. What must happen if one person is to make something clear to another? He must inject his own concept into the other person's astral substance. This concept, this thought, thus flows into the other person's astral substance. Once there, it must first of all be absorbed in the intermediary substance and [then] remake itself and become transformed [in a manner] corresponding to the forms already developed there.

Now let us assume that the one is trying to explain to the other something to do with, say, reincarnation. The other has, however, already formed a fixed idea about reincarnation. Let us assume him to be a prejudiced person who has formed for himself the idea that reincarnation is something silly and absurd. This thought has hovered in his astral substance. The new thought of the first person now arrives and dissolves itself in the intermediary astral substance of the other, and would then have to be transformed by the thought forms already existing there. This will not work, however, because his [the second person's] concepts are too rigid, too fixed. He cannot adapt the newly transmitted thought to his [own] thought forms and therefore does not understand it.

The more a person keeps his concepts flexible, so that these can always be dissolved in the surrounding intermediary substance, the more he will understand the other people he encounters. This is why it is so difficult to convey theosophical life to academically trained people. The concepts acquired at university engender structures that are rigid, fixed and enclosed within themselves, that are not easily soluable. The academic usually comes to a theosophical lecture full of such structures and is then unable to comprehend theosophical life. It would be quite different if he were educated to say about any concept: 'Yes, it could possibly be different, too, for indeed we have only a limited amount of experience, and much of what we hold to be correct will still have to be modified in the future.' If he were to do that then his soul would still be capable of improvement.

Let us take yet another situation, that of a person who encounters someone else for whom he feels reverence. How is this reverence revealed to anyone endowed with astral perception? Reverence means emitting the kind of thoughts which sink into the substance of the other person's astral body, which that substance sucks up, as it were. If, for instance, you harbour a reverent thought, this is expressed by you yourself conveying this reverence to the other person as radiating warmth. This radiating warmth of yours has its reflection in the astral world, which shows itself as the thought form of reverence and devotion with a bluish colour. The warm reverent feeling engenders a thought form which is blue in character.

But what is it that appears bluish. You can perceive this if you gaze into the infinity of the dark universe. It appears blue to you because of the light in the atmosphere. Similarly, [the reverent thought makes the astral] that was previously dark appears to you as having this bluish shade as well, because it is now lit by the bright warm feeling of reverence. If a dark place is surrounded by a feeling of reverence, then the dark centre appears to be bluish, just as a flame appears to you to have a blue core that is surrounded by light. So is it with the reverent thought as well. It is an empty space permeated by warmth. If one transmits a reverential thought to another person, one thereby offers him the opportunity of allowing his own being to stream into this empty space. This is how the interaction between the person revered and the person showing reverence works out.

If on the other hand it is with a feeling of jealousy that you encounter someone, then a different thought form exists in you, and you bring this up against him. You then emit the red thought form of egoism or self-love. This, for its part, encloses yet another thought form, which is full of the concept of [the thinker's] own self, perhaps as a result of ambition. This expresses itself not in empty space or in a hollow structure, but by a form which is completely full, which nothing else can enter. It is ringed around by a feeling of coldness and has the directly opposite thought form of an outer ring of blue around an inner core of red. The coldness of the blue colour pushes away everything that wants to enter, and the worthless red thought form stays as it is. It accepts nothing. This is how a jealous person, who cannot revere anything, stands in relation to others.

You see, what takes place in our astral body is nothing else than the product of daily life. Only someone who is trained to do so can see what is happening in the astral body. However, the effects of these processes in the astral body are continually present on the physical [plane] and anyone can satisfy himself about them in [ordinary] life. Anyone can make the following test if he says to himself: 'I will leave it undecided, whether the message of occultism is true or false, but I will test it without prejudice. I can live as if this message were based on truth. For I can behave accordingly towards my fellow men; and if I do this warily, I will indeed see whether life confirms for me what the occultist says in every individual case.' And life will [indeed] confirm it to you in every instance. You will realize a tremendous gain from that.

Whoever reflects on that for himself, whoever, say as a teacher, devotes himself not only to his own pedagogical concepts and ideas, and works not only through what he says but also through what he feels, perceives and thinks, whoever makes himself thoroughly aware that two astral bodies are interacting and knows what happens in this confrontation, whoever does all this will also know he has a duty to be continually making himself better. To the extent that he becomes better, the better his influence on the child's dispositions. He does not destroy these dispositions—on the contrary, he cultivates them.

It means something quite different from merely knowing the truth, the reality, of what we receive in return through revering another person who is worthy of it. It means something quite different to experience this: if we transmit to other people countless such thought forms enveloped in warmth, we ourselves grow thereby, through the greatness of that other person. That is something totally different again from merely grasping such things with our intellect, from simply knowing what they represent. In occultism, we learn to grasp life more earnestly, we learn to perceive that the things which are not palpable, which cannot be observed by the senses, are still a reality. We learn to understand and value the whole scope and significance of our soul world.

Perhaps someone or other may say that these are rather theoretical transformations. No, that they are not! We must become quite differently convinced about the importance of our actions and the responsibilities which life lays on our shoulders. It is the most down-to-earth aspects of life which can be influenced in this way by occultism. He who knows what results in the invisible world as a consequence of thoughts and feelings will surely grasp that it is just as important for him not to direct evil thoughts towards a person as it is to refrain from firing bullets at him. He knows that throwing the thought of hate at astral man is just as harmful for him as throwing a roofing slate is for physical man.

Understanding this is easy enough; those who meet together in groups such as the theosophical groups will feel and experience it. For they find a new source of life there. You could say to yourselves that there is [only] a simple reality for other people, a threefold one for us. Other people experience reality only through the sense world, and do not think it wicked to say that 'thoughts are free!' However, anyone who has studied the world outlook of theosophy can no longer say that thinking incurs no cost, but is convinced that he is instead responsible for what he thinks and feels about other people. You take this feeling of responsibility out into the world as the finest fruit of the theosophical conception of the world. Even if we are only beginners in rehearsal, we are still influencing the visible world through the hidden, occult world. We are refining and correcting the world through the hidden realms of existence.

That is one aspect of how we understand life. There are, however, others as well. Man does not live alone in the world as an individual; he also belongs to a family, to a tribe, to a people, that is, to a [larger] whole. Only in his physical and etheric body is he actually separate from others; the astral body, as I have already mentioned, has a porous exterior. The intermediary substance is continually disposed to receive currents from outside, and to renew itself. If we consider, however, that we belong to a nation, a tribe, a family, then the matter acquires a further dimension.

If we observe the astral bodies of individual people, we find that almost everyone differs from others in the basic colouring of the astral body. Each has a particular shade that manifests outwardly as temperament. Temperament expresses itself, then, through a particular basic colouring. A person relates to his entire surroundings in this way; the character of the family, the tribe, or the nation to which he belongs expresses itself in the basic colouring.

As an occultist one can make interesting observations if, for instance, one revisits a town which one has not seen for, say, ten years. If one observes the unsullied astral bodies of the children, one will find that they possess, in addition to their personal basic colouring, another basic colouring too. If one had carefully observed these virginal astral bodies on one's first visit and now compares them with what one finds in the astral bodies of the children ten years later, one will see that their appearance has altered. There is something in the human individual that moves with the evolution of the town or tribe or nation. This is because the currents in a collective astral body that is all around me are in continual interchange with my own [astral body], which lives within the collective astral body. Hence we have a national temperament, expressing itself in the group astral body of the nation.

Every nation, every other community, has such an astral body, and this flows into the astral bodies of the individual person. A great disharmony can develop between the individual person and the task of the whole nation, for this reason; the trends in evolution do not always all take the same course in the world. The more comprehensive often hurries ahead of the less comprehensive.

Let us consider a nation, for example. The nation, as a structure, has not been haphazardly thrown together in the world; it is not something produced by chance. Each nation, on the contrary, has its prescribed task in the course of human evolution. Anyone who contemplates a nation from a higher vantage point can reflect that every nation has a specific task, that his own nation has itself to fulfil a task which is incumbent on it. He can say to himself: 'I belong to this nation, so I must help to serve the common national task. And I am able so to serve, because an astrality lives in me that belongs to the whole nation.' This national purpose is plainly expressed on the astral plane; it is a precise thought—something that lives on higher planes than the astral plane. In order to meditate on the thoughts of the world laws, one must rise above the astral plane to the mental plane [Devachan].

For example, the fourth Sub-Race, from which our Race came, developed from a small group of people in Asia and developed into the Hebraic-Graeco-Latin Race. This had the task of fulfilling the first mission of Christianity from an ethnic standpoint. The thought [inspiring] this Race was to spread Christianity in its first stage through Europe and the adjoining regions. That is an ethnic thought.

In earlier times, the idea of reincarnation and karma was universally accepted. Then came a radical change; people were educated in the belief that the single physical life was of importance. This is very apparent in Greek art, because it developed the feeling for outward form. Therein lay the ennobling of the physical plane for the outward senses. The law then came to be developed in the Roman nation; this had its effect directly on the physical plane. Finally, Christianity permeates this law with a morality, so that one single earth life gains so much importance that a whole eternity comes to be made dependent on it. This is a one-sided thought, but it was correct and necessary. The Catholic peoples took upon themselves the mission of spreading Christianity, carrying it to Northern Europe, whereby the Germanic peoples received a new mission.

Thus we see that a national thought lives in the entire nation, and every individual [member] is fitted to this thought. What the Greeks formerly portrayed in beautiful forms in the sense world through the plastic art, what was developed as law and later deepened to morality has been developed in our days into technology for the benefit of the general public. Cities were founded; they grew and flourished and thus developed a culture of their own—the culture of the bourgeoisie. From this then evolved a utilitarian morality, which provided the impetus for the growth of a one-sided science that ought to have reached its highest point in our present time.

In this we can recognize the workings of a devachanic principle. It is the universal aspect of these changes in the course of evolution that shows us in what way a national thought has its effect. How this thought comes to expression depends on the nation's group astral body, on the national temperament. Art, for instance, with any other nation than the Greeks, would find expression in a quite different way.

Now although the national thought does live in every individual [member], the individual is much more than just his national thought. In addition, he brings his own personality to expression. Something quite remarkable and special is shown to us here. It is much easier for a person to connect himself to the thought world of his nation, in his devachanic mission, than it is to bring about the [correct] balance between his own feelings and the national feelings. This is not so easy, especially for those who have acquired higher education and sophistication of a particular kind. The adjustment between the feelings of the individual and the nation is more quickly made in the lower levels of evolution, because at those levels a greater empathy develops between individual sensibilities and the national sensibility. The lower the individual level, the stronger the expression of the national sensibility within him, rather as the animal is an expression of the species.

As man develops, however, he raises his own astral body up; it becomes more differentiated, more specific. And it is then possible for his astral body to be in a position to acquire that form of mind which lies above the mind of his nation. When what shines down from this higher level is intellectually or mentally grasped, then ideals can easily be taken up. It sometimes also happens that the feelings of a person's astral body have not developed as far as his thinking. The thoughts of a nation could influence the thinking of the individual so powerfully that they take hold of him before he has developed far enough within himself.

Individuals for whom this proves to be the case are passionate idealists; they are the martyrs for the progress of a nation. They are so because they themselves are hurrying ahead of what is actually in the rest of their astral body, because they direct their wholly elevated souls to an ideal in a selfless way.

Then, when such people come to die, their undeveloped astrality asserts itself all the more strongly; for that part of it which does not lie within the national ideal comes into play. Henceforth it is only concerned with its own development. When such a person dies, who was a great and noble idealist, who has devoted himself to the ideals of his nation, he becomes overrun by the personal element still present in him. For the lower qualities of his astral body become totally predominant. Now suppose that such a person has become a martyr. He created something noble but has been ill-treated by his nation, just as such advanced natures sometimes are. Despite this, he would indeed habitually follow his ideals boldly and spiritedly so long as he lived, looking neither to the left nor the right. But if he is persecuted, perhaps killed, on account of his ideals, then the thought of revenge comes into play immediately after his death. What he had suppressed as something personal will still be there in Kamaloka.

A nation which treats its idealists in this fashion creates for itself bad powers in Kamaloka, which rebound against it. Russia has created bad powers of this kind. For years it has ill-treated many noble personalities with the knout. The baser forces of these personalities are now active in Kamaloka as enemies of what lives in Russia, as enemies of those for whom they made sacrifices in life. Such martyrs who have recently died can now be seen fighting on the side of the Japanese, against their own people. This is a fact which becomes comprehensible to us if we look into the more deeply active powers of the life of the soul. The events of the future become clear to us if we look at them from this aspect.

We live as members of the Germanic peoples, flanked by Slavonic peoples in the east, and by Anglo-American peoples in the west. Both the Americans and the Slavs are rising races who have to fulfill their purpose in the future, races who still stand at the beginning of their national thought. The basic characteristic of the Slavonic peoples is expressed in their spiritual talents. If you try to understand the Slavonic culture, you will find that it tends towards a spiritual culture, that something spiritual is growing there. These Slavonic peoples had first to confront the races lying to the east, the Chinese and Japanese. These are the remnants of earlier races from Atlantis, as indeed all Mongolians are the residues of later Atlantean culture. They have astral bodies which intrinsically tend towards spirituality. The Slavonic peoples have to confront these.

In America we have a certain parallel. There, materialism is carried to the extreme, and has been pursued radically in all national perspectives. In modern times, that has led to the spirit itself being interpreted in a materialistic way. Whereas, among the Slavonic peoples individual personalities such as Tolstoy arose, who sought to stimulate development in a great and beautiful way, the American people took pains to conceive spirituality and the soul in a material way. Thus we find a strongly material spirituality and [indeed] spiritualism among them. With them, the spirit is sought in exactly the same way as they search after physical truths. But it is precisely in the manner of seeking that the difference lies. If you seek to see the spiritual with the eyes it becomes psychic, and this psychic aspect has been developed very strongly in America.

The American nation has to confront another ethnic element deriving from Atlantis and endowed with psychic tendencies. This ethnic element lives in the Negro peoples. The way and manner in which these two races develop together is significant: psychic has to confront psychic; spiritual has to confront spiritual. Thus we have a spiritual national thought in the east and a psychic one in the west.

We have experienced science and art on an external level; the spirit should now be raised up again. This can happen in a double way—either in a spiritual way or in a psychic way. The spiritual way leads to progress; the psychic way is retrogressive.

You can see how the world here becomes understandable, when we contemplate it from an occult basis. Again, no one need say that we cannot convince ourselves of these things. One only has to take what actually happens. One will be led to conviction through experience, when one compares the psychic view of the world and psychic research with the occult view of the world. If we seek to understand the world from the occult point of view then the world of phenomena becomes more and more comprehensible as well. Such an occult-spiritual world outlook leaves us no gaps in the comprehension of the world. That will enable us to believe in the world which the occultists report; and through that we educate an element in ourselves, which will raise us higher. This is no blind belief, but a tried and tested belief. This belief will grow stronger and more justified, firmer and surer, with every gain in experience. And when belief has engendered this sense of confidence in itself it has also developed the basis for knowledge. Man has always had to experiment before being raised to knowledge. Anyone who wants to have knowledge before investigation is like someone wanting to have the fruit before the seed. We have to *earn* our knowledge. What we already know, we need not investigate. What the investigator lacks in certainty or confidence, the certainty and confidence of belief must supply. [The two] must work together, therefore, and then in co-operation they will ultimately produce what must come to us undivided—the fruit of experience, knowledge.

But let us look on occultism as the basis of our own lives and actions; regard it as though its discoveries were useful steps in our lives. Then we shall find that it will lead us from trust to investigation, to satisfaction, and that we shall live within it in harmony.

The Royal Art in a New Form

(Lecture for a mixed audience of men and women)

Berlin, 2 January 1906

I wish to speak to you today about something which is subject to many misunderstandings and about which many extraordinary errors are spread abroad. Most of you know that I have already spoken[1] on the same subject on the occasion of our General Meeting this year, and that, at that time, following an ancient occult practice, I spoke separately to men and to women. For specific reasons which could probably become still clearer from the lecture itself, I have departed today from this ancient custom, and, indeed, because the very thing that motivated me both then and now to discuss this matter is connected with the [hope] that sooner or later—I hope sooner—this ancient custom will be abandoned altogether.

I said that many misunderstandings have circulated about the subject. I need only mention one fact out of my own life to show you that it really is not exactly easy today to get beyond what are bluntly the bizarre and superstitious notions in existence about it. On the other hand, I need only say how easily, how unbelievably, one can put one's foot in it when dealing with these extraordinary facts.

May I simply recall an incident in my life. Perhaps you will scarcely credit it, and yet it is true. It is now some 17 or 18 years ago[2] that I was in company with university professors and some particularly gifted poets. Among the professors there were also some theologians, from the theological faculty of the university in question. They were Catholics. Now in this company the following was said, not without foundation and in all seriousness—that one of these theologians, a very erudite man, would not go out at night any more, because he believed that the Freemasons would be on the loose. The man in question represented a major department, but it was not he who told the story; it was told by a colleague. He went on to relate that while he was in Rome, a number of monks of a particular order (there would have been 11, 12 or 13 of them) had vouched on oath for the [truth of the] following event.

In Paris an eminent bishop had preached a sermon in which he had spoken of the terrible danger to the world of the Order of Freemasons. After the sermon a man came to him in the sacristy and said that he was a Freemason and could give the bishop a chance to witness a meeting of the Lodge. The bishop assented, saying to himself: I will, however, take some holy relics with me, so that I am protected. Then a meeting place was arranged. The man in question led the bishop into the Lodge, where a hiding place was pointed out to him from which he could observe all that took place. He placed himself in position, held the holy relics in front of him and waited for whatever would befall. What he then saw was related in the following way. I emphasize that some of those in the company thought it all rather doubtful at the time.

The Lodge was then opened. (It bore in reality the name 'Satan's Lodge', though it had quite a different name in the outside world.) Then a remarkable figure appeared. By ancient custom (how he knew this custom, he did not relate) the figure did not walk. (It is indeed well known that spirits do not walk, but glide, so many believe.) This remarkable figure opened the session. The bishop would on no account divulge what happened next—it became too terrible—but he called upon the whole power of the relics and there was a rumbling like thunder through all the rows [of seats], the call resounding: 'We are betrayed!'—and the one who had opened the session disappeared. Briefly, a brilliant victory of episcopal powers over what was to be done, one supposes.

This was discussed as a completely serious matter[3] [in the company]. You can see from that, that there are people today, perhaps gentlemen more erudite than many others, well-known people, who nevertheless take the view that this sort of thing can happen in Freemasonry.

Now what happened was[4] that in the mid-eighties a French book appeared, which represented the secrets of the Free-masons in a most gruesome way, making them certainly more gruesome than secret. This book particularly revealed how the Freemasons celebrated Black Mass. This book was a ploy by a French journalist called Leo Taxil. He stirred up a lot of dust by bringing in a Miss Vaughan as a witness. The result of all this was that the Church found the Freemasons and their nocturnal intrigues so dangerous that they felt it necessary to found a world society against Freemasonry. A kind of council was held in Trent. Although it was not a real council, it was dubbed 'The Second Council of Trent'. It was attended by many bishops and hundreds of priests; a cardinal presided. [The Congress became a major coup for Taxil.] But afterwards rebuttals were published, after which Mr Taxil revealed that the entire contents of his books, including the people men-tioned in them, were his own invention.

You see, there are plenty of opportunities for incurring censure over such things. This was one of the worst cases of a body with a world-wide reputation doing so. From it you have to draw at least one conclusion—that hardly anything is really known about the Freemasons. For if something was known about them it would be easy to become informed, and then such rubbish could not gain currency.

Indeed, this or that opinion about Freemasonry pre-dominates in large sections of the public. Today, to be sure, it is not all that difficult to form an opinion as there is already a tolerably abundant literature written partly by those who have studied many documents, but in part also containing things which the Freemasons would say had been brought into the open by turncoats. Anyone who concerns himself to any extent with this literature will draw some sort of conclusion from what it deals with. However, one can rule out coming to a correct conclusion from it, since it is still pre-eminently true what Lessing, who was himself a Freemason, said.[5] When he was accepted, the Worshipful Master asked him: 'Now you see, don't you, that you have not been initiated into anything particularly subversive or anti-religious?' To which Lessing replied: 'Yes, I must admit that I haven't learnt any such thing. I would in fact have been glad to do so, for then, at least, I would have learned something.'

That is the statement of a man who was able to consider the matter with the right understanding, and who admitted that he had learned precisely nothing from what took place there. You can at least draw the conclusion from that, that those who are not Freemasons know nothing [about it], since even those who are Freemasons know nothing of any importance. They generally get the impression that they have gained nothing in particular from it. And yet it would be quite wrong to make such an inference.

Now there is still another opinion, which has little to do with real Freemasonry. In a text appearing in 1875,[6] the author claims that Adam became the first Freemason. One can hardly go further back than the first man in searching for the founder of an association.

Others claim that Freemasonry is an old Egyptian art; in short, that it is what has always been known as the 'Royal Art', and this is indeed placed by some back in primeval times. Finally, many rites—for thus the symbolic ways and manners of the Freemasons are designated—bear Egyptian names, and so from these names you may infer that something deriving from ancient Egyptian culture is involved. At least the opinion is widely held, both in and out of Freemasonry, that it is something very ancient.

Now Freemasonry is something which can indeed provide people with scope for reflection. The name itself connects with two perceptions differing totally from each other. Some claim—and they are not a very great party within Freemasonry—that all Freemasonry originated in the work done by masons, in the craft of erecting buildings, while the other opinion considers this to be a childish and naive conception and claims that Freemasonry was in reality always an art to do with the soul, and that the symbols taken from the work of masons (such as, for example, apron, hammer, trowel, chisel, compass, rule, square, plumb-line, spirit-level, etc.) are to be seen as symbolic of soul development. Thus, by the expression 'Masonry' is to be understood nothing else than the building of the inner person, the work on the perfection of self. If you talk with a Freemason today, you can then experience him telling you that it is a childish and naive outlook that believes that Freemasonry has ever had anything to do with the work that masons do. On the contrary, it has never concerned itself with anything else than these things: the building of the Wonder Temple, which is the theatre of the human soul, the work on the human soul itself, which has to be perfected, and the art which one must apply to all this. Now all this is expressed in these symbols so as not to expose it to profane eyes.

Looked at from our contemporary standpoint, both of these views are wholly and utterly wrong, and are so for the following reasons. As regards the first opinion, present-day man—in talking about the Freemasons having been derived from the work of building—no longer conceives himself to be as significant as he properly should. As for the second opinion, that the symbols are only there to serve as metaphors for the work on the soul, this opinion—even though it is regarded by most Freemasons as something quite irrefutable—is, when properly conceived, a nonsense. It is much more correct to link Freemasonry with the work of building, not, indeed, as architecture or construction are thought of today but in a fundamentally deeper sense.

Today there are broadly two trends in Freemasonry. The one is represented by the great majority of those calling themselves Masons today. And this majority trend claims now that all Masonry is comprised of what is known as the so-called Symbolic or Craft Masonry. Its principal outward characteristic is that it is divided into three degrees, the Apprentice, Journeyman and Master degrees; as for the inward characteristics, we will have something to say presently. Apart from these Craft Masons, there are still quite a number of Masons who maintain that Craft Masonry is only a product of the decline of the great universal Masonic idea. [They consider] it would be a falling away from this great Masonic idea, if it is claimed that Masonry comprises only these three Symbolic or Craft degrees; whereas in fact the essence, the fundamental meaning of Freemasonry lies in the so-called higher degrees, which are best preserved in the so-called Scottish or Accepted Rite, which, in a particular respect, still conserves [a relic of] what is called the Egyptian, the Misraim or the Memphis Rite.[7]

Thus we have two tendencies confronting each other: the Craft Masonry, and the Higher Degree Masonry. The Craft Masons claim that the higher degrees are nothing but a frippery based on human vanity, which takes pleasure in having something special, something spiritually aristocratic, with its ascent from degree to degree, and its pride in the possession of the eighteenth or twentieth or still higher degree.

Now you have already become acquainted with quite a number of things likely to lead to misunderstandings.

The Higher Degree Freemasonry can be traced back to the old Mysteries, to the procedures which we have described and will describe in our theosophy, as far as possible—procedures which have been in existence since primordial times and still exist today, and which have preserved the higher supersensible knowledge for mankind. This supersensible knowledge, available to mankind, was given to those who could gain access to the Mystery Schools by developing higher powers in themselves, enabling them to see into the spiritual world. Within these primordial Mysteries—they have become something else nowadays, and we do not want to speak of that now—was contained the original seed for all later spiritual culture. For what was enacted in these primordial Mysteries was not what constitutes human culture today.

If you wish to understand present-day culture and immerse yourself in it, you will find that it divides into three realms— the realm of wisdom, the realm of beauty and the realm of strength. The whole extent of spiritual culture is in fact contained in these three words. Therefore they are known as the three pillars of human culture. They are the same as the three Kings in Goethe's fairy story of the Green Snake and the Beautiful Lily[8]—the Gold King, the Silver King and the Brass King. This is connected with Freemasonry being called the 'Royal Art'. Today these three realms are separated from each other. Wisdom is essentially contained in what we call science. Beauty is essentially embodied in what we call art. And what, in Freemasonry terms, is known as strength is contained in the regulated and organized living together of humanity in the state. The Freemason subsumes all this in the relation of the will to these three principles, wisdom, beauty and strength.

What they [these three principles] were to give to humanity was in primeval times bestowed on the candidate for initiation by the revelation of the Mystery secrets. We are now looking back to a time when religion, science and art had not yet become separated, but when they were still combined. In fact, to anyone who can see supersensibly, astrally, these three principles are not for him separate; wisdom, beauty and the domain of the will impulses are for him a single unity. On the higher realms of vision there is no abstract science, only a science which exists in pictures, in that which has only a shadowy existence in the [external] world, and finds a shadowy expression in the imagination. What can [now] be read in books, in this or that record of the Creation [about the origin of the world and of humanity], was not *described*; instead it was brought before the eyes of the pupil in living pictures, in magnificent harmonious colour. And what the pupil would perceive as wisdom was art and beauty at the same time, was something which stirred his feelings to greater heights than we experience in front of an exquisite work of art. The yearning for truth and beauty, wisdom and art, and the religious impulse as well, [all] developed simultaneously. The artist's eye looked at what was enacted [in the Mysteries][9] and he who sought piety found the object of his religious ardour in these high events that were enacted before his eyes. Religion, art and science were one.

Then came the time when this unity split up into three cultural provinces—the time when the intellect went its own way. Science arose at the same time and the Mysteries which I have just described lost their importance. You know that western philosophy and science, science proper, began with Thales. That is the time when it first developed out of the former fullness of the life of the Mysteries. Then also began what in the western sense is conceived of as art; for Greek dramatic art developed out of the Mysteries. Whereas in India, up to the time of the Egyptian cult,[10] one was concerned with the suffering and death of gods, with the great Greek tragedian-poets, such as Aeschylus, Sophocles, etc., we are dealing with individual human beings who are images of the great Godhead. Through these human beings, the pupils of the Mysteries reconstructed the suffering, struggling and needy Godhead, thus displaying God to the human audience through their human imagery.

Whoever wants to understand what Aristotle meant by

purification, catharsis,[11] must interpret the concept by means of the astral, by means of the secrets of the Mysteries. The expressions which he employs for tragedy [by way of explaining it] are a dim reflection of what the pupils learnt in the Mystery [Schools]. Remember how Lessing investigated the soul forces of fear and compassion that are to be aroused through tragedy. That has furnished the material for many a great and learned discussion since the days of Lessing. [For the Mystery pupil] these emotions would be aroused in reality when God was portrayed to him in his passage through the world. The passions present [deep] in the human soul were thereby actually stirred up and drawn out, just as one induces a fever and brings it to its culmination. This led to purification so as to be able to proceed to rebirth. All this appeared in shadow images in the ancient Greek tragedies. Just as with science, so has art, too, developed out of these ancient Mysteries.

It is to these ancient Mysteries that the Higher Degree Freemasons trace back their origin. In their higher degrees they have nothing else than an imitation of the higher degrees of the Mysteries, into which the Mystery candidate was gradually initiated. Now we can also understand why the Craft Freemasons insist so much that there should be no more such higher degrees. Actually, the higher degrees have more or less lost their meaning in Freemasonry in recent centuries. What has taken place in civilization during recent centuries has been largely uninfluenced from this quarter. But there was a time when the great cultural impulses issued precisely from what Freemasonry should be. In order to understand this, we must look a little deeper into an age to which I have often referred here already, but now wish to mention in a Masonic context, that is, the twelfth century of our European cultural development.

At that time occultism, appearing under a variety of names, played a much greater role in the contemporary culture than anyone could ever imagine today. But all these different names are no longer relevant today, and I will indeed explain why. By an example from Freemasonry itself, I will show you why these names contribute nothing essential to understanding the matter.

What I am now about to relate, anyone can experience if they become an apprentice Freemason; and since these things are known, at least by name, I am able to speak about them.

A customary practice is what is known as 'tyling'. When the Lodge is opened and the Worshipful Master has taken his seat and the Outer Guard is at his post, the first question of the Worshipful Master is: Has the Lodge been tyled? The number of Freemasons who understand what this expression means are probably very few. Since the matter is simple, I can indeed give you an explanation of the term. At the time of which I am speaking, to be a Freemason meant to stand in vehement opposition to everything that commanded outward, official power. Therefore it was necessary to conduct the affairs of the Freemasons with exceptionally great caution. Precisely for this reason, it was at that time necessary for Freemasonry to appear under various names that sounded harmless. Among other names they called each other 'Brethren of the Craft' and so on. Today Freemasonry has accomplished a large part of what it then set out to do. Today it is itself officially a power in the world.

If you ask me what Freemasonry is really about, I must answer with abstract words. It consists in this, that its members aim to anticipate in thought by several centuries the events that are to occur in the world; and to perfect the high ideals of humanity in a fully conscious way, so that these ideals are not just abstract ideas.

Today, when a Freemason talks about ideals and one asks him what he means by the highest ideals, he will say that the highest ideals are wisdom, beauty and strength which, however, on further consideration, is usually nothing but a form of words. If at that time (or now indeed) the discussion about these ideals is with someone who actually understands something about this, then the discussion will be about something quite specific—about something so specific that it relates to the course of events in the coming centuries in the same way as the thoughts of an architect building a factory relate to the factory when finished.

At that time [in the twelfth century] it was dangerous to know [in advance] what was to happen later. Hence it was necessary to make use of harmless sounding words, as a cover. And that is also where the expression originated, 'Is the Lodge tyled?', which means, in effect, 'Are only those present who know the meaning of the things which have to be implanted in the future development of mankind by Freemasonry?' For each had to reflect that they must never let themselves be recognized as Freemasons when they appeared in public. This precautionary rule, then essential, has been maintained until our time. Whether many Freemasons know what is meant thereby is questionable. Most think it is some sort of verbal formality, or they interpret it more or less astutely. I could give you countless more such examples that would show you how outer circumstances have led to the adoption of practical rules for which people now try to discover some deep symbolic explanation.

But now for the very heart of what was attempted in the twelfth century. That is expressed in the deeply significant saga of the Holy Grail,[12] of that enchanted vessel which is said to have come from the distant East and to have the power to rejuvenate people, to bring the dead back to life, and so on.

Now what is the Holy Grail (in Freemasonry terms), and what is it that lies at the bottom of the whole saga? We shall best be able to understand what it is all about if we call to mind a symbol of certain Freemasonry associations, a symbol misunderstood today in the coarsest way imaginable. It is a symbol taken from sexual life. It is absolutely true that precisely one of the deepest secrets of Freemasonry has a symbol taken from sexual life and that many people who try to explain such symbols today are only following their own sordid fantasies when they understand these symbols in an impure sense. It is very likely that the interpretation of these sexual symbols will play no small role in times to come, that it is precisely this which will then reveal the parlous state into which the great ancient secrets of Freemasonry have fallen today; and on the other hand, how necessary it is in the present time for the pure, noble and profound basis of the Freemasonry symbols to be kept sacred and unblemished.

Those of you who heard my recent lecture[13] at the General Meeting will know that the true original significance of these symbols is connected with the reason for not allowing women to become Freemasons until a short while ago, and the reason for addressing men and women separately on these matters until [just] recently. On the other hand you also know that these symbols are linked—and I particularly stress this—with the two great streams running through the whole world, and rising to the highest spiritual realm; which streams we also encounter as the law of polarity in the forces of male and female.[14] Within that culture which we now have to consider, the priestly principle is expressed in Masonic terminology as the female principle in the spiritual realm—in that spiritual realm which is most closely related to cultural evolution. The rule of the priests is expressed by the female [principle]. On the other hand, the male principle is everything which is opposed to this priestly rule—however, in such a way that this opponent has to be considered as the holiest, the noblest, the greatest and the most spiritual [principle] in the world, no less. There are thus two streams with which we have to deal: a female and a male stream. The Freemasons see Abel as representing the female current, Cain, the male.

Here we come to the fundamental concept of Freemasonry, which to be sure is old, very old. Freemasonry developed in ancient times as the opponent of the priestly culture. We must now, however, make clear, in the right way, what is to be understood by priestly culture.

What is involved here has nothing to do with petty opposition to churches or creeds. Priestliness can show itself in the most completely secular [people]. Even what manifests today as science, that holds sway in many cultural groups, is nothing else than what is known in Freemasonry terms as the priestly element, though [there are?] other [such groups?] which are profoundly Masonic. We must conceive such things, then, in their entire profundity, if we want to appraise them correctly. May I explain by an example how what manifests as science can often be what is denoted in Freemasonry as the priestly element.

Who today among doctors would not scoff if told about the healing properties of the spring at Lourdes? On the other hand, what doctor would not accept as a matter of course that it is wholly reasonable for certain people to go to Wiesbaden or Karlsbad? I know I am saying something fearfully heretical, but then I represent neither the priesthood nor even medicine. However, a time is already coming when an unbiased judgement will be pronounced on both. Were there an effective medicine today, faith in the power of healing would be among the things a doctor would prescribe. One patient would be sent to Karlsbad and another to Lourdes, but both for the same reason. Whether you call it great piety on the one hand, or blatant superstition on the other, in the last analysis it is the same thing.

Understood in this way, we can characterize what underlies the priestly principle as refraining from investigating fundamentals, as accepting things as they present themselves from whatever aspect of the world, as being satisfied with what is thus given. The symbol of that for which man does nothing, the proper symbol for what is, in the truest sense of the word, donated to man, that symbol is taken from sexual life. The

human being is [indeed] productive there, but what is manifested in this productive force has nothing to do with human
art, with human science or with human ability; from it is
excluded everything which comes to be expressed in the three
pillars of the 'Royal Art'. So when some present these sexual
symbols to humanity, they want to say: In this symbol human
nature is expressed not as man has made it, but as it has been
given by the gods. This finds its expression in Abel, the hunter
and herdsman, who offers the sacrificial animal, the sacrificial
lamb, thereby offering what he himself has done nothing to
produce, which came into existence independently of him.

What did Cain, on the other hand, offer? He sacrificed what
he had obtained by his own labour, what he had won from the
fruits of the earth by tilling the soil. What he sacrificed needed
human skill, knowledge and wisdom—that which demands
comprehension of what one has done, which is based in a
spiritual sense on the freedom of man to decide things for
himself. That has to be paid for with guilt, by killing, first of all
the living things which had been given by nature or by Divine
Powers, just as Cain killed Abel.

Through guilt lies the path to freedom. Everything that is
born into the world (upon which man can, at best, act only
in a secondary way), everything given to man by Divine
Powers, everything which is there without him needing to
work at it incessantly—all this is given to us first of all in the
kingdoms of nature, over which we have no control, in *those*
kingdoms (the plant, animal and human kingdoms) the
forces of which are isolated from any human contribution
because in these kingdoms it is physical reproduction that is
involved. All the reproductory forces in these kingdoms are
given to us by nature. Inasmuch as we take what is living for
our use—because we make the world our dwelling place,
which was developed out of what is living—we thereby offer
the sacrifice given to us, just as Abel offered the sacrifice
given to him.

The symbol for these three kingdoms is the Cross. The lower beam symbolizes the plant kingdom; the middle or cross beam, the animal kingdom; and the upper beam, the human kingdom.

The plant has its roots buried in the earth and directs upwards, in the blossom, those parts which, in man, are directed downwards. It is the reproductive organs of the plant that appear in the blossom. The downward-turned part, the root, is the plant's head, buried in the earth. The animal is the plant turned half-way and carries its backbone horizontally in relation to the earth. Man is the plant turned completely round, so that the lower part is directed upwards.

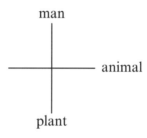

This view lies at the basis of all the mysteries of the Cross. And when theosophy shows us how man has to pass, in the course of his evolution, through the various kingdoms of nature, through the plant, animal and human kingdoms, then that is the same thing expressed by Plato in the beautiful words, 'The World Soul is nailed to the Cross of the World Body.'[15] The human soul is a spark struck from the World Soul, and the human being, as physical human being, is plant, animal and physical man at the same time. Inasmuch as the World Soul has divided itself up into the individual sparks of human souls, it is, as it were, nailed to the World Cross, nailed to what is expressed in the three kingdoms, the animal, plant and human kingdoms. Powers which man has not mastered are at work in these kingdoms. If he wants to control them, then he must create a new kingdom of his very own, which is not expressed in the Cross.

When talking about this subject I am often asked: Where is the mineral kingdom in all this? The mineral kingdom is not symbolized in the Cross, because it is that kingdom in which man can already express himself in clear and blinding clarity, where he has learnt to apply the techniques of weighing and calculating, of geometry and arithmetic—in short, everything pertaining to inorganic nature, to the inorganic mineral kingdom.

If you contemplate a temple, you know that man has erected it with ruler, compasses, square, plumb-line and spirit-level, and finally with the thinking that inorganic nature has transmitted to the architect in geometry and mechanics. And as you continue your contemplation of the whole temple, you will find it to be an inanimate object born out of human freedom and brainwork. You cannot say that, however, if you subject a plant or an animal to human observation.

So you see that what man has mastered, what he is able to master, is, up to now, the realm of the inanimate. And everything which the human being has converted to harmony and order out of the inanimate world is the symbol of his Royal Art on earth. What he has implanted into the mineral kingdom with his Royal Art started as an outflow, an incarnation of divine wisdom. Go back to the time of the ancient Chaldeans and Egyptians, when it was not only the intellect that was used in building, but when heightened perceptions permeated everything; the controlling of inorganic nature was then seen as the 'Royal Art', which is why the control of nature was denoted as 'Free masonry'. At first this may seem to be fantasy, but it is more than that.

Picture to yourselves that instant, that point in time in our earth's development when no one had yet applied his hand to the shaping of inorganic nature, when the whole planet was presented to man just as it came from nature! And what happened then? Look back to the construction of the Egyptian pyramids, in which stone was fitted to stone through human agency. Nature's creation was given a new shape as a result of human thought. Human wisdom has thus transformed the earth. That was perceived as the proper mission of free constructing man on earth. Using a wide variety of tools, guided by human wisdom, human powers have brought about in the mineral world a transformation that has unfolded between primordial times and the present day, when human powers can extend their influence over far distances without mechanical means. And that is the first pillar, the pillar of wisdom.

Somewhat later we see the second pillar established, the pillar of beauty, of art. Art is likewise a means of pouring the human spirit into lifeless matter, and again the result is an ensoulment (conquest)[16] of the inanimate to be found in nature. Try for a moment to picture in your mind how the wisdom in art gradually overcomes and masters lifeless nature, and you will see how what is there without man's participation is reshaped piece by piece by man himself. Visualize—as a fantasy, if you must—the effect of the whole earth having been transformed by the hand of man, the effect of the whole earth becoming a work of art, full of wisdom and radiating beauty, built by man's hand, conceived by man's wisdom! It may seem fantastic but it is more than that. For it is humanity's mission on earth to transform the planet artistically. You find this expressed in the second pillar, the pillar of beauty.

To which you can add, as the third pillar, the reshaping of the human race in national and state life, and you have the propagation of the human spirit in the world; you have this right here in the realm of what is lifeless.

Hence the medieval people of the twelfth century reflected, in looking back to the ancient wisdom, that the wisdom of times past was preserved in marble monuments, while contemporary wisdom is to be found in the human heart. For it is manifested through the artist, becoming a work of art through the labour of his hands. What he feels he impresses into matter that is unformed, he chisels out of the dead stone; while the inner soul of man does not of course live in this dead stone, it does manifest itself there. All art is dedicated to this purpose; there is always this mastering of unliving, inorganic nature, regardless of whether it is a sculptor chiselling marble or a painter arranging colour, light and shade. And even the statesman gives structure to nature [?][17] ... always—apart from when plant, animal or human forces come into it—you are dealing with man's own spirit.

Thus, the medieval thinker of the twelfth century looked back at the occult wisdom of the ancient Chaldeans, at Greek art and beauty, and at the strength in the concept of the state in the Roman Empire. These are the three great pillars of world history—wisdom, beauty and strength. Goethe portrayed them in his 'Fairy Story' as the Three Kings—occult wisdom in the Gold King, beauty as in Greece in the Silver King, and in the Brass King strength as it found world historical expression in the Roman concept of the state and as then adopted in the organization of the Christian Church. And the Middle Ages, with its chaos[18] resulting from the impact of the migrating nations, and with its mixed styles, is expressed in the misshapen mixed king made of gold, silver and brass; what was kept separate in the various ancient cultures, is mixed together in him. Later, the separate forces must once more develop out of this chaos to a higher level.

All those who, in the Middle Ages, took the Holy Grail as their symbol set themselves the task of using human powers to bring these separate forces to a higher stage [of development]. The Holy Grail was to have been something essentially new, even though it is closely related in its own symbolism to the symbols of a very ancient mystical tradition.

What then is the Holy Grail? For those who understand this legend correctly, it signifies—as can even be proved by literary means[19]—the following.

Till now, man has only mastered the inanimate in nature. The transformation of the living forces, the transformation of what sprouts and grows in the plants, and of what manifests itself in animal [and human] reproduction—that is beyond his power. Man has to leave these mysterious powers of nature untouched. There he cannot encroach. What results from these forces cannot be fully comprehended by him. An artist can certainly create a strangely beautiful Zeus, but he cannot fully comprehend this Zeus; in the future, man will reach a level where he can do that as well. In the same way that man has achieved control over inanimate nature, has mastered gravity with spirit-level and plumb-line, and the directional forces of nature with the aid of geometry and mechanics, so it is the case that in future man will himself control what he only receives as a gift from nature or the divine powers, namely, the living.

When in the past Abel sacrificed what he had been given by divine hand, he was thus sacrificing, in the realm of the living, only what he had received from nature. Cain, by contrast, had offered something which he had himself won from the earth by his own labour, as the fruits of effort.[20] Hence, at this time [in the Middle Ages], a radically new impulse was introduced into Freemasonry. And this impulse is that denoted by the symbol of the Holy Grail, the power of self-sacrifice. I have often said, harmony in human relationships is not brought about by preaching it, but by creating it. Once the necessary forces have been awakened in human nature, there is no more unbrotherliness. [The concepts of] majority and minority are meaningless in so far as what the Masonic symbols express; in it there can be no contention, for it is only a matter of 'can' or 'cannot'. No majority can decide whether one should use a plumb-line or a spirit-level; the facts must decide that. In that all men are brothers, there they find themselves to be at one. On that there can be no contention, if everyone treads the path of objectivity, the path which entails the acquisition of higher powers. Thus, the bond [of the Freemasons] is without doubt a bond of brotherhood, which in the broadest sense depends on what men have in common in inanimate nature.

However, not every power is still available there. Some things which were once there have disappeared again, because in the cycle of nature in which we now find ourselves, and which we call earth, it is material perception which is to the fore, while intuitive perception has been lost. I should like to indicate just one case. In architecture, the ability to design a really acoustic building has been completely lost. Yet, in the past, this art was understood. Whoever puts a building together by outward [concepts] alone will never create something acoustically sound, but anyone who thinks intuitively, with his thoughts rooted in higher realms, will be enabled to accomplish a building with these properties. Those who know that also know that, in the future, those forces of outward nature over which we have no control at present must be conquered, just as man has already conquered gravity, light and electricity in inanimate nature.

Although our age is not yet so advanced as to be able to control outwardly living nature, although that cultural epoch has not yet come in which living and life-giving forces come to be mastered, nevertheless there is already the preparatory school for this, which was founded by the movement called the Lodge of the Holy Grail. The time will, however, come—and it will be quite a specific point in time—when humanity, deviating from its present tendency, will see that deep inward soul forces cannot be decided by majority resolutions, that no vote can settle questions involving the limitless realm of love, involving what one feels or senses. That force which is common to all mankind, which is expressed in the intellect as an all-embracing unity about which there can be no conflict, is called manas. And when men have progressed so far that they are not only at one in their intellect, but also in their perceptions and feelings, and are in harmony in their inmost souls, so far that they find themselves in what is noble and good, so far that they lovingly join together in the objective, in what they have in common, in the same way that they agree that two times two makes four and three times three equals nine—then the time will have arrived when men will be able to control the living as well. Unanimity—objective unanimity in perception and feeling—with all humanity really embracing in love, such is the precondition for gaining control over the living.

Those who founded the movement of the Holy Grail in the twelfth century said that this control over living [nature] was at one time available, available to the Gods who created the cosmos and descended [to earth] in order to give mankind the germ of the capacity for the same divine forces that they already possessed themselves; so that man is now on the way to becoming a god, having something in his inner being that strives upwards towards where the Gods once stood. Today, the understanding, the intellect, is the predominant force; in the future it will be love [buddhi], and in a still more distant future, man will attain to the stage of atma.

This joint force (communal force)[21] which gives man power over what is symbolized by the cross,

is expressed—as far as the Gods' use of the force is concerned—by a symbol, namely by a triangle with its apex pointing downwards. And when it is a matter of this force being expressed in man's nature, as it germinally strives upwards towards the divine force, then it is symbolized by a triangle with its apex pointing upwards. The Gods have lifted themselves out from man's nature and have withdrawn from him. But they have left the triangle behind with him, which will develop further within him. This triangle is also the symbol of the Holy Grail.

The force as in the Gods

        The symbol of
the Holy Grail*

The force as in men

The medieval occultist expressed the symbol of the Grail—
the symbol for awakening perfection in the living—in the form
of a triangle. That does not need a communal church,
entwining itself around the planet in a rigid organization,
though this can well give something to the individual soul. But
if all souls are to strike the same note, then the power of the
Holy Grail must be awakened in each individual. Whoever
wants to awaken the power of the Grail in himself will gain
nothing by asking the powers of the official church whether
they can perhaps tell him something; rather, he should awaken
this power in himself, and should not question all that much.
Man starts from dullness [of mind] and progresses through
doubt to strength. This pilgrimage of the soul is expressed in
the person of Parzival, who seeks the Holy Grail. This is one of
the manifold deeper meanings of the figure of Parzival.

Does it further my knowledge if a corporate body, be they
ever so great, proclaims mathematical truth through its official spokesmen? If I want to learn mathematics, I must occupy
myself with it and gain an understanding of it for myself. And
of what use is it if a corporate body possesses the power of the
Cross?[22] If I want to make use of the power of the Cross, the
control of what is living, then I must achieve this myself. No
one else can tell it to me, or communicate it through words; at
best they can show it to me in the symbol, give me the shining
symbol of the Grail, but it cannot be told in an intellectual
formula.

The first accomplishment of this medieval occultism would
have been, consequently, what appeared in so many different
movements in Europe: the striving for individuality in religion,

* See note on pp. 381–382.

the escape from the rigid uniformity of the organized church. You can barely grasp to what extent this tendency underlies Wolfram von Eschenbach's *Parzival*.[23] What is manifested for the first time in the Reformation was already inherent in the symbol of the Holy Grail. Whoever has a feeling for the great meaning of what can confront us in this symbolism will understand its great and deep cultural value. The great things of the world are not born in noise and tumult, but in intimacy and stillness. Mankind is not brought forward in its development by the thunder of cannons but through the strength of what is born in the intimacy of such secret brotherhoods, through the strength of what is expressed in such world-embracing symbols, which inspire mankind.

Since that time, through innumerable channels, the hearts of men have received as an inflow what was conceived by those who were initiated into the Mysteries of the Holy Grail in the middle of the twelfth century, who had to hide from the world under pseudonyms, but who were really the leaven preparing the culture of the last four hundred years.

The guardians of great secrets, of those forces which continually influence human developments, live in the occult brotherhoods. I can only hint at what is really involved, because the matter itself goes very deeply into the occult realm.

For those who really gain access to such Mysteries, one practical result is a clearer perspective of world happenings [in the future].

Slowly but surely the organic, the living forces intervene in the present-day cycle of humanity's development. There will come a time—however fantastic this might seem to contemporary people—when man will no longer paint only pictures, will no longer make only lifeless sculptures, but will be in a position to breathe life into what he now merely paints, merely forms with colours or with a chisel.

However, what will appear less fantastic is the fact that today the first dawn is already beginning for the use of these living forces in the affairs of social life; that is the real secret surrounding the Grail. The last event brought about in the social sphere by the old Freemasonry was the French Revolution, in which the basic idea of the old Freemasonry came into the open in the social sphere with the ideas of equality, liberty and fraternity as its corollaries. Whoever knows this also knows that the ideas which emanated from the Grail were propagated through innumerable channels, and constituted the really active force in the French Revolution.

What is today called socialism exists only as an abortive and impossible experiment, as a final, I may say desperate, struggle in a receding wave of humanity's [development]. It cannot bring about any really positive result. What it sets out to achieve can only be achieved through living activity; the pillar of strength is not enough. Socialism can no longer be controlled with inanimate forces. The ideas of the French Revolution—liberty, equality, fraternity—were the last ideas to flow out of the inanimate. Everything that still runs on that track is fruitless and doomed to die. For the great evil existing in the world today, the dreadful misery which expresses itself with such frightful force, which is called the social question, can no longer be controlled by the inanimate. A Royal Art is needed for that, and it is this Royal Art which was inaugurated in the symbol of the Holy Grail.

Through this Royal Art, man must acquire control over something similar to the force that sprouts in the plant, the same force that the occultist uses when he accelerates the growth of a plant in front of him. In a similar way, a part of this force must be used for social salvation. This power, which is described by those who know something of the Rosicrucian Mysteries—as for example did Bulwer Lytton in his futuristic novel *Vril*[24]—is at present still in an elementary, germinal, stage. In the Freemasonry of the future, it will be the real content of the higher degrees. The Royal Art will in the future be a social art.

Again, I have to tell you something which will seem fantastic to the uninitiated, on account, I may say, of the comprehensive, all-embracing range of the idea. What man prints as a form deriving from his soul on the matter of this Earth Round is eternal, it will not pass away. Even though the matter thus given form outwardly decays, what the Royal Art has given form to, in pyramids, temples and churches, is imperishable. What the human spirit has given shape to, in matter, will remain present in the world as a continuing force. That is completely clear to those who are initiated in such matters. Cologne's Gothic cathedral will, for example, pass away, but it is of far-reaching significance that the atoms were once in this form. This form itself is the imperishable thing that will henceforth participate in the ongoing evolutionary process of humanity, just as the living force that is in the plant participates in the evolution of nature! The painter who paints a picture today, who prints dead matter with his soul's blood, is also creating something which will sooner or later be dispersed in thousands of atoms. What has imperishable and continuing value, what is eternal, is that he has *created*, that something from his soul has flowed into matter.

States and all other human communities come and go before our eyes. But what men have formed out of their souls, as such communities, constitute humanly-conceived ideas of eternal value, with an eternally enduring significance. And when this human race once again appears on the earth in a new form, then it will see the fruits of these elements of eternal value.

Today, whoever turns his gaze upwards to the starry heavens sees a wonderful harmony. This harmony has evolved, it was not always there. When we build a cathedral we place stone upon stone, when we paint a picture we place colour next to colour, when we organize a community we make law upon law; in exactly the same way, creative beings once worked upon what confronts us today as the cosmos.

Neither moon nor sun would shine, no animal, no plant would reproduce itself unless everything we face in the cosmos had been worked upon by beings, unless there were such beings who worked as we work today on the remodelling of the cosmos. Just as we work on the cosmos today through wisdom, beauty and strength, so too did beings who do not belong to our present human kingdom once work on the cosmos.

Any harmony is always the outcome of the disharmony of an earlier time. Just as stones were given form for a Greek temple, just as they abounded in other forms, in a perplexing variety of forms, out of which they became a co-ordinated structure, just as the profusion of colours on the palette is meaningfully arrayed in a picture, so, in just the same way, all matter was in other chaotic relationships before the creating spirit transformed it into this cosmos. The same thing is recapitulated on a new level, and only he who sees the whole can work on the details correctly and clearly. Everything that has had real significance for humanity's progress in the world has been brought about with care and judgement and through initiation into the great laws of the world plan. What the day produces is ephemeral. What is created in the day through knowledge of the eternal laws is, however, imperishable. To create in the day through knowledge of the eternal laws is the same thing as Freemasonry.

Thus you see that what confronts us in art, science and religion, beyond what is given by the gods and expressed in the symbol of the Cross, is in fact brought about by Freemasonry, from which everything that has been properly built in the world derives. Freemasonry is thus intimately involved in everything that human hand has shaped in the world, with everything that culture has created out of raw, inanimate matter. Go back to the great things the cultural epochs have produced. Consider, for example, the poems of Homer. What is contained in them?—what the initiates have taught mankind in great world-embracing ideas. The great artists did not invent their topics but rather gave form to what embraces all humanity. Is a Michaelangelo conceivable without the power of Christian concepts? Try in the same way to trace back to its origin whatever has achieved a really incisive cultural meaning, and you will in every case be led back to what has come from initiation [in the Mysteries].

Everything must in the end undergo a schooling. The last four hundred years were in fact a schooling for humanity, the school of godlessness, in which there was purely human experimentation—a return to chaos if seen from a particular point of view. Everyone is experimenting today, without being aware of the connection with higher worlds—apart from those who have once more sought and found that connection with spiritual realms. Nearly everyone lives entirely for himself today, without perceiving anything of the real and all-penetrating common design. That of course is the cause of the dreadful dissatisfaction everywhere.

What we need is a renewal of the Grail chivalry in a modern form. Anyone who can approach this will thereby come to know the real forces that today are still lying hidden in the course of human evolution.

Today so many people take up the old symbols without understanding them. What is thus made out of the sexual symbols in an uncomprehending way comes nowhere near to a correct understanding of Masonic concepts. Such understanding is to be sought in precisely those things that redeem mere natural forces—in penetrating and mastering what is living in the same way that the geometrician penetrates and masters the inanimate with his rule, compasses, spirit-level and so forth, and in working upon the living in the same way those who build a temple put the unliving stones together. That is the great Masonic concept of the future.

There is a very ancient symbol in Freemasonry, the so-called Tau:

This Tau sign plays a major role in Freemasonry. It is basically nothing else than a Cross from which the upper arm has been taken away. The mineral kingdom is excluded in order to obtain the cross at all—man already controls that. If one lets the plant kingdom come into play [*in Aktion treten*] then one obtains the cross directed upwards:*

What unfolds from the earth, from the soul, as power over the earth is the symbol of future Freemasonry.

Whoever heard my last lecture about Freemasonry[25] will remember my telling you about the Freemasonry legend of Hiram-Abiff, and how at a particular point he makes use of the Tau sign, when the Queen of Sheba wanted him to call together once more the workers engaged in building the Temple. Now the people working together in social partnership would never appear at Solomon's command, but at the signal of the Tau—which Hiram-Abiff raised aloft—they all appeared from all sides. The Tau sign symbolizes a totally new power, based on freedom, and consisting in the awakening of a new natural force.

May I be allowed to resume at the remark with which I ended last time,[26] when I told you where such great control over inanimate nature leads. Without much fantasy, one can show what is involved by an example. Wireless telegraphy works across a distance from the transmitting station to the receiving station. The apparatus can be set to work at will, it is effective over great distances, and one can make oneself

---

* See note on pp. 383–384.

understood by it. A similar force to that by which wireless telegraphy works will be at man's disposal in a future age, without even any apparatus; this will make it possible to cause great devastation over long distances, without anyone being able to discover where the disturbance originated. Then, however, when the high point of this development has been reached, it will eventually come to the point where it falls back on itself.

On the other hand, what is expressed by the Tau is a driving force that can only be set in motion by the power of selfless love. It will be possible to use this power to drive machines, which will, however, cease to function if egoistical people make use of them.

It is perhaps known to you that Keely invented a motor[27] that would only go if he himself were present. He was not deceiving people about this, for he had in him that driving force originating in the soul that can set machines in motion. A driving force which can only be moral, that is the idea of the future—a most important force, with which culture must be inoculated if it is not to fall back on itself. The mechanical and the moral must interpenetrate each other, because the mechanical is nothing without the moral. Today we stand hard on this frontier. In the future machines will be driven not only by water and steam, but by spiritual force, by spiritual morality. This power is symbolized by the Tau sign and was indeed poetically symbolized by the image of the Holy Grail.[28] Man is no longer merely dependent on what nature will freely give him to use. He can shape and transform nature; he has become the master craftsman of the inanimate. In the same way he will become the master craftsman of what is living.

As something that must be conquered, the old sexual symbol stands at the turning-point of Freemasonry. You could compare the old sexual symbol of the Freemasons with the new symbolism for future Freemasonry by the analogy of placing a rock struck from a cliff face and covered with rough grass next to a beautifully worked statue by a sculptor. Those who have been to some extent initiated into the Royal Art have been aware of this. Goethe, for instance, has expressed this marvellously in the Homunculus episode in the Second Part of *Faust*. There are still many mysteries[29] in that work, which remain to be revealed.

All this indicates that humanity faces a new epoch in the development of the occult Royal Art. Those who officially represent Freemasonry today know the least about what this future Freemasonry will be. They are the least aware that something quite new will replace the old symbols they have so often misinterpreted, and that this will have an entirely new significance.

Just as it is true that everything of real importance in the past stems from the Royal Art, so it is also true that everything of real importance in the future will derive from the cultivation of the same source. Certainly, every schoolboy today can demonstrate the theorem of Pythagoras; only Pythagoras could discover it, because he was a master in the Royal Art. It will be the same in the Royal Art of the future. Thus you see that the Masonic Art stands at a turning-point in its development, and has the closest links with the work of the Lodge of the Grail, with what can appear as salvation in the dreadful conflicts all around us.

These conflicts are only beginning. Humanity is unaware that it is dancing on a volcano. But it is so. The revolutions beginning on our earth make a new phase of the Royal Art necessary. Those people who do not drift thoughtlessly through life will know what they have to do—that they have to participate in our earth's evolution. Therefore, from a certain point of view, this very ancient Royal Art must be represented in a new form to stand alongside of what is so ancient, in which there lies an inexhaustible force. Those who can grasp the new Masonic ideas will strike new sparks from Freemasonry's ancient symbols. Then it will also become plain that contention between Craft and Higher Degree Freemasonry is meaningless set against the endeavours of real Freemasonry.

For this it is necessary to answer the question—and that brings us back to our starting-point—'What was the Royal Art up till now?' The Royal Art was the soul of our culture. And this culture of ours has two basic ingredients. On the one hand, it is built up by those forces in the human soul that concern themselves with the inanimate; and on the other hand, by the forces of those people who make it their principal task to control the inanimate simply by means of the forces summoned up by their organism—and they are the men, hence the Royal Art has hitherto been a male art. Women were therefore excluded and could not take part in it. The tasks carried on in the Lodges were set apart, kept separate—the details do not matter—from everything related to the family or to the reproduction on the purely natural basis of the human race.

In Freemasonry, a double life was led; the great ideas which came to expression in the Lodges were not to be mixed up with anything connected with the family. The work in the Lodges, being related to the inmost life of the soul, ran parallel to nurturing the social life of the family. The one current lay in conflict with the other. The women were excluded from Freemasonry. This ceased the instant that Freemasonry stopped looking backwards and turned its gaze forward. For it was precisely what flowed in from outside[?] that was seen as the female current; the Freemasons considered what came from nature as something priestly. And hitherto Freemasonry had regarded that as hostile.

Man is by his nature the representative of the force that works on the inanimate, whereas the woman is seen as the representative of the living creative force that continually develops the human race on the basis of nature. This antithesis must be resolved.

What has to be achieved in the future can only be brought about by overcoming everything in the world that relies upon the old symbols, which are expressed precisely in what is sexual. The Freemasonry that is obsolete today has these symbols but is also aware of the fact that we must overcome them. However, these sexual [symbols] must be kept in existence outside in the institutions that relate to what is natural and only in separation can the matter be resolved.

Neither the architect nor the artist nor the statesman have anything to do—in their way of thinking, that is, I ask you to consider that—with the basis of sexuality in nature. They all labour to control inanimate forces with reason, with the intellect. That is expressed in the Masonic symbols. Overcoming this basis in nature in the far future, gaining control of the forces of life—as in the far-off times of the Lemurian race man started to gain control of inanimate forces—that will be expressed in new symbols. Then the natural basis will have been conquered not only in the sphere of the inanimate but also in the sphere of the animate.

When we reflect on this, then the old sexual symbols appear to us as precisely what has to be overcome, in the broadest sense; and then we discover what in the future must be the creative and truly effective principle, in the concept of uniting both male and female spiritual forces. The outward manifestation of this progress in Freemasonry is therefore the admission of the female sex.

There is a meaningful custom in Freemasonry which relates to this matter. Everyone inducted into the Lodge is given two pairs of gloves. He puts one pair on himself; the other pair is to be put on the lady of his choice. By this is signified that the pair should only touch each other with gloves on, so that sensual impulses should have nothing to do with what applies to Freemasonry. This thought is also expressed in another symbol; the apron is the symbol for the overcoming of sexuality, which is covered by the apron. Those who do not know about this profound Masonic idea will be unable to have any inkling of what the apron really means. One cannot bring the apron into line with Freemasonry in the narrow sense.

We thus have the conquest of the natural by the free creative spirit on the one hand, but the separation by means of the gloves on the other. However, we could even take the gloves off in the end, once what is lower has been conquered by applying the immediate free spiritual forces of both sexes. Then only will what manifests itself today in sexuality be finally overcome. When human creation is free, completely free, when man and woman work together on the great structure of humanity, the gloves will no longer be distributed—for man and woman will be freely able to stretch out their hands to each other, because then spirit will be speaking to spirit, not sensuality to sensuality. That is the great idea of the future.

If anyone today wants to enter the ancient Freemasonry, then he will only be at the zenith of Masonic thinking about the future shape of mankind if he works in this spirit, and if he understands what the times demand of us, regardless of what the Order was in antiquity. If it becomes possible to gain an understanding of what is called the secret of the Royal Art, then the future will undoubtedly bring us the rebirth of the old good and splendid Freemasonry, however decadent it is today.

One of the ways in which occultism will permeate humanity will be through a revival of Freemasonry. The very best things reveal themselves precisely through the faults of their own virtues. And although we can only look upon Freemasonry today as a caricature of the great Royal Art, we must nevertheless not lose heart in our endeavour to awaken its slumbering forces again, a task which is incumbent on us[30] and which runs in a parallel direction to the theosophical movement. So long as we do not dabble in the question which weighs upon us, but really grapple with it out of the depths of our understanding of world events, make ourselves understand what is becoming manifest in the souls of the sexes, in the battle of the sexes, then we will see that it it out of these forces that the formative powers of the future must flow.

All today's chatter is nothing. These questions cannot be answered, unless the answer is drawn out of the depths. What exists in the world today as the social question or the question of woman is nothing unless it is understood out of the depths of world forces, and brought into harmony with them.

Just as it is true that the great deeds of the past had their origin in Freemasonry, so is it also true that the great practical deeds of the future will be gained from the depths of future Masonic ideas.

GOETHE AND HIS CONNECTION
WITH ROSICRUCIANISM*

There are two ways of penetrating Goethe's Rosicrucian Mystery, an exoteric way and an esoteric or occult way. The esoteric path is revealed through a study of those poems of his which are an outward expression of his Rosicrucian views and other knowledge relevant to this question.

These include:

1) The poem *Geheimnisse* ('The Mysteries'). This describes the Mystery of the Lodge of twelve with the thirteenth at their head. The contents are a reference to experiences in the outer court of the Rosicrucian Parzival Initiation (Grail Initiation).

2) The basic theme in *Faust*. Homunculus is the astral body; the journey to the 'Mothers' is a representation of the search for the Golden Triangle and the Lost Word.

3) The passages in *Wilhelm Meister* portraying the 'Journey and Transformation of the Soul' as far as the extension of consciousness to cosmic vision. (Contemplation of cosmic events. Makarius's vision is such an act of contemplation.)

4) The Fairy Story of the Green Snake and the Beautiful Lily is a portrayal of an *alchemistical initiation* as established by Christian Rosenkreutz; this is written correctly—not as in

---

* This text is only to be found in Marie Steiner-von Sivers' handwriting. It was presumably written down by Rudolf Steiner for Edouard Schuré around 1906, as Marie Steiner's transcript is found immediately following a text written down by Rudolf Steiner for Schuré in 1906, 'Zeichen und Entwickelung der drei Logoi in der Menschheit' ('Symbols and Development of the Three Logoi within Humanity'), printed in *Nachrichten der Rudolf Steiner Nachlassverwaltung*, Michaelmas 1965, and published in English in *The Apocalypse of St John*, Rudolf Steiner Press, London, 1977.

the defective tradition of the Lodges—as 030 degree (vulgarly known in Freemasonry parlance as the 30th degree. This fable contains in symbolic language *all* the secrets of this degree just as the myth of Hercules contains all the secrets of the Royal Arch degree, which is properly written 013 degree, and which is also called the fourth degree.

5) Important aspects of Rosicrucian initiation are also to be found in the poem *Pandora*.

*   *   *

The means of penetrating Goethe's Rosicrucianism in an esoteric or occult way are given in the initiation of the true 020 degree, which—to conceal the secret—is also written as 6 3 degree, being read as 6 × 3 = 18th degree (Rose Croix). In this it is shown, in an occult way, that Goethe underwent an initiation between his visits to Leipzig and Strasbourg, which only came to fruition in his life gradually, and which enabled him to fulfil a very particular Rosicrucian mission. No more about this can be *written down*; one could still say a little more about it verbally, and still more only in a *true* Rosicrucian Lodge of the 6 3 = 6 × 3 = 18th degree.

Notebook Entries by Rudolf Steiner in Connection with the Lecture in Berlin on 2 January 1906 (Archive Note No. 225)

Lessing

1875 Adam first Freemason

Building masons

Goethe's fable: Wisdom, Beauty,
                        Strength

tyling!

hl. (holy) Grail

Abel   Cain

Priesthood—Masonry

Through guilt, winning.—

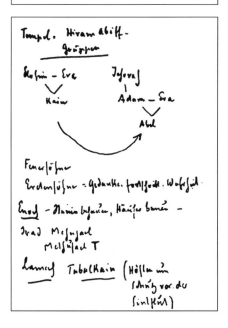

Temple   Hiram-Abiff

      groups

Elohim—Eve   Jehovah

   Cain   Adam—Eve

        Abel

Sons of Fire

Sons of Earth: Thought—Pro-
            gress—Truth.

Enoch—hew stones,
            build houses.

Irad   Mehujael
            Methusael T

Lamech   Tubal-Cain (Caves
            for protection
            from the Flood

Tubal-Cain

Nimrod—Hunting, Babylon
       Adoniram

Temple.Golden throne.
magnificent buildings

Sheba: Balkis

Adoniram: glance

T

three journeymen
       Syrian mason: Fanor
       Phoenician joiner: Amru
       Jewish miner: Methusael

Molten Sea

Benoni

Voice from above:

'Be without fear, I have made

you unburnable; hurl your-

self in the flames.'—

In the centre of the earth:
       Tubal-Cain

Hammer

Had-Had   Sarahil

NOTES

The subject matter of this abbreviated account of the beginning of human evolution must be accounted as in part an interpretation of H.P. Blavatsky's description in *The Secret Doctrine*, Vol. II, without this being obvious from the text.

Lecture 1, Berlin, 23 May 1904

Source for the text
Shorthand notes by Franz Seiler and curtailed shorthand notes by Walter Vegelahn.

1. *It was to be expected ...*
The lecture had probably been announced at short notice, as Rudolf Steiner had only just returned from a visit to London.

2. *Mrs Besant will be visiting us here ...*
Annie Besant, 1847–1933, President of the Theosophical Society from 1907, spoke once before in Berlin on the occasion of the founding of the German Section in October 1902. In September 1904, she went on a lecture tour of several German cities at the invitation of Rudolf Steiner. Her lectures, which were held in English, were reported by him in German.

3. *The next two public lectures ...*
These two public lectures of 30 May and 6 June 1904, 'History of Spiritism, Hypnotism and Somnabulism', were only exceptionally held on Mondays, otherwise Monday evenings were regularly taken up with Members' lectures.

4. *On the coming Thursdays ...*
Three lectures, 26 May, 2 and 9 June 1904 (not translated).

5. *lectures on the rudiments of theosophy.*
These lectures had been announced for April, but were not held until the autumn of 1904 (not translated).

6. *a single manuscript copy ...*
This was made public in H.P. Blavatsky's *The Secret Doctrine* (1888), Book 2, page 239. There it says: 'Now the Vatican MSS of the Kabala—a single copy of which (in Europe) is said to have been in the possession of Count Saint-Germain, contains the most complete exposition of the doctrine ...'

7. *or has been able to read it in the Astral Light.*
Dr Steiner here refers to Blavatsky's ability, known to his audience, whereby she was able to read rare manuscripts in the Astral Light, as is described by Constance Wachtmeister, among others, in *Reminiscences of H.P. Blavatsky and The Secret Doctrine* (1893).

8. *the Count of Saint-Germain,*
One of the most enigmatic and controversial personalities of the eighteenth century. His birth date and the date of his death, as well as his true name cannot be established with any certainty. According to a lecture given by Rudolf Steiner in Neuchâtel on 27 September 1911 (translated in *Esoteric Christianity and the Mission of Christian Rosenkreutz*, Rudolf Steiner Press, 1984), the name does not only refer to one personality, but to others too. In the true bearer of this name lives the individuality of Christian Rosenkreutz. See also Lecture 5 given on 4 November 1904, which is included in this volume and the notes thereto.

9. *my Atlantis lectures ...*
This refers to lectures given in January 1904, of which, however, there are no notes.

10. *To find our bearings,*
The notes of Vegelahn express this in the following way: 'To find our bearings, we must get a little insight into two currents of the present day which are hidden in the souls of men of the fifth

Root Race and are often in conflict with one another. The one current is best represented in the Indian and South European confessions and also in the outlook on life of the Jewish peoples and the Babylonians—and the other is contained in the confessions and outlook of the Persians, westward of Persia to the regions of the Teutons.'

11. *Of these two currents ...*
See *The East in the Light of the West*, fifth lecture, Munich, 27 August 1909.

12. *Devas.*
The Indian name for the gods of Devachan, the heavenly world.

13. *Outlook on life of the peoples of the Southern Zone.*
See Note 11.

14. *viewpoint of the Northern peoples ...*
See Note 11.

15. *Asuras,*
Indian—Suras = gods (from Asu = breath) became non-gods = A-suras. In the old Oriental religions, and also later by Rudolf Steiner, used as the name for satanic beings. In connection with this lecture, however, it is used in the sense of Blavatsky's *The Secret Doctrine*, Book 2 ('On the Myth of the Fallen Angel, in its various aspects'), p. 500. 'Esoterically, the Asuras, transformed subsequently into evil spirits and lower gods, who are eternally at war with the great deities—are the gods of the Secret Wisdom. In the oldest portions of the Rig Veda, they are the spiritual and the divine, the term Asura being used for the Supreme Spirit and being the same as the great Ahura of the Zoroastrians. There was a time when the gods Indra, Angi and Varuna themselves belonged to the Asuras'. Only in Atlantean times, at the transition from Lemuria to Atlantis, were these originally high gods transformed into non-gods.

In the notes of a hitherto unpublished lecture by Rudolf Steiner, given in Berlin, 17 October 1904, the following is said: 'If we wish to understand the point of view of spiritual evolution we must be clear about an important event of the Atlantean epoch. Those beings which had originally been spiritual now appeared as revolutionaries striving for independence. Suras now became Asuras. Until this time they had taken no part in evolution. They are those powers which, just as in our day, represent the intellectual and spiritual side of human nature. This side of Lucifer's nature is that which also stood for Christianity during the first centuries. There are two documents referring to that; one is in the Vatican and a copy of it is in the possession of the most thoroughly initiated Christian of the western world, The Count of Saint-Germain.'

16. *basic tendency of the Northern peoples.*
   See Note 11.

17. *We learn particulars about it ...*
   It is to be noted that the text of the paragraph beginning with these words is defective. See in this respect Blavatsky's *The Secret Doctrine*, Vol. II, 'The History of the Fourth Race', and also the lecture by Dr Steiner, Dornach, 18 January 1920 (not yet translated), in which the date of the cessation of physical incarnation is given as 6th millennium, AD.

18. *'The Sons of God saw the daughters of men ...*
   Genesis 6: 1–2. See also Blavatsky's *The Secret Doctrine*, Vol. II, Part 2, 'On the Myth of the Fallen Angel, in its various aspects'. In the story of Noah from *The Golden Legend* by Jacobus de Voragine it says of this event: '... this time men began to multiply on the earth, and the children of God, that is to say, of Seth ... saw the daughters of men, that is to say, of Cain, and were overcome by concupiscence and took them to their wives.'

19. *the saga of Prometheus.*
   This is also linked by Rudolf Steiner to Blavatsky's *The Secret Doctrine*, Book 2.

20. '*In sorrow shalt thou bring forth children.*
    Genesis 3:16.

21. '*dying and becoming ... gloomy guest'*
    Und so lang du das nicht hast,
    Dieses: Stirb und werde!
    Bist du nur ein trüber Gast
    Auf der dunklen Erde.
    Concluding verse of a poem by Goethe called *Selige Sehnsucht*
    ('Holy Longing').

22. '*And there are three that bear witness in earth,*
    First Epistle of John, v. 7. Rudolf Steiner had already
    explained this passage from the Epistle in detail in his lecture
    on 29 April 1904. According to that, the present-day materi-
    alistic concepts of blood and water must not be applied here.
    When it is said, 'There are three that bear record in heaven,
    the Father, the Word, and the Holy Ghost: and these three
    are one,' this means in theosophical terminology: atma,
    buddhi, manas, the three higher principles. And when it is
    said later on, 'And there are three that bear witness in earth,
    the Spirit, and the water, and the blood,' it means the three
    lower principles, the three soul attributes. The astral body, as
    well as the blood (not our physical blood), are the lowest
    parts of the soul. Jewish esotericism believes that movement of
    the blood is caused by the astral body and that is correct. All
    influences which do not directly pass through the soul but still
    have an effect on the body are called the 'blood' in Jewish
    esoteric teaching. It is the active principle, the motivator. We
    call only the red liquid which flows through the body 'blood'.
    By water is signified 'kama' in every occult language—feel-
    ings, emotions, passions, etc: 'And now I shall tell you why
    this is called water. You must get acquainted with the concept
    that humanity today has grown accustomed to visualizing
    everything in a much more materialistic way than he did for-
    merly. If you picture to yourself an old Cabbalist, he did not
    regard water as just a flowing element but as an image, and he
    arrived at that in the following way. He said to himself: the

water is inhabited by those animals which we reckon as the most primitive. Animals evolved originally out of the liquid element: sea animals, jelly-fish, amphibians. These then came out of the water onto the land. It was only out of water that emotions and feelings came about ... We distinguish the lower part of the soul, which stirs the blood and makes it pulsate and causes pleasure and dislike and all such other painful experiences. And that he calls water because from water is derived that element of soul. And then we have the thinking part of the soul which is Spirit.'

23. *hidden manuscripts* ...
See Note 6.

24. *the great Masters ... the founders of our spiritual movement, not our society* ...
Rudolf Steiner expressed himself in a similar way on 2 January 1905, in a letter to a member who was about to be accepted into the Esoteric School: 'You know that behind the whole theosophical movement there are highly evolved beings whom we call "Masters" or "Mahatmas". These sublime beings have already completed the path which the rest of humanity still has to tread. They are now active as the great "Teachers of Wisdom and of the Harmony of Human Perception". They are already engaged in work on higher planes to which the rest of mankind will evolve during the course of the next periods of development (so-called "Rounds"). They do their work on the physical plane through their "messengers", the first of whom was H.P. Blavatsky—I mean the first as regards the theosophical movement. The Masters never found an outer organization of society, nor would they administer one. The Theosophical Society was formed by its founder members (H.P. Blavatsky, Olcott and others) in order to promote the work of the Masters on the physical plane, but these Masters themselves have never exerted any influence on the Society as such. It is in its whole character and leadership purely and simply the work of men living on the earth.' See in this context also Lecture 16, given on 22 October 1905 (contained in this volume).

Lecture 2 Berlin, 10 June 1904

Source for the text
Shorthand notes by Franz Seiler and Walter Vegelahn and short
notes in longhand by Marie Steiner von Sivers.

1. *I mentioned already ...*
   At the end of his lecture given on 27 May 1904 with the words:
   'Next time I shall deal with one of the most important legends,
   which is one you have often heard but whose inner meaning is so
   profound that there is hardly anything to match it: the legend of
   Cain and Abel.'

2. *an allegory for very profound Mysteries*
   See in this connection: Blavatsky's *The Secret Doctrine*, Vol. II,
   'The Divine Hermaphrodite', p. 124, but also Rudolf Steiner's
   later cycle, *The Effects of Spiritual Development*, ten lectures
   given in the Hague, 20–29 March 1913 (Rudolf Steiner Press,
   1978).

3. *Enoch,*
   Apocryphal Book of the Old Testament.

4. *Take the first sentence from the fifth chapter of Genesis:*
   This is a free rendering by Rudolf Steiner of the words of the Old
   Testament. Instead of 'male *and* female created he *them*', Rudolf
   Steiner substituted: 'male-female created he *him*', with sub-
   sequent corrections of 'them', 'their', etc., into 'him', 'his', etc.
   On later occasions, Rudolf Steiner often stressed the fact that
   this first creation of man was a male-female creation. Compare
   also: *Egyptian Myths and Mysteries*, eighth lecture, and *Genesis,
   Secrets of the Bible Story of Creation*, eleventh lecture.

5. *Abel is the same as 'pneuma' in Greek,*
   See in this connection Rudolf Steiner's *The Gospel of St
   Matthew*, Lecture 5.

6. *The brain became male,*
   This passage appears to have been imperfectly preserved. One

can compare it with passages from Lectures 17, 18, 19 and 20, given on 23 October 1905 and 2 January 1906 (in the present volume).

7. *It was a sin when 'The Sons of God ...*
See Note 15 of the previous lecture.

8. *From this union resulted a race of men ...*
Genesis 6:4. 'There were giants in the earth in those days; and also after that, when the Sons of God came in unto the daughters of men, and they bare children to them, the same became mighty men, which were of old, men of renown.'

9. *It is called 'Rakshasas' in occult language ...*
According to H.P. Blavatsky's *The Secret Doctrine*, there are many explanations for this race of the Rakshasas in Oriental esoteric philosophy. See, for instance, *The Secret Doctrine*, Book 2, p. 288, where it speaks of 'Rakshasas' (giant demons) and Daityas (Titans).

A German translation of C.G. Harrison's *The Transcendental Universe*, which was among the books in Rudolf Steiner's library, may have been used by him in preparing this lecture. In the fifth lecture of the above it speaks of: 'These semi-human creatures, the progeny of the fallen angels, are known in the Hindu Scriptures as the "Asuras" and are sometimes called "Rakshasas" or demons.' This makes it plain that, in Lecture 2 held on 10 June 1904, Rudolf Steiner conferred a different meaning on the term 'Asuras' to the one he had in mind when he lectured on 23 May 1904 (Lecture 1).

10. *It is not for nothing that the Bible expresses it thus:*
An account of Christ's entry into Hell can be read in the Apocryphal Book of 'The Acts of Pilate'.

11. *The Rakshasa beings were brought thereby into a state of paralysis and lethargy.*
This passage appears in the notes of Marie Steiner von Sivers in the following form: 'The Rakshasas were brought into a state of

paralysis because they were being opposed from two sides: by the old Chela, who was deeply connected with the physical plane, and by a purely spiritual being, the Christ. Their power was thus paralysed from two sides. Something cosmic was effected. This tension, this bottled-up energy, had to be prevented from becoming effective energy. That is the Christ principle in action against the Antichrist.'

C.G. Harrison has the following to say on this subject in the aforementioned book: 'The Asuras are igneous, or dynamic, in their nature, and their power for evil was terrific. It was destroyed for ever by the advent of Jesus Christ, and they are now, as St Jude puts it, "reserved in everlasting chains until the judgment of the great day". (St Jude evidently derived his knowledge of the subject from the "Book of Enoch".) Stated in scientific terms, they are held in check, unable to move backwards or forwards, between the earth and the Eighth Sphere at the point of latency, where the attraction of both is equal on all planes, until the "great day" or axidal coincidence when they will be drawn irresistibly into the vortex of the latter. This text in St Jude has been unfortunately misunderstood, and supposed to apply to Lucifer and the first fall of the angels; hence the Miltonic and medieval myths.'

12. *Nostradamus,*
    Actually Michel de Notre Dame (1503–66). French astronomer and medical doctor. Famous on account of his *Prophecies,* written in French verse.

13. *Marie-Antoinette*
    1755–93: daughter of the Empress of Austria, Maria Theresa; became Queen of France in 1774 and ended her life on the scaffold, not heeding the warning of the Count of Saint-Germain.

14. *You know that Jesus Christ remained on the earth for ten years after His death.*
    Rudolf Steiner assumed that his audience was familiar with the work of the English theosophist G.R.S. Mead, *Pistis Sophia, A*

Gnostic Gospel (London, 1896), which begins with the words: 'It came to pass, when Jesus had risen from the dead, that He passed eleven years speaking with his disciples . . .'

15. Pistis Sophia
    The title of a work assumed to be the same as *The Apocalypse of Sophia*, composed by Velentius, the most learned doctor of the Gnosis who lived for 30 years in Egypt in the latter half of the second century.
    The only MS of the *Pistis Sophia* known to exist is the Askew manuscript, bought by the British Museum from the heirs of Dr Askew at the end of the eighteenth century.

16. *Sinnett's* Esoteric Buddhism.
    Published in 1883. See also, *The Occult Movement in the Nineteenth Century and its Relation to Modern Culture*.

17. *'Nifelheim' or 'Ymir the Giant'*
    Refer to notes for Lecture 3 given on 30 September 1904 (included in this volume), and also the first and thirty-first lectures in *Foundations of Esotericism*, Rudolf Steiner Press (1982).

18. *because it was the intention to involve man thoroughly in kama-manas*
    See twenty-third lecture in *Foundations of Esotericism*, Rudolf Steiner Press (1982).

Lecture 3, Berlin, 30 September 1904

The only source for this lecture was the short notes of Marie Steiner von Sivers. Sentences enclosed in square brackets are the amendments of the editor, where the text seemed insufficiently clear.
    Further source material has been appended below, gleaned from the writings of Charles William Heckethorn on the subject of the Druids and the Scandinavian Mysteries. A copy of Heckethorn's book in German translation was in Rudolf

Steiner's private library, and from marginal notes in Rudolf Steiner's handwriting it appears to have been used by him in connection with this lecture and other lectures included in this volume. (Charles William Heckethorn, *Geheime Gesellschaften, Geheimbünde und Geheimlehren* (Leipzig, 1900). Original English edition: *The Secret Societies of all Ages and Countries* (London, 1875).

From Charles William Heckethorn
The Secret Societies of all Ages and Countries
Vol. I, Book I, Chapter VIII, The Druids

The Druids, the Magi of the West
The secret doctrines of the Druids were much the same as those of the Gymnosophists and Brahmins of India, the Magi of Persia, the priests of Egypt, and of all other priests of antiquity. Like them they had two sets of religious doctrines, exoteric and esoteric. Their rites were practised in Britain and Gaul, though they were brought to a much greater perfection in the former country, where the Isle of Anglesey was considered their chief seat. The word Druid is generally supposed to be derived from 'an oak', which tree was particularly sacred among them, though its etymology may also be found in the Gaelic word *Druidh*, 'a wise man' or 'magician'.

Temples
Their temples, wherein the sacred fire was preserved, were generally situate on eminences and in dense groves of oaks, and assumed various forms—circular, because a circle was an emblem of the universe; oval, in allusion to the mundane egg, from which, according to the traditions of many nations, the universe, or according to others, our first parents, issued; serpentine, because a serpent was the symbol of Hu, the Druidic Osiris; cruciform, because a cross is an emblem of regeneration; or winged, to represent the motion of the divine spirit. Their only canopy was the sky, and they were constructed of unhewn stones, their numbers having reference to astronomical calculations. In the centre was placed a stone of larger dimensions

than the others, and worshipped as the representative of the Deity. The three principal temples of this description in Britain were undoubtedly those of Stonehenge and Avebury in the south, and that of Shap in Cumbria. Where stone was scarce, rude banks of earth were substituted, and the temple was formed of a high vallum and ditch. The most Herculean labours were performed in their construction; Stukeley says that it would cost, at the present time, £20,000 to throw up such a mound as Silbury Hill.

Places of Initiation
The adytum or ark of the Mysteries was called a cromlech, and was used as the sacred pastos, or place of regeneration. It consisted of three upright stones, as supporters of a broad, flat stone laid across them on the top, so as to form a small cell. Kit Cotey's House, in Kent, was such a pastos. Considerable space, however, was necessary for the machinery of initiation in its largest and most comprehensive scale. Therefore, the Coer Sidi, where the Mysteries of Druidism were performed, consisted of a range of buildings, adjoining the temple, containing apartments of all sizes, cells, vaults, baths, and long and artfully-contrived passages, with all the apparatus of terror used on these occasions. Most frequently these places were subterranean; and many of the caverns in this country were the scenes of Druidical initiation. The stupendous grotto at Castleton, in Derbyshire [Peak Cavern], called by Stukeley the Stygian Cave, as well as the 'Giants Caves' between Luckington and Badminton [in Wilts.], certainly were used for this purpose.

Rites
The system of Druidism embraced every religious and philosophical pursuit then known in these islands. The rites bore an undoubted reference to astronomical facts. Their chief deities are reducible to two—a male and a female, the great father and mother, Hu and Ceridwen, distinguished by the same characteristics as belonged to Osiris and Isis, Bacchus and Ceres, or any other supreme god and goddess representing the two principles of all being. The grand periods of initiation were quar-

terly, and determined by the course of the sun, and his arrival at the equinoctial and solstitial points. But the time of annual celebration was May-eve, when fires were kindled on all the cairns and cromlechs throughout the island, which burned all night to introduce the sports of May-day, whence all the national sports formerly or still practised date their origin. Round these fires choral dances were performed in honour of the sun, who, at this season was figuratively said to rise from his tomb. The festival was licentious, and continued till the luminary had attained his meridian height, when priests and attendants retired to the woods, where the most disgraceful orgies were perpetrated. But the solemn initiations were performed at midnight, and contained three degrees, the first or lowest being the Eubates, the second the Bards, and the third the Druids. The candidate was first placed in the pastos bed, or coffin, where his symbolical death represented the death of Hu, or the sun; and his restoration in the third degree symbolized the resurrection of the sun. He had to undergo trials and tests of courage similar to those practised in the Mysteries of other countries, and which therefore need not be detailed here.

The festival of the 25th of December was celebrated with great fires lighted on the tops of the hills, to announce the birthday of the god Sol. This was the moment when, after the supposed winter solstice, he began to increase, and gradually to ascend. This festival indeed was kept not by the Druids only, but throughout the ancient world, from India to Ultima Thule. The fires, of course, were typical of the power and ardour of the sun, whilst the evergreens used on the occasion foreshadowed the results of the sun's renewed action on vegetation. The festival of the summer solstice was kept on the 24th of June. Both days are still kept as festivals in the Christian church, the former as Christmas, the latter as St John's Day, because the early Christians judiciously adopted not only the festival days of the pagans but also, so far as this could be done with propriety, their mode of keeping them, substituting, however, a theological meaning for astronomical allusions. The use of evergreens in churches at Christmas time is the Christian perpetuation of an ancient Druidic custom.

Doctrines

The Druids taught the doctrine of one supreme being, a future state of rewards and punishments, the immortality of the soul and a metempsychosis. It was a maxim with them that water was the first principle of all things, and existed before the creation in unsullied purity, which seems a contradiction to their other doctrine that day was the offspring of night, because night or chaos was in existence before day was created. They taught that time was only an intercepted fragment of eternity, and that there was an endless succession of worlds. In fact, their doctrines were chiefly those of Pythagoras. They entertained great veneration for the numbers three, seven, nineteen (the Metonic cycle), and one hundred and forty-seven, produced by multiplying the square of seven by three. They also practised vaticination [prophecy], pretending to predict future events from the flights of birds, human sacrifices, by white horses, the agitation of water, and lots. They seem, however, to have possessed considerable scientific knowledge.

Political and Judicial Power

Their authority in many cases exceeded that of the monarch. They were, of course, the sole interpreters of religion, and consequently superintended all sacrifices; for no private person was allowed to offer a sacrifice without their sanction. They possessed the power of excommunication, which was the most horrible punishment that could be inflicted next to that of death, and from the effects of which the highest magistrate was not exempt. The great council of the realm was not competent to declare war or conclude peace without their concurrence. They determined all disputes by a final and unalterable decision, and had the power of inflicting the punishment of death. And, indeed, their altars streamed with the blood of human victims. Holocausts of men, women, and children, enclosed in large towers of wicker-work, were sometimes sacrificed as a burnt-offering to their superstitions, which were, at the same time, intended to enhance the consideration of the priests, who were an ambitious race delighting in blood. The Druids, it is said, preferred such as had been guilty of theft, robbery, or other crimes, as most acceptable to their gods; but when there was a scarcity of criminals, they made no scruple to supply their place with innocent persons. These dreadful sacrifices were offered by the Druids, for the public, on the eve of a dangerous war, or in the time of any national calamity; and also for particular persons of high rank, when they were afflicted with any dangerous disease.

Priestesses
The priestesses, clothed in white, and wearing a metal girdle, foretold the future from the observation of natural phenomena, but more especially from human sacrifices. For them was reserved the frightful task of putting to death the prisoners taken in war, and individuals condemned by the Druids; and their auguries were drawn from the manner in which the blood issued from the many wounds inflicted, and also from the smoking entrails. Many of these priestesses maintained a perpetual virginity, others gave themselves up to the most luxurious excesses. They dwelt on lonely rocks, beaten by the waves of the ocean which the mariners looked upon as temples surrounded with unspeakable prodigies. Thus the island of Sena or Liambis, The Saints, near Ushant, was the residence of certain of these priestesses, who delivered oracles to sailors; and there was no power that was not attributed to them. Others, living near the mouth of the Loire, once a year destroyed their temple, scattered its materials, and, having collected others, built a new one—of course a symbolical ceremony; and if one of the priestesses dropped any of the sacred materials, the others fell upon her with fierce yells, tore her to pieces, and scattered her bleeding limbs.

Abolition
As the Romans gained ground in these islands the power of the Druids gradually declined; and they were finally assailed by Suetonius Paulinus, governor of Britain under Nero, A.D. 61, in their stronghold, the Isle of Anglesey, and entirely defeated, the conqueror consuming many of them in the fires which they had kindled for burning the Roman prisoners they

had expected to make—a very just retaliation upon these san-
guinary priests. But though their dominion was thus
destroyed, many of their religious practices continued much
longer; and so late as the eleventh century, in the reign of
Canute, it was necessary to forbid the people to worship the
sun, moon, fires, etc. Certainly many of the practices of the
Druids are still adhered to in Freemasonry; and some writers
on this Order endeavour to show that it was established soon
after the edict of Canute, and that as thereby the Druidical
worship was prohibited *in toto*, the strongest oaths were
required to bind the initiated to secrecy.

Chapter IX, Scandinavian Mysteries

Drottes

The priests of Scandinavia were named Drottes, and instituted
by Sigge, a Scythian prince, who is said afterwards to have
assumed the name of Odin. Their number was twelve, who were
alike priests and judges; and from this order proceeded the
establishment of British juries. Their power was extended to its
utmost limits, by being allowed a discretionary privilege of
determining on the choice of human victims for sacrifice, from
which even the monarch was not exempt—hence arose the
necessity of cultivating the goodwill of these sovereign pontiffs;
and as this order, like the Israelitish priesthood, was restricted to
one family, they became possessed of unbounded wealth, and at
last became so tyrannical as to be objects of terror to the whole
community. Christianity, promising to relieve it from this yoke,
was hailed with enthusiasm; and the inhabitants of Scandinavia,
inspired with a thirst for vengeance on account of accumulated
and long-continued suffering, retaliated with dreadful severity
on their persecutors, overthrowing the palaces and temples, the
statues of their gods, and all the paraphernalia of Gothic
superstition. Of this nothing remains but a few cromlechs; some
stupendous monuments of rough stone, which human fury
could not destroy; certain ranges of caverns hewn out of the
solid rock; and some natural grottos used for the purpose of
initiation.

Rituals

The whole ritual had an astronomical bearing. The places of initiation, as in other Mysteries, were in caverns, natural or artificial, and the candidate had to undergo trials as frightful as the priests could render them. But instead of having to pass through seven caves or passages, as in the Mithraic and other Mysteries, he descended through nine—the square of the mystic number three—subterranean passages, and he was instructed to search for the body of Baldur, the Scandinavian Osiris, slain by Loki, the principle of darkness, and to use his utmost endeavours to raise him to life. To enter into particulars of the process of initiation would involve the repetition of what has been said before; it may therefore suffice to observe that the candidate on arriving at the sacellum had a solemn oath administered to him on a naked sword, and ratified it by drinking mead out of a human skull. The sacred sign of the cross was impressed upon him, and a ring of magic virtues, the gift of Baldur the Good, delivered to him.

Astronomical Meaning Demonstrated

The first canto of the Edda, which apparently contains a description of the ceremonies performed on the initiation of an aspirant, says that he seeks to know the sciences possessed by the Aesas or gods. He discovers a palace, whose roof of boundless dimensions is covered with golden shields. He encounters a man engaged in launching upwards seven flowers. Here we easily discover the astronomical meaning: the palace is the world, the roof the sky; the golden shields are the stars, the seven flowers the seven planets. The candidate is asked what is his name, and replies Gangler, that is, the wanderer, he that performs a revolution, distributing necessaries to mankind; for the candidate personates the sun. The palace is that of the king, the epithet the ancient Mystagogues gave to the head of the planetary system. Then he discovers three seats; on the lowest is the king called Har, sublime; on the central one, Jafuhar, the equal of the sublime; on the highest Tredie, the number three. These personages are those the neophyte beheld in the Eleusinian initiation, the hierophant, the daduchus or torchbearer, and the epibomite or attendant on the altar; those he sees in Freemasonry, the master, and the senior and junior wardens, symbolical personifications of the sun, moon, and Demiurgus, or grand architect of the universe. But the Scandinavian triad is usually represented by Odin, the chief deity; Thor, his first-born, the reputed mediator between god and man, possessing unlimited power over the universe, wherefore his head was surrounded by a circle of twelve stars; and Freya, a hermaphrodite, adorned with a variety of symbols significant of dominion over love and marriage. In the instructions given to the neophyte, he is told that the greatest and most ancient of gods is called Alfader (the father of all), and has twelve epithets, which recall the twelve attributes of the sun, the twelve constellations, the twelve superior gods of Egypt, Greece, and Rome. Among the gods of the Scandinavian theogony there is Baldur the Good, whose story, as already hinted above, formed the object of the initiatory ceremonies. Baldur is Mithras, the sun's love. He foresees the danger that threatens him; he dreams of it at night. The other gods of Valhalla, the Scandinavian Olympus, to whom he reveals his sad forebodings, reassure him, and to guard against any harm befalling him, exact an oath from every thing in nature on his behalf, except from the mistletoe, which was omitted on account of its apparently inoffensive qualities. For an experiment, and in sport, the gods cast at Baldur all kinds of missiles, without wounding him. Hoder the blind [that is, Fate], takes no part in the diversion; but Loki [the principle of evil, darkness, the season of winter] places a sprig in the hands of Hoder, and persuades him to cast it at the devoted victim, who falls pierced with mortal wounds. For this reason it was that this plant was gathered at the winter solstice by the Druids of Scandinavia, Gaul, and Britain, with a curved knife, whose form symbolized the segment of the zodiacal circle during which the murder of Baldur took place. In the Edda of Snorro we have another legend of Odin and Freya, the Scandinavian Isis or Venus, giving an account of the wanderings of the latter in search of the former, which, of course, have the same astronomical meaning as the search of

Isis for Osiris, of Ceres for Proserpine, etc. One of the chief festivals in the year, as with the Druids, was the winter solstice; and this being the longest night in the year, the Scandinavians assigned to it the formation of the world from primeval darkness, and called it 'Mother Night'. This festival was denominated 'Yule', and was a season of universal festivity.

Lecture 4, Berlin, 7 October 1904

Source for the text
Shorthand report from Franz Seiler, together with longhand notes by Marie Steiner von Sivers. Rudolf Steiner spoke about the Prometheus saga on later occasions, e.g. in: *Egyptian Myths and Mysteries*, Anthroposophic Press (1971) (tenth lecture); *Earthly and Cosmic Man*, Rudolf Steiner Publ. Co., 1948 (seventh lecture); *Things of the Present and of the Past in the Spirit of Man* (sixth lecture), typescript. Following the lecture on 'Prometheus', Rudolf Steiner spoke about the 'Argonaut saga and the Odyssey', 'Siegfried', and the 'Wars of Troy'. These were once translated with the present lecture in the typescript copy Z 331.

1. *Friday lectures*
During 1904 Rudolf Steiner not only spoke at the regular Group Meetings, which took place on Mondays, but occasionally also on Fridays to a very small circle which gathered in the flat of Fräulein Klara Motzkus in the Schlüterstrasse. The main subject dealt with was the myths and sagas. We do not have reports from all the lectures which were held there; at the most they are very fragmentary notes. These lectures of 1904, except for Lecture 1 of 23 May 1904, were all held for this small circle of friends. The May and June lectures of 1905 (Lectures 11 to 14), and Lecture 20 of 2 January 1906 were held on the Mondays for the official Berlin Group. The October lectures of 1905 (Lectures 15 to 19) were held for the General Meeting audience of the German Section.

2. *Manu*
   The name 'Manu' comes from the Sanskrit root 'man' =
   'thinking'. In Indian theosophical terminology this denotes high
   spiritual beings, who have the task of forming new cultures or
   epochs. For further details concerning the Manu of the fifth
   epoch, see Rudolf Steiner's *Cosmic Memory*, Rudolf Steiner
   Publications (1971); *Occult Science*, Rudolf Steiner Press (1969),
   and a lecture given in Heidelberg on 21 January 1909, 'Some
   Aspects of Reincarnation and the Life After Death', typescript
   copy Z 360.

3. *The consciousness of the fact that man of the fifth Root Race
   himself stood under the Fire Sign*
   This is expressed in H.P. Blavatsky's *The Secret Doctrine*, Vol.
   III, 'Esotericism', p. 330, in the following way: 'Prometheus is a
   symbol and a personification of the whole of mankind in relation to an event which occurred during its childhood—"Baptism
   by Fire"—which is a Mystery within the great Promethean
   Mystery, one that may be at present mentioned only in its broad
   general features.'

4. *as described by Scott-Elliot*
   The Story of Atlantis by W. Scott-Elliot, The Theosophical
   Publishing Society (London). See also *Cosmic Memory, Atlantis and Lemuria* by Rudolf Steiner, Rudolf Steiner Publications.

5. *our seven principles*
   These seven principles and the organs with which they are
   occultly connected are enumerated as follows:
   1. Physical body—base of the nose.
   2. Etheric body—liver.
   3. Kama or kama-rupa (astral body)—digestive system, sto-
      mach.
   4. Kama-manas (astral-ego)—umbilical cord.
   5. Higher Manas (spirit-self)—heart and blood circulation.
   6. Buddhi (life-spirit)—larynx.
   7. Atma (spirit man)—the Akasha.

6. *Adam Cadmon*
Compare also: *Man's Life on Earth and in the Spiritual Worlds*, second lecture, Oxford, 22 August 1922.

7. [*Here follow a few unclear sentences*]
The unclear sentences are as follows: 'Every saga undergoes change. It derives from the most ancient tradition and undergoes change at a certain definite point. It is the same in the case of every saga, even those which can again be taken literally.'

Lecture 5, Berlin, 4 November 1904

Source for the text
Notes by Mathilde Scholl, together with longhand notes by Marie Steiner von Sivers.

1. *At the beginning of the fifteenth century ...*
In the original notes this was given as fourteenth century. Rudolf Steiner sometimes reckoned centuries as the Italians do (Quattrocento = fifteenth century). In a handwritten document from 1907, however, Rudolf Steiner writes: 'In the first half of the fifteenth century Christian Rosenkreutz ...' etc. (*Letters and Documents 1901–1925*).

2. *Christian Rosenkreutz.*
Christian Rosenkreutz is a personality of the fourteenth to fifteenth centuries, not considered historical by modern investigators, who became known through two legendary anonymous writings: *Fama Fraternitatis* and *Confessio Fraternitatis*, published in Cassel in 1614 and 1615 respectively, in which it is stated that Christian Rosenkreutz was of German aristocratic descent and lived from 1378 to 1484. The name first became known through an anonymous handwritten document of 1604, which appeared in 1616 under the title: *Chymische Hochzeit: Christian Rosenkreutz, Anno 1459*, whose author, Johann Valentin Andreae, was declared by Rudolf Steiner to have been inspired by Christian Rosenkreutz him-

self. According to Rudolf Steiner, Christian Rosenkreutz was a real historical personality.

See: *A Commentary on the Chymical Wedding of Christian Rosenkreutz*, Temple Lodge (1989); *Chymical Wedding of Christian Rosenkreutz*, E. Foxcroft translation of 1690, Camphill Village Trust (1969); *A Christian Rosenkreutz Anthology*, compiled and edited by Paul M. Allen, Rudolf Steiner Publications, Blauvelt (New York 1968); *The Chymical Wedding of Christian Rosenkreutz. A Commentary* by E.E. Pfeiffer, Mercury Press.

3. *it was embodied in a kind of myth.*
It is worth noting that Rudolf Steiner here attributes the origin of the Temple Legend to Christian Rosenkreutz in the fourteenth and fifteenth centuries, but he never mentions how it came to be transferred to the Freemasons. Among Freemasons themselves its origin remains obscure. It is generally accepted that it arose in the eighteenth century, because that is the time of its first appearance in literature. Even though it is suspected that it formed a part of Masonic knowledge at an earlier period, this cannot be proved from documents. For this lecture, too, Rudolf Steiner seems to have made use of the account given by Charles William Heckethorn in his *Secret Societies*, namely, Quotation from Vol. I, Book VIII, Ch. 1.

The Legend of the Temple

Ancestry of Hiram Abiff
Solomon, having determined on the erection of the temple, collected artificers, divided them into companies, and put them under the command of Adoniram or Hiram Abiff, the architect sent to him by his friend and ally Hiram, King of Tyre. According to mythical tradition, the ancestry of the builders of the mystical temple was as follows. One of the Elohim, or primitive genii, married Eve and had a son called Cain; whilst Jehovah or Adonai, another of the Elohim, created Adam and united him with Eve to bring forth the family of Abel, to whom were subjected the sons of Cain, as a punishment for the

transgression of Eve. Cain, though industriously cultivating the soil, yet derived little produce from it, whilst Abel leisurely tended his flocks. Adonai rejected the gifts and sacrifices of Cain, and stirred up strife between the sons of the Elohim, generated out of fire, and the sons formed out of the earth only. Cain killed Abel, and Adonai pursuing his sons, subjected to the sons of Abel the noble family that invented the arts and diffused science. Enoch, a son of Cain, taught men to hew stones, construct edifices and form civil societies. Irad and Mehujael, his son and grandson, set boundaries to the waters and fashioned cedars into beams. Methusael, another of his descendants, invented the sacred characters, the books of Tau and the symbolic T, by which the workers descended from the genii of fire recognized each other. Lamech, whose prophecies are inexplicable to the profane, was the father of Jabal, who first taught men how to dress camels' skins; of Jubal, who discovered the harp; of Naamah, who discovered the arts of spinning and weaving; of Tubal-Cain, who first constructed a furnace, worked in metals, and dug subterranean caves in the mountains to save his race during the deluge; but it perished nevertheless, and only Tubal-Cain and his son, the sole survivors of the glorious and gigantic family, came out alive. The wife of Ham, second son of Noah, thought the son of Tubal-Cain handsomer than the sons of men, and he became progenitor of Nimrod, who taught his brethren the art of hunting, and founded Babylon. Adoniram, the descendant of Tubal-Cain, seemed called by God to lead the militia of the free men, connecting the sons of fire with the sons of thought, progress, and truth.

Hiram, Solomon, and the Queen of Sheba

By Hiram was erected a marvellous building, the Temple of Solomon. He raised the golden throne of Solomon, most beautifully wrought, and built many other glorious edifices. But, melancholy amidst all his greatness, he lived alone, understood and loved by few, hated by many, and among others by Solomon, envious of his genius and glory. Now the fame of the wisdom of Solomon spread to the remotest ends of the earth; and Balkis, the Queen of Sheba, came to Jerusalem, to greet the great king and behold the marvels of his reign. She found Solomon seated on a throne of gilt cedar wood, arrayed in cloth of gold, so that at first she seemed to behold a statue of gold with hands of ivory. Solomon received her with every kind of festive preparation, and led her to behold his palace and then the grand works of the temple; and the queen was lost in admiration. The king was captivated by her beauty, and in a short time offered her his hand, which the queen, pleased at having conquered this proud heart, accepted. But on again visiting the temple, she repeatedly desired to see the architect who had wrought such wondrous things. Solomon delayed as long as possible presenting Hiram Abiff to the queen, but at last he was obliged to do so. The mysterious artificer was brought before her, and cast on the queen a look that penetrated her very heart. Having recovered her composure, she questioned and defended him against the ill will and rising jealousy of the king. When she wished to see the countless host of workmen that wrought at the temple, Solomon protested the impossibility of assembling them all at once; but Hiram, leaping on a stone to be better seen, with his right hand described in the air the symbolical Tau, and immediately the men hastened from all parts of the works into the presence of their master; at this the queen wondered greatly, and secretly repented of the promise she had given the king, for she felt herself in love with the mighty architect. Solomon set himself to destroy this affection, and to prepare his rival's humiliation and ruin. For this purpose, he employed three fellow-craftsmen, envious of Hiram, because he had refused to raise them to the degree of masters, on account of their want of knowledge and their idleness. They were Fanor, a Syrian and a mason; Amru, a Phoenician and a carpenter; and Metusael, a Hebrew and a miner. The black envy of these three projected that the casting of the brazen sea, which was to raise the glory of Hiram to its utmost height, should turn out a failure. A young workman, Benoni, discovered the plot and revealed it to Solomon, thinking that sufficient. The day for the casting arrived, and Balkis was present. The doors that restrained the molten metal were opened, and torrents of liquid poured into the vast mould wherein the brazen sea was to assume its form.

But the burning mass ran over the edges of the mould, and flowed like lava over the adjacent places. The terrified crowd fled from the advancing stream of fire. Hiram, calm, like a god, endeavoured to arrest its advance with ponderous columns of water, but without success. The water and the fire mixed, and the struggle was terrible; the water rose in dense steam and fell down in the shape of fiery rain, spreading terror and death. The dishonoured artificer needed the sympathy of a faithful heart; he sought Benoni, but in vain; the proud youth perished in endeavouring to prevent the horrible catastrophe when he found that Solomon had done nothing to hinder it.

Hiram could not withdraw himself from the scene of his discomfiture. Oppressed with grief, he heeded not the danger, he remembered not that this ocean of fire might speedily engulf him; he thought of the Queen of Sheba, who came to admire and congratulate him on a great triumph, and who saw nothing but a terrible disaster. Suddenly he heard a strange voice coming from above, and crying, 'Hiram, Hiram, Hiram!' He raised his eyes and beheld a gigantic human figure. The apparition continued: 'Come, my son, be without fear, I have rendered thee incombustible; cast thyself into the flames.' Hiram threw himself into the furnace, and where others would have found death, he tasted ineffable delights; nor could he, drawn by an irresistible force, leave it, and asked him that drew him into the abyss: 'Whither do you take me?' 'Into the centre of the earth, into the soul of the world, into the kingdom of great Cain, where liberty reigns with him. There the tyrannous envy of Adonai ceases; there can we, despising his anger, taste the fruit of the tree of knowledge; there is the home of thy fathers.' 'Who then am I, and who art thou?' 'I am the father of thy fathers, I am the son of Lamech, I am Tubal-Cain.'

Tubal-Cain introduced Hiram into the sanctuary of fire, where he expounded to him the weakness of Adonai and the base passions of that god, the enemy of his own creature whom he condemned to the inexorable law of death, to avenge the benefits the genii of fire had bestowed on him. Hiram was led into the presence of the author of his race, Cain. The angel of light that begat Cain was reflected in the beauty of this son of love, whose noble and generous mind roused the envy of Adonai. Cain related to Hiram his experiences, sufferings, and misfortunes, brought upon him by the implacable Adonai. Presently he heard the voice of him who was the offspring of Tubal-Cain and his sister Naamah: 'A son shall be born unto thee whom thou shalt indeed not see, but whose numerous descendants shall perpetuate thy race, which, superior to that of Adam, shall acquire the empire of the world; for many centuries they shall consecrate their courage and genius to the service of the ever ungrateful race of Adam, but at last the best shall become the strongest, and restore on the earth the worship of fire. Thy sons, invincible in thy name, shall destroy the power of kings, the ministers of the Adonai's tyranny. Go, my son, the genii of fire are with thee!' Hiram was restored to the earth. Tubal-Cain before quitting him gave him the hammer with which he himself had wrought great things, and said to him: 'Thanks to this hammer and the help of the genii of fire, thou shalt speedily accomplish the work left unfinished through man's stupidity and malignity.' Hiram did not hesitate to test the wonderful efficacy of the precious instrument, and the dawn saw the great mass of bronze cast. The artist felt the most lively joy, the queen exulted. The people came running up, astounded at this secret power which in one night had repaired everything.

One day the queen, accompanied by her maids, went beyond Jerusalem, and there encountered Hiram, alone and thoughtful. The encounter was decisive, they mutually confessed their love. Had-Had, the bird who filled with the queen the office of messenger of the genii of fire, seeing Hiram in the air make the sign of the mystic T, flew around his head and settled on his wrist. At this Sarahil, the nurse of the queen, exclaimed: 'The oracle is fulfilled. Had-Had recognizes the husband which the genii of fire destined for Balkis, whose love alone she dare accept!' They hesitated no longer, but mutually pledged their vows, and deliberated how Balkis could retract the promise given to the king. Hiram was to be the first to quit Jerusalem; the queen, impatient to rejoin him in Arabia, was to elude the vigilance of the king, which she accomplished by withdrawing from his finger, while he was overcome with wine, the ring wherewith she had plighted her troth to him. Solomon hinted to the fellow-craftsmen that the removal of his rival, who refused to give them the master's word, would be acceptable unto himself; so when the architect came into the temple he was assailed and slain by them. Before his death, however, he had time to throw the golden triangle which he wore round his neck, and on which was engraven the master's word, into a deep well. They wrapped up his body, carried it to a solitary hill and buried it, planting over the grave a sprig of acacia.

Hiram not having made his appearance for seven days, Solomon, against his inclination, but to satisfy the clamour of the people, was forced to have him searched for. The body was found by three masters, and they, suspecting that he had been slain by the three fellow-craftsmen for refusing them the master's word, determined nevertheless for greater security to change the word, and that the first word accidentally uttered on raising the body should thenceforth be the word. In the act of raising it, the skin came off the body, so that one of the masters exclaimed 'Mac-benach!' (the flesh is off the bones!) and this word became the sacred word of the master's degree. The three fellow-craftsmen were traced, but rather than fall into the hands of their pursuers, they committed suicide and their heads were brought to Solomon. The triangle not having been found on the body of Hiram it was sought for and at last discovered in the well into which the architect had cast it. The king caused it to be placed on a triangular altar erected in a secret vault, built under the most retired part of the temple. The triangle was further concealed by a cubical stone, on which had been inscribed the sacred law. The vault, the existence of which was only known to the 27 elect, was then walled up.

4. *Before the outbreak of the French Revolution a personality appeared to Madame d'Adhémar,*
The historical basis for this lies in the work of the writer, Etienne-Léon, Baron de Lamothe-Langon, who published the *Souvenirs sur Marie-Antionette, Archiduchesse d'Autriche, Reine de France, et sur la cour de Versailles par Madame la Comtesse d'Ahémar, Dame du Palais* (Paris, 1836). About 50 years later these memoirs were rescued from oblivion by H.P. Blavatsky and her friends. One of the very rare copies of these memoirs

was to be found in the library of H.P. Blavatsky's aunt who lived in Odessa. Henry Steel Olcott, who founded the Theosophical Society with Blavatsky in 1875, wrote in his *Old Diary Leaves—The True Story of the Theosophical Society* (1895), Vol. 1, p. 24: 'If Mme. de Fadeef—H.P.B.'s aunt—could only be induced to translate and publish certain documents in her famous library, the world would have a nearer approach to a true history of the pre-revolutionary European mission of this Eastern Adept than has until now been available.'

The English theosophist Isabel Cooper-Oakley published all the parts of the *Souvenirs de Madame d'Adhémar* relevant to Saint-Germain in her book *The Comte of Saint-Germain—The Secret of Kings* (Milan, 1912). (See also Note 11 to Lecture 9 of 16 December 1904).

5. *the Count of Saint-Germain,*
    The spiritual identity of Christian Rosenkreutz and the Count of Saint-Germain is a result of Rudolf Steiner's own investigations. See also the lecture of 27 September 1911, translated in *Esoteric Christianity and the Mission of Christian Rosenkreutz* (Rudolf Steiner Press, 1984).

6. *'For they have sown the wind, and they shall reap the whirlwind.'*
    Quotation from Hosea 8: 7. See also Note 7 to Lecture 9 of 16 December 1904.

7. *the Cross of the World Body.*
    See Note 10 to Lecture 12 of 22 May 1905.

8. *only exists secretly.*
    The German rendering is: 'exists only in between [?]' (*dazwischen*). The sense is somewhat obscure.

Lecture 6, Berlin, 11 November 1904

Source for the text
Rechecked shorthand notes by Franz Seiler; notes by Mathilde Scholl; longhand notes by Marie Steiner von Sivers.

About the text

All sources concur that we are here dealing with a shortened version of this lecture. The conclusion especially is preserved in only a very fragmentary fashion. In a handwritten copy of the notes of Mathilde Scholl there is a marginal reference to the fact that the contents of this lecture were later included in the third degree of the section dealing with cult and symbolism of the Esoteric School. The main value these notes have for us today is that they form the only full account of Manichaeism in the whole of Rudolf Steiner's work. As literary source material Rudolf Steiner made use of the work of Eugen Heinrich Schmitt: *Die Gnosis—Grundlagen der Weltanschauung einer edleren Kultur*, Vol. 1 (Leipzig, 1903), a book which Rudolf Steiner had in his private library and which he had commended in his periodical *Luzifer* (see Note 2). In the chapter of this work dealing with Manichaeism the extracts that Rudolf Steiner used for his lecture were marked by him. This lecture was held in the same year when the first fragments of the original Manichaean manuscripts from Turfan were published.

1. *the problem of Faust*
   See: *Goethe's Standard of the Soul*, Anthroposophical Publishing Co. (1925); *Goethe's Secret Revelation and the Riddle of Faust*, Rudolf Steiner Publishing Co. (1933); 'The Problem of Faust', (R. 55)—especially lecture of 3 November 1917.

2. *the first number of* Luzifer.
   The first number of Rudolf Steiner's *Luzifer*, a periodical concerned with soul life, spiritual development and theosophy, with its opening article on *Luzifer*, appeared in June 1903.

3. *St Augustine,*
   The famous Church Father (354–430 AD) was, according to his own confession, a disciple of Manichaeism for nearly nine years until his 'conversion'. See lecture of 26 December 1914, in *Festivals of the Seasons*.

4. *a person who called himself Mani . . .*
   Originally Mani is said to have been called 'Corbicius'. 'Mani' was the name that he gave himself and, according to Schmitt (see note concerning the text), this has the significance: 'an Aeon of the Mandaeans: Mana raba, which is as much as to say: the promised Comforter, the Paraclete'. The date of Mani's life is usually considered to be 215/16–276/7 AD.

5. *The Albigenses, Waldenses and Cathars . . .*
   According to Charles William Heckethorn (see note to lecture 3 of 30 September 1904): 'The sect of the Albigenses, the offspring of Manichaeism, fructified in its turn the germs of the Templars and Rosicrucians, and of all those associations that continued the struggle and fought against ecclesiastical and civil oppression.' The relationship between Manichaeism and Freemasonry is expressed thus by Heckethorn: 'Masons in this degree call themselves the "children of the widow", the sun on descending into his tomb leaving nature—of which Masons consider themselves the pupils—a widow, but the appellation may also have its origin in the Manichaean sect, whose followers were known as the "sons of the widow".'
   According to Joseph Schauberg in his book (*Vergleichendes Handbuch der Symbolik der Freimaurerei mit besonderer Rücksicht auf die Mythologien und Mysterien des Altertums*) on the symbolism of Freemasonry, a copy of which was in Rudolf Steiner's library: '. . . nearly all Freemasonry symbols show that the Masons of old believed in and dedicated their service to a worship of the light after the manner of the oriental sects of the Parsees, Sabaeans, perhaps also of the Manichaeans'.

6. *the Knights Templar, of whom we shall speak separately,*
   There is no evidence to show when this could have taken place in this context. See also sixth lecture (25 September 1916) in *Inner Impulses of Evolution* (Anthroposophic Press, 1984), and lecture of 2 October 1916 (Z 425).

7. *Freemasonry really belongs to this stream, though it is connected with others, for instance with Rosicrucianism.*

The origin of Freemasonry and its connection with Rosicrucianism is a much debated and unsolved theme, even in the literature of Freemasonry itself, whereas it has hardly even been touched on in serious historical studies. A first attempt in this direction, if exclusively from a rational and a spiritual point of view, is the work of Frances A. Yates: *The Rosicrucian Enlightenment*.

8. *What outer history has to say about Mani is very simple.*
   At this point the contents of Rudolf Steiner's lecture seem to have been very inadequately reported. He based what he had to say on a legend which he later repeated in a lecture for members (according to notes lacking date or indication of locality). In the aforementioned notes the literal transcript is as follows: 'Mani, or Manes, the founder of Manichaeism appeared in the third century AD in Babylon. An unusual legend has the following to say about him: Skythianos and Terebinthus, or the Buddha, were his predecessors. The latter was the pupil of the former. After the violent death of Skythianos, Terebinthus fled with the books to Babylon. He also suffered misfortune; the only one to accept his teachings was an elderly widow. She inherited his books and left them, at her death, to her foster-child, a twelve-year-old boy whom she had adopted out of slavery when he was seven years old. The latter, who might also be called a "Son of the Widow", came to public notice at the age of 24 as Manes, the founder of Manichaeism.'

   This legend is dealt with at length and with full references as to source in the work of D. Schwolsohn: *Die Ssabier und der Ssabismus* (Petersburg and Leipzig, 1856). (The detailed source references are not quoted in what follows.)

   'Now that it has been established that Manichaeism has been derived from Mandeaism, we shall attempt to throw light on the account given of Mani by another of the Church Fathers. According to Epiphanius, Cyrillus Hierosolymitanus, Socrates and the author of the *Acta Disputationis S. Archelai* (*Acta Archelai*) with whom Theodoretus Suidas and Cedrenus in part agree, Mani was not the real founder of Manichaeism but had as his predecessor a certain Scythianus and the latter's pupil,

Terebinthus, who afterwards called himself the Buddha. It goes on to say that anyone who wished to make a denial of the heresy of Manichaeism must at the same time abjure Zarades (Zoroaster), the Buddha and Scythianus. According to the *Acta Archelai*, the last-named was a Scyth from Scythia—which accounts for his name, which was not really Scythianus—and he appeared at the time of the Apostles, when he started to spread his doctrine of the two principles. He is said to have been a Saracen by birth and married a woman from upper Thebes, for whose sake he settled in Egypt where he became acquainted with the wisdom of the Egyptians. Epiphanius, Socrates and Cyrillus Hierosolymitanus give similar accounts, only the first of these says that he was a Saracen by birth, was educated in Arabia and journeyed to India and Egypt, and the last mentioned says emphatically that his teachings had nothing in common with either Judaism or Christianity. He, or his pupil Terebinthus, was the author of four books, which the latter, after his emigration to Babylon, left to a widow when he died. Mani, the slave of this widow, inherited these writings from her and proclaimed their doctrines as his own. Theodoretus, Suidas and Cedrenus have the same to say of Terebinthus and Mani, only they identify the latter with Scythianus; Theodoritus even goes so far as to say that the reason why Mani was called Scythianus was that he was a slave, and Suidas and Cedrenus say that by birth he was a Brahmin. Bauer maintains that these two predecessors of Mani, Scythianus and Terebinthus-Buddha, could not possibly be held to be historical personages: "Alone the obvious anachronism that Scythianus is reckoned as belonging to the time of the Apostles, and then to make his successor, Mani, appear soon after, is enough to make us suspicious of the historical truth of the whole story." This, however, is quite a wrong supposition. The time of the Apostles lasted until Trajan, who died in 117, for, according to Eusebius, John the Evangelist only died during Trajan's reign. When it is said that Scythianus appeared during the time of the Apostles, it is only the last years of the said Apostle which are meant. As proof of this a point made by Suidas will serve, to the effect that the Emperor Nerva (who reigned from AD 97 for 1 year and 4 months) recalled the

Evangelist, John, from Patmos, where he had been in exile, to Ephesus; at that time, adds Suidas, the dogma of the Manichaeans became known through the public proclamation of Mani's heresy. The latter statement, however, is almost certainly founded on mistaken identity; for, in another place, Suidas himself says that Manes lived at the time of the Emperor Aurelian (reigned 271–75). Without doubt, Suidas gleaned from his source that Scythianus proclaimed his dualistic doctrine at the time of Nerva and as he, as mentioned above, confused Manes with Scythianus, he substituted the former for the latter. According to that Scythianus started proclaiming his doctrine at the time of Nerva, that is to say, in AD 97. His pupil, Terebinthus-Buddha, may therefore have lived until AD 170 or 180, or even longer. Mani appears to have been born about AD 190. En-Nadim informs us (on the authority of Mohammed ben Is'haq Sahrmani, who is otherwise unknown) that Mani came before Schabur Ardsir (Sapores I) in the second year of the reign of the Roman Emperor Gallus (Trebonianus), who commenced his rulership November AD 251. As en-Nadim further adds, this took place on April 1 according to the Manichaeans, that is to say, on 1 April AD 253. But as Mani, according to en-Nadim, had been wandering the land and gathering pupils for 40 years before he came before Schabur and was already 24 years old before he started to preach his doctrines, it follows from this that he must have been born around the year AD 190. According to the reports of the above mentioned Church Fathers, Mani did not come into direct personal contact with Terebinthus, but arrived as a seven-year-old boy at the house of the widow, in whose possession were the writings of the already deceased Terebinthus. The chronology therefore fits in very well and Scythianus and Terebinthus-Buddha can very well both be historical personages; only Bauer makes the conjecture, for reasons which have much in their favour, that Scythianus and Terebinthus-Buddha are identical, which could be so, as Mani, as stated above, never came into personal contact with either of them. But the questions remain: who was Scythianus and whence did he obtain his dualistic teaching? The *Acta Archelai* states specifically that he was a Scyth from Scythia and yet he is generally called a Saracen. We explain this contradiction in the following way. He was born in a north-eastern province of Parthia, which in later times went under the general name of Scythia. Afterwards he wandered to the Near East, namely, southern Mesopotamia and north-eastern Arabia (whence the name "Saracen") and, at the time of Nerva, he was proclaiming his dualistic teaching and became the precursor of Mani. Bauer expressed himself likewise. El'hasai'h, or Elchasai', or Elkasai' (founder of the sect of the Ssabiers or Sabians, mentioned in the Koran—otherwise Mandaeans) also came from north-eastern Parthia and proclaimed his dualistic doctrine in the same region and at the same time as Scythianus and was also, in certain respects, a precursor of Mani, as has been shown above. Does it not appear to be a reasonable conjecture to suppose that Scythianus, who was named after his birthplace, is identical to the El'hasai'h of en-Nadim, the Elchasai' of the Pseudo-Origines and the Elkasai' of Epiphanius and Theodoretus?

'After what has been said there can be no further doubt about the influence of Parsism on Mandaeism, a fact which was already suspected by Lorsbach. Bauer would see indications of the spread of Buddhism—with its consequent influence on Manichaeism—in the accounts of Scythianus and Terebinthus-Buddha, whom he identifies, but to whom he attaches no historical reality. This he would see substantiated in many ways, one of which is the abjuration formula of the Manichaeans who, on conversion to the Church, were required to denounce the Buddha among others. An influence of Buddhism in the Near East at such an early date is certainly a possibility; for en-Nedim states specifically that Buddhism had penetrated into Transoxiana even before Mani's time. Weber also finds it "highly probable that Buddhist missionaries, urged on by their fresh religious zeal, had spread over the further parts of western Iran" at the time of which he was speaking (the time of the Greek rulership of India). Weber adds, however, that data on the subject are wanting. In another place he remarks, "the important influence which Buddhism had on the teaching of Mani is easily explained by the flowering of the same under the Yueitchi-Princes of Indo-Scythia, whose rulership spread temporarily over a large part of the eastern provinces of Iran". We are also of the opinion that the account which Mas'udi gives of the journeys of Budasp (Buddha) to Seg'estan, Zabulistan and Kerman point to an early spread of Buddhism in Persia. If, then, according to this, Scythianus, who in our opinion is a well-authenticated historical personality, was the disseminator of Buddhist doctrines, so, according to the above arguments, we would have to look for Buddhist elements and Buddhist influences among the Mandaeans. Perhaps the many assertions of Mohammedan writers to the effect that Budasp (Buddha) was the founder of the cult of the Ssabiers arose out of an actual historical influence of Buddhism on the Mandaeans, who were originally called Ssabiers by the Mohammedans. The genetic origin of both Buddhism and Mandaeism is still insufficiently known for us to be able to form conclusive views about the influence of the former on the latter. We will therefore content ourselves with gentle hints and indications to future investigators, which may perhaps help towards clearing up the problem.'

Even though the latest research no longer pays heed to this legend, because it ascribes a different origin to Mani, it is not thereby invalidated as a description of Mani's 'spiritual' origin. Compare Note 13, 'why it was that Mani called himself the "Son of the Widow"', and Rudolf Steiner's ninth lecture of the cycle given in Munich in 1909: *The East in the Light of the West*, Rudolf Steiner Publishing Co., and Anthroposophic Press.

9. *was also initiated into the Mithraic Mysteries.*
   According to Franz Cument, *The Mithras Mysteries*, Manichaeism was the inheritor of the Mithras Mysteries and the continuator of their mission.

10. *Mani described himself as the 'Paraclete',*
    Compare once more with Lecture 9 of *The East in the Light of the West*, quoted above.

11. *Augustine opposed his Catholic views to the Manichaean teaching which he saw represented in a personality whom he called Faustus.*
    In his writing *Contra Faustum*. Regarding Faustus, compare

Bruckner, *Faustus von Mileve* (Basle, 1901), where Faustus is described as an important representative of Manichaeism in Roman cultural circles.

12. *the legend of Manichaeism is a great cosmic legend,*
The legend is given as follows by Eugen Heinrich Schmitt (see notes referring to text above referring to Schmitt on p.324).

' "While the Powers of Darkness were chasing and devouring one another in a wild rage they arrived one day at the borders of their territory. Here they glimpsed a few beams of the Kingdom of Light and were so struck by the splendid sight that they decided to relinquish their quarrels among themselves and took counsel together as to how they could gain mastery over the Good which they had just seen for the first time and of which they formerly had no notion. Their desire thereafter was so great that all of them, as many as there were, armed themselves for battle." This is the description of events given by Titus of Bostra. In a similar way Alexander of Lycopolis presents it to us: "In the Hyle (Matter) desire arose to climb to the upper regions; there was espied the Divine Ray of Light which engendered so much amazement that a decision was immediately formed to get the same into its power." Of the measures taken by the threatened Kingdom of Light we are informed by the Acts of Archelaus (*Acta disputationis cum Maneta*, Chap. 7): "As the Father of Light became aware that the Darkness was about to attack his holy Domain, he allowed a force to emanate from him which is called the Mother of Life, this, in its turn, produced from itself Archetypal Man who, arrayed with the five pure Elements, Light, Fire, Wind, Water, Earth, descended to the earth like an armed warrior to do battle against Darkness." Manes himself gives the name of the Universal or World-Soul to this force which emanates from God. We can recognize here the same force which is called the Heavenly Mother or Holy Spirit by Bardesanes and other Gnostics (According to Titus of Bostra 1.29. Compare Bauer: *Manichaeism*).

'When Hyle made its attack, God held counsel to decide on a punishment, says Alexander of Lycopolis. But, as he had no means of punishment—there being no Evil in the House of

God—he sent forth a force, a Soul Force, against Matter, so that Matter was penetrated through and through and death consumed it with the force of this separation, with the force of this inner division and confusion which resulted from being mixed together in this way. It reminds us of the saying of Christ: "Every kingdom divided against itself is brought to desolation." (Luke 11:17). The latter interpretation contains the deeper esoteric meaning of the above battle. Not force against force, not evil against evil can be the recompense of the gentle light of heaven of which the moral was proclaimed by Christ. His victory must be achieved in quite a different way: in the form of a quiet disintegration in which the Forces of Light act as a kind of ferment to leaven the dough of matter; thus the Gospel describes the battle of the Light in such a wonderfully meaningful fashion. The pictures which Mani gives describe exactly the same event as the Gospel, but in more detail and with a depth which corresponds to the more mature historical setting.

'Therefore it is exactly the same thought which is expressed in the further unfolding of this Manichaean hero-tale. In the struggle against the opposing forces of Hyle the heavenly hero is not able to prevail, although, like Proteus of the Greek saga, he constantly disguises himself and takes on the shape of the various elements. The Demons overcome him and gain possession of his armour; yes, they appropriate many pieces of his radiant, sun-like nature to themselves and he would have been entirely at their mercy had he not called out to the Father, the Primeval Source of Light! The latter sent him the help of the Spirit of Life (*pneuma zoon*), who stretched forth the succour of his right hand and drew him up again out of darkness into the Heights of Light. "That is why," adds the *Acta Archelaus*, Chapter 7, "when Manichaeans meet one another they give each other the right hand, as a token that they have been rescued out of darkness; for, in darkness, says Mani, live all heresies." This point is of particular interest, because it quite openly states the object of this allusion, "heresy", which in this case refers to the ecclesiastical, satanic doctrine, which has known how to appropriate the Garment of Light, the outward form of Christianity, to itself to deceive and captivate the nobler souls. These are the plundered sun-like parts of Archetypal Man, which have come under the dominion of depravity-seeking mankind; a depravity which took on the appearance of sanctity through this act of plunder. It is, however, only one aspect of the meaning of this myth, which embraces both evolution and history. The noblest parts of Archetypal Man, his Sons, as it were, were fixed in the heavens as sun and moon by the Spirit of Life. These are the symbols of the all-illuminating Light and Life of Christ and the Paraclete, whereas the other stars, as scattered, expired light, are fixed in the heavens as the Demons of the Night. This Spirit of Life makes his appearance as the tamer of material existence, as the Spirit who brings measure and sets a limit to matter. He was therefore given the name "Architect of the Universe" by the Manichaeans and essentially he plays the part of Horos, or Horothathos, the boundary-marker of Valentius. That part of divine Life and Light, however, which is held captive in the nature forms of the plants, animals and man, is given the name "suffering Jesus", "the Man of Sorrows", "Jesus Patibilis". In the sense of Manichaeism, however, Jesus only represents this divine figure when He surmounts the restricted sufferings within the narrow limits of the body, when it was nailed to the Cross on the hill near Jerusalem. He becomes the Saviour of the World only when He identifies His Divine Life with that of all the suffering beings of a world yearning for his redeeming, light-shedding thoughts. And nothing is more characteristic of the crudity of the basic views of the Constantinian Church than that its chief exponent, the great Augustine, was morally unable to find anything in these thoughts but a calumny and defilement and humiliation which would have been sufficient to make the Manichaeans blush. On the other hand, we have seen with what delicacy Mani discharged himself of his task of rendering tangible a struggle between the forces of the Divine and the forces of Matter, of Evil, of Violence and the Demonic, and how beautifully he is able to honour the holy majesty of powerless mildness and to bring forth the dawning of a more noble culture of which the rough Roman mind of an Augustine had no inkling.'

13. *why it was that Mani called himself the 'Son of the Widow'*
The Manichaeist scholar Hans Heinrich Schaeder writes in his study of *Origin and Development of the Manichaean System*, from his collection of lectures, 1924–25, from the Warburg Library: 'We do not know what "Son of the Widow" means.' Rudolf Steiner, by contrast, explains the meaning still more profoundly than in the lecture under consideration as being a 'Mystery' title. *Mysteries of the East and of Christianity*, Rudolf Steiner Press (1972).

14. *my description of Lemuria*
His description in the periodical *Luzifer*. Contained in *Cosmic Memory*, Rudolf Steiner Publications (1971).

15. *Manu . . .*
See Note 2 to Lecture 4 of 7 October 1904.

16. *Beautiful words have been handed down from Mani . . .*
Rudolf Steiner here gives a free rendering of a quotation from Eugen Heinrich Schmitt, *Die Gnosis* (already mentioned at the beginning of these notes). Schmitt's text is as follows: 'It would therefore be a notable test of the fact that Manichaeism, as understood by initiates and as inner secret doctrine, is not just a retelling of Persian fables but a genuine Gnostic teaching based on spirit-vision, if we could only prove in a single case that the Manichaeans sought the source of their knowledge and warranty for their truth not in outward belief in authority (Mani said this or that) but directly through inner soul-vision. And this evidence is actually forthcoming. Mani himself introduces his foundation letter (*epistola fundamenti*) with the following words:
' "These are the words of healing and the eternal fountain of life. He who hears them and believes in them first of all and keeps their message will never more be prey to death but will enjoy a truly immortal and splendid life. For truly he is blessed who, through this divine doctrine, partakes of the knowledge (Gnosis) which sets him free to pass over into eternal life. The peace of the Invisible God and a knowledge of Truth will be with their brothers and loved ones who believe in the laws of heaven

even as they put them into practice in their daily lives. And they will behold you sitting on the right hand of the Light and will take away from you all malevolent attacks and all snares of this world; the gentleness of the Holy Spirit will in truth open your inner sense, so that you shall behold your own soul with your very eyes." The last words of this sentence, "*Pietas vero Spiritus Sancti intima vestri pectoris adaperiat, ut ipsis oculis videatis vestras animas,*" appear in the Latin of Augustine (*De actis cum Felixe L. 1 C. 14 Migne Aug. Opp. omnia Tomas VIII).'

17. '*I would not accept the teachings of Christ if they were not founded on the authority of the Church.*'
   (*Contra epist. Manich*, 5).

18. *The Manichaean Faust said,*
   (In Augustine's work *Contra Faustum*, VI, 8). After Augustine (basing his statement on John 20:29) calls those blessed who have not seen and yet have believed, Faustus makes the reply: 'If you imagine that we are called upon to believe without reason or reckoning, then you may well be happier without reasoning, but I prefer to get my blessedness through insight.' Quoted from Eugen Heinrich Schmitt: *Die Gnosis—Grundlagen der Weltanschauung einer edleren Kultur*, and marked in Rudolf Steiner's copy.

19. *the Faust saga.*
   Compare Herman Grimm: 'Die Entstehung des Volksbuches von Dr Faustus', in *Fifteen Essays*, third edition (Berlin, 1882).

20. *the Luther saga.*
   It is a well-known legend that Luther, while staying in hiding at the Wartburg in Thuringia under the protection of Frederick the Wise (1521–22), threw an ink-bottle at the Devil.

21. *Luther carries on the principle of authority,*
   Martin Luther, 1483–1546. The great inaugurator of the German Reformation was an Augustinian monk prior to leaving the monastic life. See Rudolf Steiner's two lectures: 'Luther' and 'Luther the Janus-head', in *The Karma of Materialism*.

22. *harmonization of life with form.*
Rudolf Steiner had spoken on several occasions about the concepts life and form at the time he gave this lecture. See lecture of 3 November 1904: 'Theosophy and Tolstoy' copy Z 332. Also twenty-seventh lecture in *Foundations of Esotericism*, Rudolf Steiner Press (1983).

23. *a spiritual current which goes beyond the Rosicrucian current,*
In a note of 1907 Rudolf Steiner writes that, within the Rosicrucian current, the initiation of Manes was looked upon as one of the Higher Degrees which consisted of understanding the true function of Evil.

24. *the fifth Round ...*
See diagram in connection with Lecture 10 of 23 December 1904. Compare also: *The Apocalypse of St John*, Rudolf Steiner Press (1977).

25. *Nietzsche's 'blonde beast',*
'Blonde beast' in his *Zur Genealogie der Moral*, which was widely praised. However, Rudolf Steiner said in his lecture of 6 October 1917, 'Elemental Spirits of Birth and Death', copy Z 400, ... 'people understood very little about it. It was the Devil himself who inspired people with the wish, as Nietzsche devotees, to become "blonde beasts" themselves ... but even though people never became "blonde beasts" in Nietzsche's sense— something took place in this century as a result of this socially disturbing impulse of the nineteenth century.'

26. *the Eighth Sphere.*
This difficult occult concept had already been explained by Rudolf Steiner, shortly before this time, as for instance on 31 October 1904, in the following way: 'In the first half of the fourth Round mankind developed the capacity for adapting his senses to the mineral kingdom for the first time. In the second half of the fourth Round he redeemed the mineral kingdom. But a part of this remained behind and was excluded, because it was no longer of any use to mankind. That constitutes the Eighth

Sphere, which is no longer of use to the development of man, but can be used by higher beings.' (From previously unpublished notes.) In the year 1915, Rudolf Steiner again went very thoroughly into the concept of the Eighth Sphere. See *The Occult Movement in the Nineteenth Century*, especially the fourth and fifth lectures, Rudolf Steiner Press (1973).

27. *that of Jesuitism (pertaining to Augustine) and that of Free-masonry ...*
Rudolf Steiner spoke in much more detail on this subject, which is here only briefly mentioned, in his lecture given in Dornach on 3 July 1920 (as yet untranslated). But he also spoke about Jesuitism on 20 May and 3 and 6 June: 'Three Lectures on Roman Catholicism'. Copy Z 65.

28. *The two run parallel to one another but they point in quite dif-ferent directions.*
In the shorthand version of Franz Seiler a few sentences occur at the end. It is not quite clear if this is the answer to a question 'Christ appears in person during the sixth Root Race (great epoch)—the Thousand-years Reign, originally it was Aeon, in Latin *saeculum saeculorum*. In the sixth Root Race, therefore, both the Bad and the Good will have evolved ... [Gap] ... The Keely Motor came too early, no doubt. An individual will possess so much power during the seventh Root Race that he will be able to kill thousands and thousands at a stroke.' Compare this with Note 29 to Lecture 20, the last lecture in this volume.

Lecture 7, Berlin, 2 December 1904

Source for the text
Newly checked shorthand notes by Franz Seiler, as well as longhand notes by Marie Steiner von Sivers.

1. *about whom I have already spoken in connection with the Rosi-crucian Order.*
Lecture 5 of 4 November 1904.

2. *secret of Freemasonry and its tendency is expressed in this Temple Legend.*
See Note 3 to Lecture 5 of 4 November 1904.

3. *Craft Masonry.*
Craft Masonry covers the three degrees of Entered Apprentice, Fellow Craftsman and Master Mason. It is referred to by Heckethorn as 'Blue Masonry' and by Rudolf Steiner as 'Johannesmaurerei'. See Notes 2 and 11 to the succeeding lecture (Lecture 8, 9 December 1904).

4. *I will now describe what happens to a novice about to be initiated into the first degree,*
For this description Rudolf Steiner again drew on the account given in Charles William Heckethorn's *Secret Societies* (pp. 267–71), some passages of which were marked by him accordingly.

5. *I shall still speak about the connection between Manichaeism and Freemasonry.*
It is not known whether this intention was carried out.

6. *they were known as Dionysiacs.*
Dionysiacs are mentioned by Heckethorn, pp. 79 and 250.

7. *Vitruvius*
Vitruvius Pollio, royal architect under Caesar Augustus, wrote his ten-volume work *De Architectura* between 16 and 13 BC, drawing from Greek sources and from his own experiences.

8. *Luzifer*
Rudolf Steiner refers here to articles which he at that time contributed to his periodical *Luzifer*, later known under the title *Luzifer Gnosis*, which were then published in book form and are available in English under the title *Cosmic Memory*, (Rudolf Steiner Publications, Chapter 'Lemuria').

9. *Regarding connections with Manichaeism ... [Gap]*
See Note 5.

10. *the 'Royal Arch',*
Since the Tolerance Agreement of 1813 the 'Royal Arch Degree' has passed as the Fourth Degree. See Note 16 to the succeeding lecture, and also the notes about 'Goethe's relationship to Rosicrucianism' which appear as an appendix to these lectures.

Lecture 8, Berlin, 9 December 1904

Source for the text
Shorthand notes by Franz Seiler, re-edited for publication.

1. *I am speaking to you as a non-Mason ...*
Rudolf Steiner entered later (1906) into a purely formal relationship with the Memphis-Misraim Freemasonry. See *The Course of My Life*, Chapter 36.

2. *the Charter of Cologne in 1535.*
According to a work by Friedrich Heldmann, contained in Rudolf Steiner's private library, *Die drei ältesten geschichtlichen Denkmäler der teutschen Freymaurerbrüderschaft* ('The three oldest historical documents of the German Freemasonry Brotherhood'). The Charter of Cologne of 1535, together with the oldest statutes of the Strasbourg Lodge of 1459 and its revision of 1563 form the oldest documents of German Freemasonry. Heckethorn, however, among others, holds it to be apocryphal, otherwise spurious. (See also Note 11 of this lecture.)

3. *The Freemason of whom I speak is Goethe.*
Goethe became a member of the 'Amalia' Lodge in Weimar. See also the commentary on Goethe's relationship to Rosicrucianism at the end of this volume.

4. *two verses of his Freemasonry poem ...*
The last two verses of his Freemasonry poem *Symbolum.*

5. *Royal Arch Degree,*
In his description of this degree Rudolf Steiner is again basing himself on Heckethorn, *Secret Societies*, Book 8, Chapter 7.

6. *The first, who represents the most important in the circle of twelve, is called Zerubbabel.*

   According to Heckethorn, p. 180, the name Zerubbabel is 'a compound word, meaning: "the bright Lord, the Sun". He rebuilds the temple and therefore represents the sun, risen again'. It supposedly is connected with the Zerubbabel of the Old Testament, a noble from the family of David, who, on return from captivity in Babylon, completed the building of the Temple of Jerusalem.

7. *I am talking about an ideal situation, in fact, which only very rarely arises when suitable people happen to be present.*

   At the end of this sentence a very unclear statement follows, which could be rendered as follows: 'Only a kind of memory is there, an indication of a memory of it, but the effect is missing.'

8. *The next officer is Jeshua, the high priest;*

   According to Heckethorn, p. 180: 'The next officer is Jeshua, the high priest; the third, Haggai, the prophet. These three compose the grand council. Principals and senior and junior sojourners form the base; Ezra and Nehemiah, senior and junior scribes, one on each side; janitor or tyler without the door.'

9. *The arrangement of the Lodge—though this is not always the case—is a large square hall with a vaulted ceiling,*

   According to Heckethorn, p. 260: 'The Lodge must have a vaulted ceiling, painted blue and covered with golden stars, to represent the heavens'. '... the brethren take their places according to their rank; the grandmaster in the east, the master in the south, and the novices at the north.'

10. *And those who take their places in the south are roped together. Each of them has the rope wound around him three times, uniting him with his fellows at a distance of three or four decimeters.*

    According to Heckethorn, p. 281: 'Nine companions must be present at the opening of a Royal Arch Chapter; not more nor less than these three are permitted to take this degree at the same time, the two numbers making up the twelve, the number of zodiacal signs. The candidates are prepared by tying a bandage over their eyes, and coiling a rope seven times round the body of each, which unites them together, with three feet of slack rope between them.'

11. *He who is initiated into this fourth degree, the first of the higher degrees, which in certain regions [?] still provides an inkling of the significance of the Temple Legend, has to pass three veils.*
According to Heckethorn, p. 265: 'Without the Royal Arch Degree, Blue Masonry is incomplete'. The 'Blue Masonry' of Heckethorn is what Rudolf Steiner calls 'Johannesmaurerei' (St John Masonry) and is usually known simply as Craft Masonry in this country. This Order got its name 'St John Masonry' from the Charter of Cologne, 1535 (see Note 2). Heckethorn, Book 8, Chapter 2 (end), says: 'The Freemasons have also frequently been said to be descended from the Knights Templars, and thus to have for their object to avenge the destruction of that Order, and so to be dangerous to Church and state; yet this assertion was repudiated as early as 1535 in the "Charter of Cologne", wherein the Masons call themselves the Brethren of St John, because St John the Baptist was the forerunner of the Light.' To continue the quotation from Heckethorn regarding 'Blue Masonry': 'Without the Royal Arch Degree, Blue Masonry is incomplete, for we have seen in the Legend of the Temple that, through the murder of Hiram, the Master's word was lost; that word is not recovered in the Master's Degree, its substitute only being given; hence the lost word is recovered in the Royal Arch Degree. Blue Masonry, in fact, answers to the lesser Mysteries of the ancients wherein, in reality nothing but the exoteric doctrines were revealed; whilst "spurious Masonry", or all subsequent degrees—for no one can be initiated into them who has not passed through the first three degrees—answers to the greater Mysteries.'

12. *The history of Freemasonry is related to them in the following way: The first true Mason was Adam,*
According to Heckethorn, p. 248, Freemasons claim to be '... not contemporary with the creation of man, but with that of

the world; because light was before man, and prepared for him a suitable habitation, and light is the scope and symbol of Freemasonry.' Edward Spratt, an Irish author, described Adam as the first Freemason, who, even after his expulsion from Paradise, possessed great knowledge, especially in the field of geometry. Edward Spratt: *Konstitutionenbuch für irländische Logen* (1751).

13. *Desaguliers …*
John Theophilus Desaguliers, 1683–1744. From 1719 he was the Grand Master of the first English Grand Lodge. Desaguliers passes for the strongest personality of the so-called 'Revival' movement in Freemasonry. As a renowned scientist (pupil of Isaac Newton) he is numbered among those who prepared the way for the founding of the theory of electricity.

14. *Oriental or Memphis Masonry.*
See Note 1 to next lecture (Lecture 9, 16 December).

15. *In Germany, where there is a branch of the Memphis-Misraim Freemasonry with world-wide Masonic connections,*
Rudolf Steiner bases his statement here on an assertion in the *Historische Ausgabe der Oriflamme. Der Schottische, Memphis- und Misraim-Ritus der Freimaurerei, AD 1904, Berlin,* according to which, at that time, friendly relationships existed between the twelve Grand Orients and Supreme Grand Councils of the Ancient and Accepted Scottish Rite and the Sovereign Sanctuaries of America, Egypt, Rumania, Spain, Cuba, Naples and Palermo. In Germany, however, the Memphis and Misraim Freemasonry was at that time considered 'irregular' and was not recognized.

16. *Articles of Union of 1813 between Craft Masonry with its three degrees and those branches of Masonry that recognize the higher degrees.*
In the last Article of 1 December 1813, it is stated that: 'It is explained and expressed that the pure and ancient Freemasonry shall consist of only three Degrees and no more, namely, the

Degrees of Entered Apprentice, Fellow Craftsman and Master Mason, with the addition of the High Grades of the Holy Royal Arch. But this Article shall not bind any Lodge or any Chapter to hold a gathering in accordance with the constitution of the said Order.' (*History of Freemasonry* by Heinrich Boos. From Rudolf Steiner's own library.)

17. *the manifesto which has been given by the Grand Orient of the Memphis and Misraim Rite ...*
    Rudolf Steiner read out the whole of the manifesto in the present lecture.

18. *Vitruvius*
    See Note 7 to Lecture 7 (2 December 1904).

19. *The speech which the English Prime Minister Balfour has made ...*
    The speech made by Balfour to the British Association on 17 August 1904 appeared the same year in translation under the title *Unsere heutige Weltanschauung* ('Our present outlook') (Leipzig 1904). At the time of the present lecture this speech had already been discussed in the November issue of *Luzifer-Gnosis*, under the heading: 'Present-day culture as reflected in Theosophy', in which the relevant passages from Balfour and Blavatsky are set over against one another. This discussion has been published in German in the complete edition of Rudolf Steiner's works as Volume 34, *Luzifer-Gnosis*. (For the text of Balfour's speech, see Note 22 to the next lecture, 16 December 1904.)

20. *This has been known to occultists since 1879. I emphasize this, although I cannot prove it.*
    At a later date Rudolf Steiner has often spoken in greater detail about the decisive importance of the year 1879, as for instance in *The Fall of the Spirits of Darkness*, Rudolf Steiner Press (1993).

21. *There are two tendencies, a left and a right tendency,*
    See in this connection Rudolf Steiner's detailed description in

The Occult Movement in the Nineteenth Century. For this statement Rudolf Steiner apparently made use of the publication by the Englishman C.G. Harrison, *The Transcendental Universe.*

Lecture 9, Berlin, 16 December 1904

Source for the text.
Shorthand report of Franz Seiler and longhand notes by Marie Steiner von Sivers. For the press the text by Seiler was newly revised.

1. *combined Rite of Memphis and Misraim.*
   According to legend the Memphis Rite is supposed to have originated with a man called Ormus, who was converted to Christianity by St Mark in the year 46. It is said that the Crusaders carried this Masonic knowledge with them from the Holy Land and founded a Grand Lodge in Scotland in the twelfth century. The legend derives the name Misraim from Mizraim, one of the sons of Ham. He came to Egypt, possessed himself of the country and called it after his name (Misraim or Mizraim—an old name for Egypt). The teaching about Isis, Osiris, Typhon, etc., is supposed to have come from him, cf. Schuster: *Die geheimen Gessellschaften, Verbindungen und Orden*, Vol. 2 (Leipzig 1906). According to Heckethorn (*Secret Societies*, Book 8, Chapter 20), the Egyptian Masonry was founded by Cagliostro. The Rite of Misraim is attributed (Heckethorn, Book 8, Chapter 10) to a foundation in Milan of 1805, i.e. ten years after the supposed death of Cagliostro, which foundation was laid by several Masons 'who had been refused admission into the Supreme Grand Council'. The Rite of Memphis is said to be a copy of the Rite of Misraim and was founded in Paris in 1839. It is supposed to have been combined with the Misraim Rite towards the end of the nineteenth century, since when it has been known as the 'Memphis-Misraim Rite'. John Yarker (see Note 16), the 'Absolute Sovereign Grand Master in and for Great Britain and Ireland of the

Combined Scottish, Memphis and Misraim Rite', established a Grand Orient (Grand Lodge) for Germany in 1902.

2. *The so-called Count Cagliostro,*
   Count Alexander Cagliostro, allegedly identical with the Sicilian Joseph Balsamo—a fact which he himself, however, always vigorously denied—died in the Vatican prison in 1795. He is regarded, along with the Count of Saint-Germain, as one of the most controversial figures of the eighteenth century. In an account of his life by François Ribadeau Dumas, *Cagliostro*, Allen and Unwin (1967), the attempt was made to put the record straight. For instance, it was quoted out of the Protocol of the trial by the Inquisition that 'it has not been possible to find a single witness among Cagliostro's accusers who had known Balsamo'. Furthermore, a passage is quoted from the book by Cagliostro's 'learned historian', Dr Marc Haven, *Le Maître inconnu Cagliostro*: 'No one has proved that Balsamo and Cagliostro are one and the same person; neither Morands, nor Goethe, not the Commissary Fontaine, nor even the trial of the Holy Inquisition have produced a document which precludes all doubt.'

3. *To prolong human life to a span of 5,527 years.*
   In the notes of Marie Steiner von Sivers it is said to be 5,530 years. According to Heckethorn (Book 8, Chapter 20), 5,557 years (see Note 13). Ribadeau Dumas (in the work quoted above) states that Cagliostro left many works behind him, among which is one entitled *The Art of Prolonging Life*. All of them, apart from his *Egyptian Ritual*, have disappeared. As Ribadeau Dumas says, 'If they haven't been burned, they must reside in the Vatican archives. Let us hope that, in the light of the new ideas of the oecumenical movement and reconciliation with the "separated Brethren", the Vatican Library will one day release these curious documents to which Cagliostro so often referred and through which he might be vindicated.'

4. *I remarked earlier that the French Revolution arose out of the secret societies ...*

This almost certainly happened during Lecture 5 given on 4 November 1904, though it is not recorded in the notes.

5. *What Mabel Collins depicted in her novel* Flita ...
Mabel Collins (pseudonym for Mrs Kenningdale-Cook), 1851–1927, was one of the best authors of the Theosophical Society. Rudolf Steiner wrote an appreciation of her novel *Flita, True Story of a Black Enchantress*, when it first appeared in German translation. This was published in March 1905 in the periodical *Luzifer-Gnosis* and is recorded in the complete edition in German of Rudolf Steiner's works in Vol. 34, *Luzifer-Gnosis*.

6. *in the writings of the Countess d'Adhémar ... Count of Saint-Germain.*
See Note 4 to Lecture 5 given on 4 November 1904.

7. *'They who sow the wind shall reap the whirlwind'* ...
According to the account of Madame d'Adhémar, the Count said to her: 'Madame, they who sow the wind shall reap the whirlwind; this is what Jesus said in the Gospels, perhaps not before I did but, anyway, his words have been preserved in writing, only mine could have been made use of.' Quoted from Heyer, *Aus dem Jahrhundert der Französischen Revolution* (1956 ed.) These words, however, do not appear in the New Testament, but in the Old Testament, Hosea 8:7. (See also the statement in Lecture 5 of 4 November 1904.)

8. *In books about the Count of Saint-Germain you can read that he died in 1784,*
He is reputed to have died in Eckernfoerde on 27 February 1784. As proof of this is the death register of the St Nicholas Church in Eckernfoerde, according to which he was 'quietly interred' on 2 March 1784.

9. *the Landgrave of Hessen,*
Prince Karl, 1744–1836, son of the ruling Landgrave Frederick II, Danish General and Governor of the Dukedoms of Schleswig and Holstein. His Freemasonry writing *La Pierre Zodiacale*

du temple de Denderah appeared in 1824. His memoires, which were dictated 1816/17, appeared in Copenhagen in 1861 and, in German translation, in Cassel in 1866. In the latter is to be found a report concerning the Count of Saint-Germain.

10. *the Countess d'Adhémar recounts in her memoires . . .*
See Karl Heyer's *Aus dem Jahrhundert der Französischen Revolution.*

11. *In reality he was at that time, in 1790, with some Rosicrucians in Vienna . . .*
Rudolf Steiner apparently bases his statements on an article by Isabel Cooper-Oakley in the periodical *Gnosis*, of 15 December 1903, the pertinent passage of which reads (quoted from *The Count of Saint-Germain* by Isabel Cooper-Oakley, Rudolf Steiner Publications, p. 145 and p. 140 *et seq.*):

'Franz Graeffer left us the curious account of a journey by Saint-Germain to Vienna. Unfortunately this description is not quite satisfactory. Graeffer himself confesses that it was written on 15 June, long after the event. He says: "A peculiar irresistible feeling has compelled me to set down these transactions in writing once more, after so long a time, just today June 15th 1843." Further, I make this remark, that these events have not been hitherto reported.

'One day the report was spread that the Comte de Saint-Germain, the most enigmatical of all incomprehensibles, was in Vienna. An electric shock passed through all who knew his name. Our Adept circle was thrilled through and through: Saint-Germain was in Vienna!

'Barely had Graeffer, his brother Rudolf, recovered from the surprising news, than he flies to Hiniberg, his country seat, where he has his papers. Among these is to be found a letter of recommendation from Casanova, the genial adventurer whom he got to know in Amsterdam, addressed to Saint-Germain.

'He hurries back to his house of business; there he is informed by the clerk: "An hour ago a gentleman has been here whose appearance has astonished us all. This gentleman was neither tall nor short, his build was strikingly proportionate, everything about him had the stamp of nobility ... He said in French, as it were to himself, not troubling about anyone's presence, the words: 'I live in Fedalhofe, the room in which Leibnitz lodged in 1713.' We were about to speak, when he was already gone. This last hour we have been, as you see, Sir, petrified ..."

'In five minutes Fedalhofe is reached. Leibnitz's room is empty. Nobody knows when "the American gentleman" will return home. As to luggage, nothing is to be seen but a small iron chest. It is almost dinner time. But who would think of dining! Graeffer is mechanically urged to go and find Baron Linden; he finds him at the "Ente". They drive to the Landstrasse, whither a certain something, an obscure presentiment, impels them to drive post-haste.

'The laboratory is unlocked; a simultaneous cry of astonishment escapes both; at a table is seated Saint-Germain, calmly reading a folio, which is a work of Paracelsus. They stand dumb at the threshold; the mysterious intruder slowly closes the book, and slowly rises. Well know the two perplexed men that this apparation can be no other in the world than the man of wonders. The description of the clerk was a shadow against reality. It was as if a bright splendour enveloped his whole form. Dignity and sovereignty declared themselves. The men were speechless. The Count steps forward to meet them; they enter. In measured tones, without formality, but in an indescribably ringing tenor, charming the innermost soul, he says in French to Graeffer: "You have a letter of introduction from Herr von Seingalt; but it is not needed. This gentleman is Baron Linden. I knew that you would both be here at this moment. You have another letter for me from Bruehl. But the painter is not to be saved; his lung is gone, he will die July 8th 1805."

'Saint-Germain then gradually passed into a solemn mood. For a few seconds he became rigid as a statue, his eyes, which were always expressive beyond words, became dull and colourless. Presently, however, his whole being became reanimated. He made a movement with his hand as if in signal of his departure, then said: "I am leaving (*ich scheide*); do not visit me. Once again will you see me. Tomorrow night I am off; I am much needed in Constantinople; then in England, there to prepare two inventions which you will have in the next century—trains and steamboats. These will be needed in Germany. The seasons will gradually change—first the spring, then the summer. It is the gradual cessation of time itself, as the announcement of the end of the cycle. I see it all; astrologers and meteorologists know nothing, believe me; one needs to have studied in the Pyramids as I have studied. Towards the end of this century I shall disappear out of Europe, and betake myself to the region of the Himalayas. I will rest; I must rest. In exactly 85 years people will again set eyes on me.* Farewell, I love you." After these solemnly uttered words, the Count repeated the sign with his hand. The two Adepts, overpowered by the force of such unprecedented impressions, left the room in a condition of complete stupefaction. In the same moment there fell a sudden heavy shower, accompanied by a peal of thunder. Instinctively they return to the laboratory for shelter. They open the door. Saint-Germain is no more there . . .'

12. *the Sovereign Sanctuary, who is identical with what is known as the Grand Orient in Freemasonry, and is in possession of the real occult knowledge.*

It would seem that a *person*, rather than a *body of people*, is here meant. Heckethorn, in talking about the Order of Memphis, says that 'it works 33 degrees and embraces a far more extensive ritual of workable degrees than any other rite, every one of its 33 degrees having its appropriate and elaborate ceremonial easily arranged for conferment and its titles are purged of ridiculous pretensions. Its government is strictly representative, as in our own political constitution. The 32 and 31 are the first, second, third and fourth Officers of the Chapter, Senate and Council and form the Mystic Temple and Judicial Tribunal, the presiding Officer, or Grand Master of Light, having the 33rd degree *to enable him to represent the Province in the Sovereign Sanctuary* (33–95) or *ruling body.*'

Dr Steiner speaks at the beginning of this lecture about the

---

* Said in 1790. Exactly 85 years later (1875) the Theosophical Society was founded.

Combined Rite of Memphis and Misraim having a great number of degrees, that 95 out of the 96 degrees have to be undertaken by its members and that the Supreme Leaders of the Grand Orients usually possess the *96th degree*. It seems likely that it is this Supreme Leader who is in possession of the actual occult knowledge and knows the path and the language of the Freemasonry Manifesto, through which is revealed the voice of the 'Wise Men of the East'.

13. *Masonic Manifesto,*
See preceding lecture of 9 December in which the text of the Manifesto is given in full.

14. *where this should have come in the discussion about Atlantean times in the* Luzifer *article, a row of dots was printed in place of those things which may not yet be communicated.*
This relates to the articles which appeared in the periodical *Luzifer-Gnosis* in December 1904 under the title 'From the Akashic Records'. See *Cosmic Memory*, Chapter 4, 'Transition of the Fourth into the Fifth Root Race', Rudolf Steiner Publications Inc. (New York, 1961), p. 66.

15. *the* Theosophical Review
The article in question appeared in the December issue of the *Theosophical Review* of 1904 signed only 'E'. Its contents were the result of a combined exercise undertaken by 'E', the interrogator, and 'T', the medium employed to transmit by automatic means the communications of 'F', the spirit guide. What follows comprises only a few extracts of the original article. '"F", though a politician and a man of the world, is an enthusiastic humanitarian ... He added that he felt very anxious, for soon an important discovery would be made which would give the doctors a greater power than they had even now, and that it would lead to more cruelty in experiments on animals, for the man who found it out would think he had learned it by vivisection. "But remember, it is not so, it is not a *discovery*, only a remembrance; for the man who will find it out was an Atlantean, and the Atlanteans were far more learned in

medicine than we are; indeed the body had no secrets for them."
I then began to question him about Atlantis . . .

'They commanded the elements, made fine weather or storm
as it pleased them. There were no children, for by an effort of
unnatural power they attained to the great secret of causing life
without material union of the two forces. The soul returned and
reincarnated by an effort of will, taking its form from the natural elements without any other medium. This was what ultimately ended their power, for it could not be allowed to
continue. It is dimly figured in a late Hebrew legend by the "tree
of life". There was nothing left of progression, and therefore a
cataclysm had to overtake this civilization, and destroy even its
memory.

'They overset the balance of creation, and so ruined their
civilization. The material cause was that they withdrew the life-
force of the earth, and exhausted all the supplies of the life-
current. This caused convulsions of nature, and the storm broke,
irremediable, terrible, and swamped them. The Titans vied with
the gods but were defeated. All religions tell this tale as a note of
warning.

'Your earth is a living creature, and if you can tap its life-
current you can work all miracles. The Atlanteans are the souls
of today in some cases, but they have been discrowned . . . They
had to return into ordinary life by the simple way of being born
as an ordinary infant.

'I will now tell you a little more about the wonderful power of
Atlantis, so as to make you realize what man has been, and will
be in the future ages; for to tell the truth Atlantis was *material
perfection*, to *this* man can never return, but to *perfection* he will
come in future time.

'The ways of life of the highest classes were most simple, for
nourishment was obtained almost from the air alone. Like
orchids, the rulers, and more especially the priests, drew all their
sustenance from the substance contained in the atmosphere.
Consult any botanist you like and you will see that I am right.
You cannot do this, for you are not self-materialized; you are
creatures *born*, and not *made by your own will* . . .

'It was only the discovery of the *great secret*, that of the "tree of life", which simplified matters, and that you will never regain until you cease to care for the power for its own sake. I mean the secret of death and birth. There is no need for men to die. There is no reason for men to be born. I know the secret in part, but not fully, for I am not good enough to be permitted to recall the wonderful power. If I could do this I should at once be tempted to reveal it to you, for it would be, God willing, an eternity of happiness.

'I will, however, try and define somewhat and give you an example. A man is entirely renewed each seven years; after a while, however, he deteriorates and slowly decomposes. This is owing to ignorance, for if he knew how to regulate the inflow of new particles, he would never choose worse but rather better particles, and the atoms would remain permanently polarized by his will. Man is really held in a single cell; this cell is immortal and descends from generation to generation, creating ever new forms in which a human spirit can manifest. If this cell is retained in the body, and there is no procreation or waste of conservative power, then there is no reason why man should not exist for ever, during the cycle. By his children, however, man reproduces himself, and so destroys his material self. To an adept, to marry is to become a lower creature subject to death. This is truth. Every man or woman who creates can only do so by handing on his immortality. Man is a spirit, and the spirit is the central point of the materialized form. The whole of mankind accepts death as a necessity, and therefore people hypnotize themselves into a belief that they must die, but there is no reason for it if the *cell* is still intact in them.

'Think it over and understand that this is one of the chief Christian teachings that has been corrupted. Christ rose from the dead to be the first fruits of life.

'I want to refer to the new discovery which will be made, and of which I have previously spoken. It was well known once, and will return to the fated man's memory, and he will be hailed as a benefactor of humanity. In the old days of Atlantis when the secrets of the body were entirely unveiled to the caste of rulers and priests, they learnt it in a far more terrible way even than that of vivisection, namely, by the stultification of the soul, thus

destroying or distorting the power of evolution in a creature.
You do not know this, thank God! or the earth would be once
more a land of devils ...'

16. *There is a man at the head of the American Misraim movement,
    whose significant character constitutes a sure guarantee of con-
    stancy in the advance. This is the excellent Freemason, John
    Yarker.*
    Yarker, 1833–1913, was an Englishman who was active within
    English Freemasonry. When it is here said that he was at the
    head of the 'American' Misraim movement, this is on the
    grounds of a statement made in the *Historical Edition of the
    Oriflamme* (Berlin 1904), co-edited by him, to the effect that
    only America possessed a legitimate Charter and that Yarker
    had been appointed in New York in 1872 'by S.G.C. 33° as
    "Chief Representative" and "Guarantor of Friendly Relation-
    ships" with the Manchester Grand Orient of the Scottish Rite
    and Sovereign Sanctuary of the Memphis and Misraim Rite.' As
    significant Masonic author he had obtained high degrees in
    many different connections. (See end of Note 1 to this lecture.)

17. *a certain Reuss,*
    Theodore Reuss, 1855–1923. Authorized by Yarker to inaugu-
    rate the setting up of the Memphis-Misraim Rite in Germany.
    Rudolf Steiner did not know Reuss at that time. An account of
    this is going to appear in the documentation of the history of
    Rudolf Steiner's 'Esoteric School' (untranslated).

18. *the well-known Carl Kellner*
    Carl Kellner, 1851–1905, Austrian inventor and big business-
    man. According to Hugo Göring in the January 1895 issue of the
    periodical *Sphinx* (official organ of the German Theosophical
    Society, edited by Hübbe-Schleiden), he invented the process for
    the manufacture of cellulose and worked together with the
    medical doctor Franz Hartmann. Kellner was the Sovereign
    Honorary General Grand Master for the Memphis and Misraim
    Rite in Great Britain and Germany and signed himself as such for
    the *Historical Edition of the Great Oriflamme* of 1904.

19. *Dr Franz Hartmann.*
Franz Hartmann, 1838–1912. After an adventurous life and personal acquaintance with H.P. Blavatsky, he founded the so-called 'Leipzig' Theosophical Society. He was the editor of the theosophical periodical *Lotusblüten.* He is mentioned by Rudolf Steiner in his autobiography *The Course of My Life* and in the second volume of Rudolf Steiner's letters.

20. *There are four kinds of instruction given in the Misraim Rite.*
The four kinds of instruction described by Rudolf Steiner are enumerated by Heckethorn (p. 299), where he deals with the 'Organization of the Rite of Misraim'. He says: 'Then arose the Rite of Misraim with 90 degrees arranged in four sections, viz. 1. Symbolic, 2. Philosophic, 3. Mystical, 4. Cabbalistic, which were divided into 17 classes.' 'The Rite of Memphis', he says (p. 301), 'is a copy of the Rite of Misraim and was founded in Paris in 1839. It was composed of 91 degrees, arranged in three sections and seven classes'. Where Heckethorn speaks of the 'Ancient and Primitive Rite of Masonry or Order of Memphis' (pp. 253–256), he states: 'The Ancient and Primitive Rite of Masonry works 33 degrees, divided into three sections, embracing modern, chivalric and Egyptian Masonry, as the latter was worked on the continent last century ... It embraces a far more extensive ritual of workable degrees than any other rite, every one of its 33 degrees having its appropriate and elaborate ceremonial easily arranged for conferment, and its titles are purged of ridiculous pretensions'.

On the other hand, when speaking about the Egyptian Rite in connection with Cagliostro, Heckethorn says (p. 352): 'The Egyptian Rite invented by Cagliostro is a mixture of the sacred and profane, of the serious and laughable; charlatanism is its prevailing feature.'

From this it appears that the 'Memphis and Misraim Rite', referred to by Rudolf Steiner, is a complex mixture of those rites which confer the higher degrees. Heckethorn refers to these as 'spurious Masonry' (p. 265), in contradistinction to 'Blue' or 'Symbolic' Masonry, which restricts itself to the three lowest degrees only.

21. *Last time I read to you from a speech by the English Prime Minister Balfour.*

   This has not been recorded in the notes at our disposal. In connection with the speech itself, see Note 19 to the previous lecture and the succeeding note to this.

22. *The physical atom is condensed electricity. I regard Balfour's speech as something of extreme importance.*

   The following extract of Balfour's speech is the part referred to. Under the heading: 'Reflections Suggested by the New Theory of Matter'.

   'But today there are those who regard gross matter, the matter of everyday experience, as the mere appearance of which electricity is the physical basis; who think that the elementary atom of the chemist, itself far beyond the limits of direct perception, is but a connected system of monads or sub-atoms which are not electrified matter, but are electricity itself; that these systems differ in the number of monads which they contain, in their arrangement, and in their motion relative to each other and to the ether; that on these differences, and on these differences alone, depend the various qualities of what have hitherto been regarded as indivisible and elementary atoms; and that while in most cases these atomic systems may maintain their equilibrium for periods which, compared with such astronomical processes as the cooling of a sun, may seem almost eternal, they are not less obedient to the law of change than the everlasting heavens themselves.

   'But if gross matter be a grouping of atoms, and if atoms be systems of electrical monads, what are these electrical monads? It may be that, as Professor Larmor has suggested, they are but a modification of the universal ether, a modification roughly comparable to a knot in a medium which is inextensible, incompressible and continuous. But whether this final unification be accepted or not, it is certain that these monads cannot be considered *apart* from the ether. It is on their interaction with the ether that their qualities depend; and without the ether an electric theory of matter is impossible.

   'Surely we have here a very extraordinary revolution'.

   It is interesting to note that Balfour does not use the term 'frozen' electricity or 'coagulated' electricity as the German translation does. He merely states that matter is the 'mere appearance of which electricity is the physical basis'.

23. *something which has been in publication since 1875 [1879?]*
See Note 20 to the preceding lecture.

Lecture 10, Berlin, 23 December 1904

Source for the text
Derived *only* from shorthand notes by Franz Seiler, rechecked for the 1979 publication in German.

1. *A week from now I shall speak about the meaning of the days connected in the Church calendar with the Christmas festival— most especially about Epiphany, which follows on the less important New Year festival.*
The German text, as handed down, reads: '. . . an Weihnachten, vor allen Dingen an das minder bedeutende Fest Neujahr anschliessen, das Fest der Epiphanie', which could be rendered as follows: '. . . about Christmas, most especially about the less important New Year's festival, the festival of Epiphany.' One must assume that the shorthand copy of Seiler intended the following: '. . . das minder bedeutende Fest Neujahr anschliessende Fest der Epiphanie', which would give the rendering as in the text of the lecture above. The said lecture was held on 30 December 1904 and its subject was the 'Three Kings' festival'.

2. *it is quite unjustifiable to speak in public in the style of the Manifesto of the Freemasons which I read to you a fortnight ago.*
In the lecture given on 9 December 1904 (Lecture 8 in this volume). Regarding the style of speaking appropriate to lecturing in public, see *The Course of My Life*, Chapter 32.

3. Theologia Deutsch.
Written about 1380. First published by Luther (fragmentary edition) Wittenberg, 1516. Complete edition 1518. First German

translation by Johannes Arndt, 1597. Translation into modern German by Franz Pfeiffer, Gütersloh, 1875.

4. *the Masters, as a rule, are not personages known to history;*
   See Note 21 to the lecture given on 23 May 1904 (Lecture 1 in this volume).

5. *You were first physically incarnated in the preceding races [after] the time of the Hyperborean and Polarian epochs.*
   The word *nach* ('after') is missing from the German edition, but to leave it out would be to negate the sense given in Lecture 1 of this series, 'Whitsuntide', given on 23 May 1904, which reads: 'It is a wrong conception when theosophists believe that reincarnations had no beginning and will have no ending. Reincarnation started in the Lemurian Age and will cease again at the beginning of the sixth Root Race or Age.' (See diagram opposite.) The German would then read: 'In physischer Inkarnation waren Sie in den vorhergehenden Rassen erst zur Zeit *nach* der hyperboräischen und polarischen Rasse vorhanden.'

6. *we are living in the fifth period of the fifth great post-Atlantean epoch;*
   See diagram opposite.

7. *This base colour gives rise to a certain substance ... [Gap] ... [called Kundalini, which holds together, within the human being, the forces that lead eventually to the spirit.]*
   The latter part of this sentence (within square brackets) was a correction made for the earlier edition of this lecture, published on 23 November 1947, in the members' newsletter of the German Anthroposophical Society, No. 47.

Lecture 11, Berlin, 15 May 1905

Source for the text
Shorthand notes by Franz Seiler, Walter Vegelahn and Berta Reebstein-Lehmann.

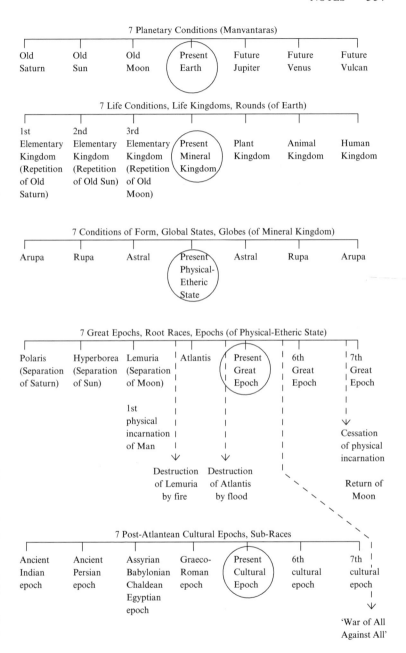

1. *in earlier lectures ...*
   For example, Lectures 3 and 5 of 30 September and 4 November 1904.

2. *in the Laocoon.*
   In this connection see lecture held in Munich, 14 March 1910.

3. *Livy's account ...*
   Titus Livius (59 BC–AD 17), Roman historian, author of a history of Rome (*Annales*) from the foundation of the city to the death of Drusus (9 BC); of the 142 books of this history, 35 of them and epitomes of most of the rest are extant.

4. *alb*
   A white vestment reaching to the feet, worn by the celebrant at Mass over the cassock and having long pointed sleeves. The oldest type of vestment derived from Egyptian and Hebrew times.

5. *the Prometheus saga.*
   See Lecture 4 of 7 October 1904 in the present volume.

6. *Jehovah is also called the God of [created] form,*
   See lecture of 25 October 1905, in *Foundations of Esotericism*, Rudolf Steiner Press (London 1983).

7. *the Eighth Sphere.*
   See Note 26 to Lecture 6 given on 11 November 1904.

8. *the Freemasons themselves no longer understand this, and believe that man should work on his own ego.*
   At this point the texts diverge. According to Seiler it is 'ego- istical' egos; according to Vegelahn and Reebstein 'spiritual' egos, which might have resulted from a mis-hearing or mistake in writing and could have been 'own' egos—(*geistigen* = *eigenen*).

9. *If we could bring people to engage in social reform from a theo- sophical basis,*

Rudolf Steiner was working towards establishing a reform of the social life soon after the end of the Great War. See 'The Threefold Order of the Body Social', RSE 252 and 253.

10. *Albert Schäffle.*
Albert Eberhard Friedrich Schäffle, 1831–1903, sociologist, wrote much on this subject. In another connection Rudolf Steiner mentions his work *Bau und Leben des sozialen Körpers* ('Construction and Life of the Body-Social'), a four-volume work published in Tübingen (1875–78).

Lecture 12, Berlin, 22 May 1905

Source for the text
Shorthand notes from Walter Vegelahn and from Berta Reebstein-Lehmann.

1. *each word in the Bible's account of it ...*
First Book of Kings, Chapters 5–7.
Second Book of Chronicles, Chapters 3–4.
Ezekiel, Chapters 40–42.

2. *Jean Paul recounts the following incident:*
Jean Paul (pseudonym for Jean Paul Friedrich Richter), 1763–1825, poet, writer of novels, and thinker. The episode here related was recorded in his childhood reminiscences.

3. *only the anointed priest in the Holy of Holies was allowed to utter the name 'Yahveh'.*
This took place once a year on the Day of Atonement. Leviticus 16:29–34: 'And this shall be an everlasting statute unto you, to make an atonement for the children of Israel, for all their sins, once a year.'

4. *Noah's Ark, and the other is the Temple of Solomon.*
According to notes of a lecture by Rudolf Steiner given in Cologne on 28 December 1907 (not yet published in German,

but intended for inclusion in Volume 101 of the complete edition) he there states:

'Were we to take millennia into account rather than centuries, we would observe how the form of the human body undergoes change according to the thoughts, feelings and conceptual criteria of previous millennia; and the mighty leading powers of evolution give to man the right concepts at the right time, so that even the human form becomes transformed ...

'How did the whole length, breadth and height of the physical body of today actually evolve? It is a result of what was at first contained in the astral and etheric bodies. That was where the thoughts, pictures, feelings, etc. at first resided. You will better be able to understand what I have to say if you call to mind a process which takes place immediately after physical death. It happens then that the physical body is at first forsaken by the etheric and astral bodies. Sleep consists in the fact that the astral body and ego withdraw leaving the physical body and ether body lying in bed. Death is differentiated from sleep through the fact that in the former state the physical body alone remains behind on the bed and the ether body withdraws along with the other two members of man's being. A strange phenomenon then takes place which could be described as a sensation, but which is connected with a kind of concept. The person feels as if he were expanding—and then the memory-tableau occurs, but before that happens he feels himself expanding in all directions—he gains dimension on all sides.

'This viewing of his ether body in huge dimensions is a very important concept; for it had to be induced into Atlantean man at a time when his etheric body was not so closely knit up with his physical body as it was to be in post-Atlantean times. This concept which occurs in man at death today had first to be aroused in him at that time. If a person were to visualize the approximate dimensions which are experienced by man today when he expands at death, then he has built up the motive, the thought form, which is able to bring his physical body into approximately its present form. If, therefore, the true measurements were held up in front of a person whose etheric body was at times separated from his physical body, they would take on the form that the physical body has today. And this form would have been induced into man primarily by those who are leaders of mankind's development. The exact account of this is contained in the various stories of the flood, particularly the biblical account. If you were to visualize man more or less surrounded by those forms which the etheric body must have in order that the physical body can be built up acccording to its proper dimensions, then you would have the same dimensions as Noah's Ark.

'Why are the exact measurements of Noah's Ark given in the Bible?' So that man, who was to be the bridge from Atlantean times to post-Atlantean times, would have a structure 300 cubits long, 50 cubits broad, 30 cubits high, which he must have around him in order to build up the proper thought form, to develop the right motive, out of length, breadth and height, to build up the post-Atlantean body in the right way. There you have a symbol from which the dimensions of your present-day body have been taken and which are the result of the thought form which Noah experienced in the Ark. It is not for nothing that Noah was placed in the Ark and that the Ark was described in this way. The Ark was built thus so that the human body could be properly formed in post-Atlantean times. The whole of mankind was educated by means of the use of effective symbols. Man carries with him at the present day the measurements of Noah's Ark. When man stretches his hands upwards the measurements of the Ark come to expression in the measurements of man's present-day body. Now man has evolved from Atlantis to post-Atlantis. In the epoch which will follow ours, the sixth epoch, man's body will again be quite differently formed; and today, too, man must experience those thought forms which will enable him to create for the next epoch the motives to provide the proper measurements for the bodies. That must be presented to man. Today the measurements of man's body are in the proportion 300 to 50 to 30. In the future his body will be built up quite differently. What will supply present-day man with the thought form for building up his future body? That is also told us. It is the measurements of the Salomonic Temple. And these measurements of the Salomonic Temple, when realized in physical form, represent, with profound symbolical significance, the whole physical organization of the man of the next epoch, the sixth great epoch.

'Everything which is effective in mankind takes its start from inside the human being, not from outside. What appears as thought and feeling at one period is outward form in the next. And the individualities who guide mankind must implant the thought forms into him many thousands of years in advance, if they are to become outward reality later. There you have the working of the thought forms which are activated by such symbolical figures. They have a very real meaning.'

5. *its proportions correspond to those of the human body, and also with those of Solomon's Temple.*
It has not been possible to identify the literary source to which Rudolf Steiner here refers.

In the *Cabbala* of Agrippa von Nettesheim (Scheible edition, Stuttgart, 1855), it is stated in the chapter concerning 'The Measurement, Relationship and Harmony of the Human Body': '... Yes, God Himself instructed Noah in the building of the Ark according to the measurements of the human body, just as He Himself incorporated into the whole world-mechanism the symmetry of man; and therefore the latter is called the macrocosm, the former the microcosm. With reference to the above some microcosmologists determine the measurements of the human body as being six foot, the foot being ten degrees and the degree being five minutes; this amounts to 60 degrees or 300 minutes, the same number of geometrical cubits as, according to the description of Moses, were contained in the length of the Ark. Just as the human body, however, has a length of 300 minutes, a breadth of 50 and a thickness of 30, so had the Ark of Noah not only a length of 300 cubits, but also a width of 50 and a depth (or height) of 30, from which it will be seen that there is a relationship of 6 to 1 of the length to the breadth, 10 to 1 of the length to the depth and 5 to 3 of the breadth to the depth.'

Further to this, Franz Coči in his work *Detailed Calculation of the Three Dimensions of Noah's Ark from the Standpoint of Geometry and Mechanics* (translated from Polish into German by Wenzel Bauernöpl, Bilin, 1899), demonstrated mathematically that: 'The only fitting and possible relationship of width to height of a four-sided hollow body, which combines the use of the least amount of material with the greatest stability, would be to take 5 (more exactly 5.322232) for the width and for the height 3 (more exactly 2.967768) equal parts. And this is the ratio in which the Ark actually was built.'

6. *The inner divine Temple is so formed as to enclose the fivefold human being. The square is holy. The door, the roof and the side pillars together form a pentagon.*
The version here translated is the version from the notes of Berta Reebstein-Lehmann. Walter Vegelahn's version is only fragmentary. It is rendered thus: 'The ... temple is so formed that it encloses the fivefold human being. That ... is the most important thing about the temple. The square is holy, the roof, the roof-covering and the side pillars together form ... In front of the altar stood two cherubim.'

7. *the door, the roof and the side pillars together form a pentagon.*
First Book of Kings, Chapter 6, verse 31:
    'And for the entering of the oracle he made doors of olive tree: the lintel and side posts were a fifth part of the wall.' The gloss referring to 'fifth part' gives the alternative 'five-square'.
    Emil Bock in his *Old Testament History*, Vol. 3, in speaking about the Temple of Solomon says:
    'The third, inmost chamber in the west, the Holy of Holies (*Debir*), was screened by a wooden partition containing a pentagonal doorway and covered by a curtain of four colours.'

8. *Knights Templars,*
See in this connection Rudolf Steiner's later and more detailed accounts of the Templars, e.g. lecture of 2 October 1916 in Dornach ('The Templars', copy Z 156); also the lecture of 25 September 1916 in *Inner Impulses of Evolution*, Anthroposophic Press (1984).

9. *We have traced the time from the first to the fourth cultural epoch.*
The text is quite plainly only preserved in an incomplete form. In

connection with the cultural epochs and the course of the sun through the zodiac, see Rudolf Steiner's lecture given in Dornach on 8 January 1918, in the lecture course entitled *Ancient Myths*, Anthroposophic Press, 1994.

10. *Plato said of it that the World Soul is crucified on the World Body.*
Rudolf Steiner often quotes this passage from Plato's Timaeus, but his formulation is closer to that of Vincenz Knauer, a Viennese philosopher personally known to him, whose book *Die Hauptprobleme der Philosophie...* ('The Development and Partial Solution to the Main Philosophical Problems from the Time of Thales to Robert Hamerling'), formed part of his personal library. In this particular version the passage here quoted has the following wording: 'God laid this soul in cross-formation through the universe and spread out over it the world body.' In the English translation of this passage (Penguin Classics, 1971, p. 48) it reads as follows: 'He then took the whole fabric and cut it down the middle into two strips, which he placed crosswise at their middle points to form a shape like the letter X; he then bent the ends round in a circle and fastened them to each other opposite the point at which the strips crossed, to make two circles, one inner and one outer.'

However, neither Plato's Timaeus, nor Vincenz Knauer's book in which he had underlined the pertinent passage, appears to be the source for the description used here. It seems rather that Rudolf Steiner has discovered in these philosophers something which put him onto the track of what he himself had found out, which would explain the deviation from the descriptions of both of these writers. This way of enlivening and verifying his spiritual revelations with historical records is described by him in his autobiography, chap. 26:

'My relationship to Christianity should make it clear that my science of spirit is not attained through research of the kind ascribed to me by many people. They intimate that I have put together a theory of spirit on the basis of ancient traditions. I am supposed to have elaborated Gnosticism and other teachings. The spiritual insight gained in *Christianity as Mystical Fact* is brought directly out of the world of spirit. It was only because I wished to demonstrate to the audience at these lectures, and to the readers of the book, the harmony between what can be perceived in spirit and the records of history that I examined the latter and incorporated them in the content. But I took nothing from these documents unless I had *first* experienced it in the spirit.'

11. *But this Temple ... [Gap in text]*
    This passage is very incomplete. In the Vegelahn text there are only the words as given above. In the text given by Reebstein it continues: 'But the Temple is not yet understood by man.' Perhaps the correct rendering should be: 'But the building of the Temple is not yet understood by man.'

12. *These two streams were already current when our race began ...*
    [Gap]
    In the Vegelahn text this sentence finds an incomplete continuation: 'These two streams already made themselves felt at the beginning of our race—the old stream which entered evolution at a time when the gods were still engaged in creating the world, and the second ... which must always continue to build in this Temple of Wisdom ...'

Lecture 13, Berlin, 29 May 1905

Source for the text
Shorthand notes by Franz Seiler, Walter Vegelahn, Berta Reebstein-Lehmann and longhand notes by Marie Steiner von Sivers.

1. *The Christian legend about the Cross ...*
   Parts of this legend are to be found in *The Golden Legend or Lives of the Saints*, a collection of legends from the thirteenth century by Jacobus de Voragine, translated into English by William Caxton (edited by F.S. Ellis, Temple Classics, 1939). In this the death of Adam is described and how he sent 'Seth his son into Paradise for to fetch the oil of mercy, where he received certain grains of the fruit of the tree of mercy by an angel ...

'And then he laid the grains or kernels under his father's tongue and buried him in the vale of Hebron; and out of his mouth grew three trees of the three grains, of which trees the cross that our Lord suffered his passion on was made ...'

In another place in the same work we are told more about the history of the wood of the cross. Under the section headed 'The Invention of the Holy Cross' it is stated:

'... it is read in the Gospel of Nicodemus that when Adam waxed sick Seth his son went to the gate of Paradise terrestrial for to get the oil of mercy for to anoint withal his father's body ...

'In another place it is read that the angel brought him a branch, and commanded him to plant it in the Mount of Lebanon. Yet find we in another place that he gave him of the tree that Adam ate of, and said to him that when that bare fruit he should be guerished and all whole. When Seth came again he found his father dead and planted this tree upon his grave, and it endured there unto the time of Solomon. And because he saw that it was fair, he did hew it down and set it in his house named Saltus. And when the Queen of Sheba came to visit Solomon she worshipped this tree, because she said the Saviour of all the world should be hanged thereon ...

'Then, after this history, the cross by which we be saved came of the tree by which we were damned.'

This extract of *The Golden Legend* by William Caxton differs from the German version in that some details given by Caxton are omitted in the German and vice versa. The fact that the tree was not found suitable for the building and was used as a bridge over which the Queen of Sheba was to pass is not mentioned in the English text.

In *Bilder okkulter Siegel und Säulen. Der Münchner Kongress, Pfingsten 1907, und seine Auswirkungen*, Bibl. 284, there is a comprehensive note dealing with the source of the Temple Legend. It is there said that, according to the research of Otto Zöckler (*Das Kreuz Christi*, chapter headed 'Medieval Legends concerning the Wood of the Cross', Gütersloh 1875, preserved in the University Library, Basle), the legend about the three seeds from the Tree of Life forms part of a complicated series of legends from the twelfth century onwards. The earliest literary mention of Adam being buried on Golgotha is quoted by the Alexandrian Church Father Origen, from a tradition out of the second century, to which was added the tradition of Seth's journey to Paradise which is recorded in the third century in the Nicodemus Gospel, which originally contained an account of the fetching of the oil of mercy for the healing of Seth's sick father, Adam. It was only in later centuries that the genealogical connection between the wood of the Tree of Paradise and the Cross of Christ was established in its various forms.

This legend, including the elaborations concerning Seth's journey to Paradise for the three seeds, was freely quoted by Rudolf Steiner on many occasions including: the present lecture on 29 May 1905; lectures in Leipzig on 15 December 1906 (Bibl. 97); in Berlin on 17 December 1906 (Bibl. 96); in Munich on 21 May 1907 (Bibl. 284); in Cassel on 29 June 1907 and in Basle on 25 November 1907 (both in Bibl. 100); and in Dornach on 19 December 1915 (Bibl. 165).

In his lecture in Cassel, *The Golden Legend* was characterized as having provided a subject for occult instruction since the most ancient times and, referring to Seth, it interprets his mission as of one who could see 'into the end times, when the harmony between the two principles of mankind would be re-established'. By the two principles is meant the two trees pertaining to the red and purple blood which are represented in the two pillars of the temple.

As is evident from the interpretation of the legend by spiritual science the pictures which it presents are symbolic of the fourth degree in the Rosicrucian initiation, which is characterized by the 'Finding of the Philosopher's Stone' and is also known as the *güldene*, or 'golden degree'. This gives us an esoteric explanation of why it was usually referred to by Rudolf Steiner as *The Golden Legend*.

There is a much longer and more detailed version of this legend in an old Cornish legend (*The Ancient Cornish Drama*, edited and translated by Edwin Norris, Oxford University, 1859).

In this version there is not only the account of the fetching of the oil of mercy by Seth, but also of the attempt by Solomon to incorporate the wood from this tree into the temple and its final rejection.

The portion of this drama relating to the oil of mercy is also to be found in *Lyra Celtica*, an anthology of Celtic poetry edited by E. A. Sharp and J. Matthay (John Grant, Edinburgh, 1932).

2. *The famous rod of Moses ...*
Also, according to a mystic Hebrew source, the rod of Moses inscribed with the unutterable name of God is nothing else than the Tree of Life. In the *Midrasch Wojoscha* (the smaller Midrasch commentary on the later legends of the Old Testament) it is said: 'I (Moses) asked her (Zippora) where he (Jithro) obtained this tree. She answered: It is the rod which the Holy One, Blessed may He be! created on the sabbath eve after having created His world. The Holy One, Blessed may He be! handed it to the first man, who handed it to Chanoch, who handed it to Noah, who handed it to Sem, who handed it to Abraham, who handed it to Jacob, who brought it with him to Egypt and gave it to Joseph his son. When Joseph died, the Egyptians plundered his house and brought this rod to Pharoah's palace. My father Jithro was one of Pharoah's great astrologers, he saw the rod, conceived a desire for it, stole it and brought it to his own house. On this rod was inscribed the unutterable name of God and the ten plagues which the Holy One, Blessed may He be! would one day cause to fall on the Egyptians in the land of Egypt ... And how many days and how many years did this rod lie already in my father's house until the day when he took it in his hand, went out into the garden and planted it in the ground. When he returned to the garden to fetch it he found that it had already sprouted and grown blossoms.' (Quoted from Hans Ludwig Held: 'Von Golem und Shem', from the periodical *Das Reich*, January 1917.)

3. *as Giordano Bruno, for example, called it.*
Philotheus Giordano Bruno (1548–1600), *De rerum Principiis Elementis et Causis*, Second Dialogue: 'Universal reasoning is the most inward, real and individual faculty and a potential part of the World Soul.'

4. *Now Plato said about this, that the World Soul has been crucified on the World Body.*
See Note 10 to the preceding lecture.

5. *as Goethe says,*
Second part of *Faust*, end chorus: 'All things transitory are but a likeness.'

6. *'Fairy Story of the Green Snake and the Beautiful Lily',*
Goethe: *The Fairy Tale of the Green Snake and the Beautiful Lily*, Floris Books, 1979. See also *Goethe's Standard of the Soul as illustrated in Faust and in the Fairy Story of the Green Snake and the Beautiful Lily*, Anthroposophical Publishing Company (London, 1925); and *Goethe's Secret Revelation and the Riddle of Faust*, Rudolf Steiner Publishing Company (London, 1933).

7. *'With the law sin came into the world.'*
The Epistle of Paul to the Romans, Chapter 5, verse 13 and Chapter 8, verse 2.

Lecture 14, Berlin, 5 June 1905

Source for the text
Shorthand report of Walter Vegelahn and Berta Reebstein-Lehmann, and also longhand report by Marie Steiner von Sivers.

It is to be taken into account that the notes are in part very deficient and may not be regarded as being verbatim reports.

1. *I did speak about some of the things to be mentioned today, a year ago.*
In his lecture of 23 May 1904 (Lecture 1).

2. *You know that our Earth evolution was cosmologically preceded by the Moon evolution.*
In connection with the following description, see the fundamental works of Rudolf Steiner: *Cosmic Memory*, Rudolf

Steiner Publications (New York, 1971), and *Occult Science, An Outline*, Rudolf Steiner Press (London, 1969).

3. *The initiates tread the path in advance* ... [*Gap*]
A few very inadequately recorded sentences follow this in all texts. In Vegelahn's text it is as follows: 'Then the astral body was permeated by manas, buddhi appeared in the etheric body and the Father-principle in the physical body. This working went so far that a brain could be formed, up to the point where the being learned to say "I". That was the case with the Ur-Semites.'

4. *in* Light on the Path:
Light on the Path, by Mabel Collins (1851–1927), a theosophical writer acknowledged by Rudolf Steiner by an exegesis to the work in question (printed in his *Guidance in Esoteric Teaching*, Rudolf Steiner Press, London, 1994).

5. *If, in escaping from the earthly,*
Rudolf Steiner here draws his Heraclitus quotation from a work on philosophy by Vincent Knauer.

Lecture 15, Berlin, 21 October 1905

Source for the text
Longhand notes by Anna Weissmann, Stuttgart, and Marie Steiner von Sivers. (To the notes by Anna Weissmann was added the remark that this lecture was held in a very restricted circle).

To the theme in general.
In order to avoid a possible source of grave misunderstanding regarding the various statements made by Rudolf Steiner about the atom and future new forces of nature, it is necessary to point out that these varying statements must be considered in their context. It is especially necessary to differentiate between Rudolf Steiner's criticism of the atomic theory as a philosophy

of life and his views about the nature of the atom from an occult point of view.

His criticism of the atomic theory as a philosophy of life was first expressed in his essays 'Einzig mögliche Kritik der atomistischen Begriffe', 1882 (Only possible View of the Atomistic Concepts), and 'Die Atomistik und ihre Widerlegung', 1890 (Atomic Theory and its Refutation), which have as their purpose to show that it is impossible to regard the atom as being the 'basic principle of all existence'. Just as telegraph wires and electricity are only conveyors of what is the essential, so atoms, too, are only the agents or bearers of effects produced by the spirit. This basic view runs through the whole of Rudolf Steiner's work. Even in one of his last works, in his autobiography (*The Course of My Life*, Chapter 32) it is stated: 'Atoms, or atomic structure, can only be the result of spiritual action or organic action.'

Something quite different is involved in the statements about the atom which he made in the present lectures. Here he was speaking from an occult point of view to a very restricted circle about the atom as nature's archetypal building material, in connection with Freemasonry. For, in the same way as nature was to have been sanctified through Masonic cultic symbolism, so Rudolf Steiner wished to awaken through the cultic-symbolic section of his Esoteric School, for which these lectures were a preparation, the knowledge that the 'laboratory table should become the altar of the future' and that the impulse of selflessness must be implanted into the social order if our utilitarian culture is not to perish through egoism. That is why he published simultaneously with that his 'Fundamental Social Law' which states:

'In a community of human beings working together, the well-being of the community will be the greater the less the individual claims for himself the proceeds of the work he has himself done, i.e. the more of these proceeds he makes over to his fellow workers, and the more his own requirements are satisfied not out of his own work done but out of work done by the other.' (Quoted from: *Anthroposophy and the Social Question*.)

The occasion, which was provided not by occult promptings but by external science, was the result of insight into the effects which the latest discoveries of physics at the turn of the nineteenth to twentieth centuries could have for mankind. The perception of the fact that modern science and technology were fast approaching a stage where they could only contribute to the welfare of mankind if human souls are enriched and deepened by a theosophical view of life prompted Rudolf Steiner to come out in support of the publication of spiritual truths. That the physics of the period was beginning to investigate the connection between the atom, electricity and etheric forces was recognized by Rudolf Steiner as a tremendously important turning-point in the development of human thought because, as occultist, he knew that 'a new point of departure will be made from the atom to the mineral-physical world'. (See also Lecture 9 of 16 December 1904 and Note 22 thereto.)

For this reason he ascribed tremendous importance to the speech of the then Prime Minister Balfour, which pointed in this direction. (In the British Association, 14 August 1904.)

With the prophecy given in the three lectures of 9, 16 and 23 December 1904, that man would learn to 'think into the atom' and would acquire the ability to make use of its inner force, was combined not only a warning of the grave dangers which would threaten him if this force were not used selflessly in the service of the whole but also an allusion to the fact that, as something of greatest importance for the future, man will be able to build with atoms as 'the smallest of building stones' in the future.

This latter, not further elaborated suggestion, gets a firmer outline through the notes of Lecture 15 of 21 October 1905 and the supplementary notes of the lecture of 21 October 1907, according to which the occultist is capable of making the atom 'grow'.* At the same time mention is also made of his capacity

---

* Many years later, in a lecture in Berlin on 22 June 1915 (in 'Thoughts for the Times', C 39), Rudolf Steiner again came to speak of the atom in connection with the Jupiter evolution and mentioned the above lectures. A literal rendering of what he said there would be as follows: 'I have spoken formerly about the atom as being built up out of the whole cosmos. You can find it again in those earlier lectures which were held right at the beginning of our Berlin activities.'

to make it 'shrink'. To his audience at that time these thoughts were not quite new. For in the literature of the Theosophical Society, especially that by C.W. Leadbeater and Annie Besant, there was a great deal concerning the power of growing and shrinking as a faculty particularly to be developed in the case of etheric clairvoyance; this was usually found in connection with a description of the clairvoyant investigation of atoms. It was just in the year 1905 that Annie Besant had spoken and written on this subject on various occasions. There was also a study done by Leadbeater and Besant in collaboration in 1895 which appeared anew at this time under the title *Occult Chemistry*. Rudolf Steiner rejected this manner of presentation as 'materialistic spiritualism', just as he rejected the atomism of natural science as a basis for a philosophy of life, for in this theosophical literature, too, the atoms were regarded as the underlying principle of all existence, instead of recognizing them as being the result and agents of definite spiritual effects.

For the same reason he did not speak about a mere outward technique of etheric enlargement and diminution but about the fact that from the twentieth century onward an etheric clairvoyance would gradually develop as a new natural ability of mankind, whereby the reappearance of Christ in the etheric realms would become perceptible (see *The Etherization of the Blood* and *The True Nature of the Second Coming*.) Then there will be chemists and physicists who will no longer preach the doctrine that the world consists of only material atoms, but they will teach that matter is built up 'in the way that Christ arranged it'. (See *Spiritual Guidance of the Individual and Humanity*, Chapter 3.)

It can be inferred from lecture 20, given on 2 January 1906 (in this volume), that when it is said that man will use the atom in future times for building purposes, that is connected with gaining mastery over the etheric, over the life forces. In a slightly later lecture (Munich, 4 December 1907, published in Vol. 98 of the complete edition), this fact is stated again very clearly in the following words:

'... When man has developed so far that he has reached the first stage of clairvoyance, then the life of the plants, the laws governing life, will be just as clear to him as the laws of the mineral world are at present.

'When you put together a machine or build a house you are acting in accordance with the laws of the mineral world. A machine is constructed according to the laws of the mineral world, but a plant cannot be built in this fashion. If you wish to have a plant you must leave it to those beings who underlie the structure of nature. In future times man will be able to create plants in a laboratory, but only when it has become a sacrament to him, a holy office which he performs. All creation of living things will only be permitted to man when he has become so sincere and pure minded that for him the laboratory bench has become an altar. Before that time not the slightest hint will be revealed to him of how living things are composed. In other words: the ego as an organ of con-sciousness lives in the mineral world and will ascend to the plant kingdom, which it will learn to understand just as it now understands the mineral world. Later on it will learn to com-prehend the laws of the animal kingdom and after that those of the human kingdom. All human beings will learn to com-prehend the inner life of plants, of animals and of man; that is a perspective of the future. Whatever one is truly able to com-prehend, one can demonstrate—for instance a watch. Present-day man will never be able to demonstrate anything taken from living nature without the help of the beings who stand behind nature—so long as it is not a sacramental operation that he is performing.'

1. *Devas.*
   The gods of Devachan, or the heavenly world.

2. *The time it takes for the sun to traverse one zodiacal sign is about 2,600 years.*
   Later Rudolf Steiner gave more precise figures for this, according to which the precession of the equinox through the whole zodiac takes $12 \times 2,160 = 25,920$ years, which is a Platonic or world year. Human incarnations are generally connected with these epochs of 2,160 years.

3. *If one goes back a million years in Germany,*
   It is unusual for Rudolf Steiner to give specific figures for such distant events. If we go back in time beyond the end of the Ice Age (10,000 years ago), there is a great discrepancy between the figures given by modern science and those of spiritual science. For instance, modern science sets the date of the commencement of the Ice Age at one million years ago. Spiritual science, on the other hand, puts the commencement of the Ice Age into the middle of Atlantis—'The cosmos became calculable for the first time around 13,500 BC. At that time most of Atlantis was already submerged' (Blavatsky). The trouble with chronology is that modern science still takes present-day conditions as its norm for calculating (e.g. rate of disintegration of matter) and projects it into the past. Spiritual science, on the other hand, calculates according to cosmic rhythms (progression of the sun through the zodiac).

4. *Yet, occult books, however, give descriptions and pictures of the atom.*
   Rudolf Steiner obviously refers here to the representations of atomic structures as they appeared in theosophical literature. Just at the time of these lectures a new edition of *Occult Chemistry*, written in 1895 by C.W. Leadbeater and Annie Besant, had appeared with illustrations. Many of the latter were also depicted in Annie Besant's most popular work, *The Ancient Wisdom* (1899). The first to represent atomic forms in this way was the American, Babbit, in his work *The Principle of Light and Colour* (1878), which was referred to in the Besant-Leadbeater study.

5. *the fifth Round ...*
   In explanation of the terms 'Round', 'Globe', etc., see diagram at end of Lecture 10, 23 December 1904.

6. *Dionysius, the pupil of the Apostle Paul ...*
   Dionysius is mentioned in the Acts of the Apostles, Chapter 17, verse 34. Two works appeared under his name at the end of the fifth century in Syria: *Concerning the Heavenly Hierarchy* and

Concerning the Ecclesiastical Hierarchy, which were translated from Greek into Latin in the ninth century by John Scotus Erigena.

7. *Nicolaus Cusanus.*
Nicholas of Cusa, 1401–64, German mystic. Compare: *Die Mystik im Aufgange des neuzeitlichen Geisteslebens und ihr Verhältnis zur modernen Weltanschauung*, translated variously as 'Mysticism and Modern Thought', 'Mystics of the Renaissance' and 'Eleven European Mystics'.

8. *When Goethe speaks of the Spirit of the Earth ...*
In the first part of *Faust*, Scene I.

Lecture 16, Berlin, 22 October 1905

Source for the text
Shorthand notes by Franz Seiler; made ready for publishing by Marie Steiner von Sivers.

1. *May I once more make it known ...*
The first announcement was most probably given during the General Meeting of the German Section which had taken place beforehand.

2. *the Besant Branch ...*
The then name of the Berlin Branch which held its usual evening meetings.

3. *the Music of the Spheres ...*
The principle teaching of Pythagoras (*c.* 580–500 BC) was that the universe was conceived in the form of a harmoniously ordered whole (the Harmony of the Spheres).

4. *the ancient Indian Vedas.*
Veda (Sanskrit word for 'sacred knowledge'). The Vedas are the complete collection of the oldest religious documents of the

Hindus, written in Sanskrit, to which a supersensible origin has been attributed. They contain a comprehensive literature which was handed on by word of mouth for many ages. The Vedic manuscripts are divided mainly into the following: 1) the Sanhitas; 2) the Brahmanas; 3) the Aranyakas and Upanishads. The Sanhitas are the anthologies of songs, sacrificial formulae and magical incantations. Four such anthologies are distinguished, usually referred to simply as 'the four Vedas'.

5. *the animals in the dark caves of Kentucky lost their ability to see...*
   This example is often cited by Rudolf Steiner. The phenomenon of the rudimentary organs was first observed in the American caves. See Darwin's *Origin of Species*, Chapter 5, 'The Laws of Mutation'.

Lecture 17, Berlin, 23 October 1905

Source for the text
Shorthand notes by Franz Seiler; newly checked for publication.

1. *any kind of female member was, for Freemasonry, strictly taboo.*
   See Note 6.

2. *the outward compilation of the Bible is rightly ascribed to only a few hundred years before the birth of Christ.*
   This was at the time of the return of the Jews from the Babylonian captivity in the fifth century BC by the Hebrew scribe Ezra.

3. *In ancient Greek mythology Zeus is portrayed with ample female breasts.*
   There is a Zeus type, several examples of which are still preserved in Asia Minor, in which the upper part of the body is covered by a number of breasts or humps similar to the famous statue of *Artemis Ephesia* (e.g., relief sculpture of the *Stratios Zeus* and the figures on coins, among which is the 'Labrandeus Zeus' from Caria).

4. *That is a process in man himself.*
See in this connection the later descriptions which Rudolf Steiner gave in *The Effects of Spiritual Development* (Rudolf Steiner Press, 1978).

5. *I have retained . . .*
Franz Seiler's shorthand report was expressed in the following way:
'I have reserved for myself a wish (*Neigung*) to speak (*erzählen*) about those of the race of Abel and those of the race of Cain.'
In checking over the shorthand notes once more it became clear that the sentence could also be interpreted as follows:
'I have reserved for myself the aim of bringing about (*erzielen*) a reconciliation (*Einigung*) between Abel's race, etc.

6. *The founding of the Adoption Lodges in the eighteenth century paved the way for the sexes to come together.*
In *Secret Societies of all Ages and Countries* by Charles William Heckethorn (Book 8, Section 21) we learn that:
'According to one of the fundamental laws of Masonry—and a rule prevailing in the greater Mysteries of antiquity—women cannot be received into the order . . .
'But we have seen that Cagliostro admitted women to the Egyptian Rite; and when at the beginning of the eighteenth century several associations sprang up in France that in their external aspect resembled Freemasonry, but did not exclude women, the ladies naturally were loud in their praise of such institutions, so that the Masonic brotherhood, seeing it was becoming unpopular, had recourse to the stratagem of establishing "Adoptive" Lodges of women, so called because every such Lodge had finally to be adopted by some regular Masonic Lodge. The Grand Orient of France framed laws for their government, and the first Lodge of Adoption was opened in Paris in 1775 . . .
'Similar Lodges spread over Europe, Great Britain excepted, but they soon declined and are at present confined to the place of their origin.'

7. *The founder of our Society was indeed a [female] member of such
   an Adoption Lodge.*
   This refers to H.P. Blavatsky (1831–91) who was awarded the
   highest Adoption degree of the Memphis-Misraim Freemasonry
   in 1888 by John Yarker (see Note 16 to Lecture 9 of 16
   December 1904) after she had published her first great work, *Isis
   Unveiled.*

Lecture 18, Berlin, 23 October 1905

Source for the text
The text was taken from the most complete of four, supplemented by the other three.

1. *until it was put into documentary form,*
   See Note 2 to the preceding lecture.

2. *Zeus, who was worshipped as the progenitor of the human race,
   was portrayed in the oldest [versions of] Greek mythology as
   having female breasts.*
   See Note 3 to the preceding lecture.

3. *So, with Hiram, we have arrived at the transition from the third to
   the fourth post-Atlantean epoch,*
   Hiram was living during the reign of King Solomon, which is
   reckoned as being 993–53 BC. The fourth Sub-Race had its
   beginning in 747 BC according to Rudolf Steiner.

4. *Manvantara.*
   This is the Indian theosophical term for a great cosmic epoch of
   evolution. A period of manifestation such as the planetary states
   (Old Moon, Old Sun, etc.).

5. *In the ancient Hebrew language there is a Word, a mantra, which,
   it is said, will create the world if uttered sufficiently strongly.*
   This possibly refers to the 'Ineffable name of God' which,
   according to Hans Ludwig Held ('Von Golem und Shem' in *Das*

Reich, January 1917), 'is a difficult formula sequence corresponding to the 12-, 42-, or 72-letter name, the knowing of which reveals the secret of God's works or God's activity from beginning to end.'

6. *'I will put enmity between thee and the woman and between thy seed and her seed';*
Genesis 3:15.

7. *in 1775 the first of the so-called Adoption Lodges was founded; a lodge for women . . . H. P. Blavatsky belonged to such an Adoption Lodge.*
See Notes 6 and 7 to the preceding lecture.

Lecture 19, Berlin, 23 October 1905

Source for the text
Shorthand notes by Franz Seiler with supplementary material supplied by three other anonymous members of the audience.

1. *I already indicated a week ago that I wished to say a few words precisely on this subject*
At the previous Members' meeting of the Berlin Branch (on Monday 16 October), Rudolf Steiner made the following remark during the announcement of the forthcoming activities: 'At next Monday's meeting I shall speak about occultism, esotericism and theosophy. I wish to draw your attention to the fact that this subject will be dealt with in conjunction with current happenings. I would beg you to invite as many members as possible, also those living at a distance.'

Lecture 20, Berlin, 2 January 1906

Source for the text
(a) Writing from an unknown hand (the most complete).
(b) The typed clean copy of Franz Seiler's shorthand. The

original shorthand copy of this was also available and on renewed scrutiny was found to be incomplete and to have been supplemented and restored during the process of typing by Seiler, sometimes with the help of text (a) which apparently stood at his disposal.

(c) A very much shortened version by an unknown hand in close textual agreement with (a).

(d) A much shortened text with gaps noted by Berta Reebstein.

(e) Notes by Marie Steiner von Sivers.

(f) Notes from an unknown hand.

The basis used for the printed version was copy (a) with the additional consideration of (b) after comparison with its shorthand copy and other texts.

Places in the text that are deficient in all versions are indicated in the following notes.

To the symbols in the Text

The hexagram as symbol of the Holy Grail

It seems that the texts at this point have not been clearly conceived. It is significant that only the triangle is mentioned and nothing is said of the hexagram. But after the words in Seiler's shorthand copy, 'The medieval occultist expressed the symbol of the Grail ... in the form of a triangle,' he has drawn a hexagram which could only have been inserted at the time he was writing.

The two triangles and hexagram have been reproduced in the present volume as taken from Reebstein's text (d) which provides the greatest number of diagrams.

In text (f) the diagram with its pertinent text are rendered thus:

Human 'This triangle is the symbol of the Holy Grail and also
Strength the symbol for awakening perfection in the living.
That is the Power of Christ which is described as
✡ "Vril" in *Zanoni*. It exists at present in an elementary
germinal state and will become in the future that
Divine which will form the true content of the higher

Power   degrees, namely, the Royal Art. Man must attain this for himself, quite alone, without too much questioning.'

Text (f) also contains a variant which is not found in the other texts: 'Everything which is expressed through art, science and religion, inasmuch as it is not given by the Gods—and therefore standing under the sign of the Cross—is derived from Freemasonry. Hence, therefore, the sign of Freemasonry: ✡ Cain and † Abel.'

The other texts have none of these diagrams. For an explanation of the hexagram as a symbol, see Rudolf Steiner's lecture of 12 January 1924, contained in *Rosicrucianism and Modern Initiation*, Rudolf Steiner Press (London, 1965). A personal remark relating to the hexagram was recorded by Alexander Strakosch (*Mitteilungen aus der anthroposophischen Arbeit in Deutschland*, Christmas, 1958). In the house which was built for the anthroposophical work in Stuttgart, Landhausstrasse 70, in 1911, the hexagram was displayed in the upper parts of the windows of the main hall. Strakosch, who had expected to find the pentagram, asked Rudolf Steiner about it and received the reply: 'The hexagram is actually the sign for the Christ and the Venus evolution.'

The Tau Symbol
The explanations of the Tau symbol are fragmentary and the texts differ in their wording.

Text (a) has the following: 'The Tau sign plays an important role in Freemasonry. It is basically nothing else than a Cross with the upper arm taken away. In a figurative sense, therefore, the mineral realm has been omitted. But in order to arrive at the Cross at all, the plant kingdom must be brought into play, whereby one arrives at the upward pointing Cross ⊥.'

Text and symbol of (a) both seem questionable. Marie Steiner, who once made some preparatory corrections of (a), left off the symbol in its original form and replaced it with the following: 'In order to arrive at the Cross at all, the plant kingdom must be brought into play, whereby the upward pointing Cross is obtained (↓↑T).'

In *text (b)* the following version is given: 'This Tau sign plays an important role in Freemasonry. It is nothing else but the Cross. Only one of the beams is left off. The mineral kingdom has been left off in order to arrive at the Cross at all. If you allow the plant kingdom to come into play you get the upward pointing cross ⊥.' In the shorthand version of this there is a gap after the words: 'in order to arrive at the Cross at all'. Instead, the symbol ⊥ is inserted after 'upwards pointing Cross', whereas it has been left out of the fair copy.

The *text (d)* only has: 'The Tau plays an important role T. It is nothing else than the Cross. If the productive forces of the plant ...' It is significant that the Tau symbol has been drawn, but not the reverse form, in a text which otherwise provides the greatest number of diagrams.

Text (f) has the following: 'The Tau is the Cross, from which the upper beam has been removed. The mineral realm has been left off; man controls it already. For if one lets the plant realm come into play one arrives at ⊥. What develops out of the earth, out of the soul as power over the earth, is the symbol of future Freemasonry.'

The other texts do not contain a reference to this.

1. *Most of you know that I have already spoken ...*
In the two lectures 17 and 18 in this volume on 23 October 1905, to men and women separately.

2. *It is now some 17 or 18 years ago ...*
Rudolf Steiner here refers to his association with the circle around Marie Eugenie della Grazie in Vienna during the eighties of the last century. See in this connection *The Story of My Life*.

3. *This was discussed as a completely serious matter ...*
The occasion for this lay in the discussions prevailing at that time between the Church and Freemasonry concerning the sensational work by Leo Taxil on satanic practices of the

Freemasons which had already appeared in 100,000 copies at the time of these discussions, *Die Drei-Punkte-Brüder*. And see the following note.

4. *Now what happened was ...*
Rudolf Steiner refers here to the now famous Taxil-Vaughan swindle. Leo Taxil (pseudonym for Gabriel Jogand Pagès), 1854–1907, brought up by Jesuits and known since the seventies as an anti-clerical writer and founder of several free-thinking societies, became a member of the Paris Lodge 'Le Temple de l'Honneur Français' in 1881, but was excluded from it soon afterwards because he was supposed to have forged letters of Brothers Victor Hugo and Louis Blanc. In April 1885 he staged his repentant return to the Church. In obedience to the encyclical of Leo XIII of 20 April 1884, *Humanum Genus* in which the unmasking of Freemasons as confederates of the Devil was required, he commenced his main work, *Les Frères Trois-Points* (Paris, 1885; German, H. Gruber, S.J., *Die Drei-Punkte Brüder*, Paderborn 1886–87), started his unmasking campaign with other writings concerned with his fabricated Freemasonry system of 'Palladism' and was even called to a private audience with Leo XIII in 1887. The unparalleled success of Leo Taxil and his two other accomplices, the German Karl Hacks (pseudonym, Dr Bataille, brother-in-law of the publisher of the ultramontane *Kölnischen Volkszeitung*) and the Italian Domenico Margiotta, in Catholic Church circles reached its climax when Taxil invented the witness Miss Diana Vaughan (*Miss Diana Vaughan. Mémoires d'une Expalladiste. Publication mensuelle*). With the co-operation of the highest Church dignitaries, Taxil founded an Anti-Freemasonry Union which summoned a first Anti-Freemasonry Congress in Trient, September 1896. Thirty-six bishops, 50 episcopal delegates and over 700 opponents of the Lodges, most of them priests, took part in the Congress. The Sovereign Bishop Cardinal Haller of Salzburg and the leader of the Catholic nobility in Germany, Prinz Karl zu Löwenstein, chaired the meeting. The Congress was a public declaration of the revelations of Taxil and Miss Vaughan; only a few sceptics demanded proof. The first to start questioning the

Taxil affair was the Freemason Gottfried Joseph Findel, who published his *Katholischer Schwindel* as early as 1896. In general, however, H. Gruber, S.J., who had long been a believer in Taxil, is credited with being the first to raise doubts about him with his three-volume work *Leo Taxils Palladismus-Roman*. This work only appeared in 1897, however. A.E. Waite, with his *Devil Worship in France or the Question of Luzifer* (London, 1896) is also said to have this distinction.

By this time Taxil admitted in a great assembly in Paris, 19 April 1897, that everything was a deliberate swindle on his part and that the Devil Bixtru and his satanic Bride, Miss Vaughan, had never existed. According to the *Allgemeines Handbuch der Freimaurerei*, Taxil's confession came about earlier than was intended 'because, according to his own admission, he could not carry the mystification any further after the appearance of Findel's work'. Bibliographical references: Graf von Hoensbroech, *Das Papsttum in seiner sozial-kulturellen Wirksamkeit* (Leipzig, 1900); Karl Heise, *Entente-Freimaurerei und Weltkrieg* (Basle, 1920); Friedrich Hasselbacher, *Entlarvte Freimaurerei* (Berlin, 1939).

5. *what Lessing, who was himself a Freemason, said . . .*
According to Mönckeberg (*G.E. Lessing als Freimaurer*, Hamburg, 1880), Lessing, on his enrolment in the Hamburg Lodge on 15 October 1771, was asked by the Worshipful Master, von Rosenberg: 'Now, you see indeed, I have told the truth! You have not discovered anything anti-religious or politically dangerous, have you?' Lessing is said to have replied: 'Ha, I wish I had discovered something of the sort. It would have pleased me better.'

6. *In a text appearing in 1875, the author claims that Adam became the first Freemason.*
It cannot be determined what text Rudolf Steiner was referring to. However, according to Heckethorn, quoted previously, this notion already appeared in 1751 in the *Konstitutionenbuch für irländische Logen*.

7. *Scottish or Accepted Rite, which, in a particular respect, still conserves [a relic of] what is called the Egyptian, the Misraim or the Memphis Rite.*
This is Seiler's shorthand version. In text (a) it is rendered: 'so-called Scottish? or the same rite as that which corresponds, in a particular respect, to what is called the Egyptian, the Misraim, or the Memphis Rite.' The Reebstein text (d) only has: 'Scottish or Accepted Rite—Memphis Rite.'

8. *Goethe's fairy story ...*
On this, see Note 6 to the lecture given on 29 May 1905 (Lecture 13).

9. *The artist's eye looked at what was enacted [in the Mysteries]*
In text (a) 'in the Mysteries' is replaced by 'in the spiritual world'. In the shorthand version of Seiler these words are missing. For his fair copy he apparently made use of text (a).

10. *Whereas in India, up to the time of the Egyptian cult ...*
This sentence is incomplete in all versions. It is given in the published version as corrected by Marie Steiner from text (a).

11. *Whoever wants to understand what Aristotle meant by purification, catharsis ... how Lessing investigated ...*
Compare also: 'Aristotle on the Mystery Drama' (NSL 420, *Anthroposophical Monthly*, Vol. 4, No. 9); *Speech and Drama*, Anthroposophical Publishing Company (London, 1960).

12. *in the symbolically deeply significant saga of the Holy Grail ...*
Rudolf Steiner often spoke about the Grail Mysteries at the time of these lectures, for instance in Berlin on 19 May 1905 (*Anthroposophical News Sheet*, Vol. 5, No. 11), and in Landin (Mark), on 29 July 1906 (typescript copy Z 307).

13. *my recent lecture ...*
The double lecture given on 23 October 1905 to men and women separately (Lectures 17 and 18 in the present volume).

14. *On the other hand you know ... forces of male and female.*
    This sentence is not word for word as transcribed. The various
    texts are different. Text (a) omits from this sentence the words
    'great streams' and has in their place 'forces of male and female',
    and ends at the word 'realms', omitting the rest. Seiler's fair
    copy has the same wording, but the shorthand version has a gap
    here. In Reebstein's text (d) we find the following: 'The symbols
    are connected with questions running through the whole world,
    which meaning ... basic forces of male and female.' The notes of
    Marie Steiner von Sivers give the following: 'The two sexes are
    only an expression of the two great currents, which confront us
    as the Law of Polarity.' The printed version has been revised by
    the editor to give a meaningful rendering.

15. *The World Soul is nailed to the Cross of the World Body.*
    See Note 10 to lecture given on 22 May 1905 (Lecture 12).

16. *ensoulment (conquest) ...*
    'Ensoulment' (*Beseelung*), 'conquest' (*Besiegung*). Texts (a) and
    (b) have the former; text (d) the latter.

17. *And even the statesman gives structure to nature [?]*
    The questionable word 'nature' was given in texts (a) and (b) but
    was missing in the other texts.

18. *And the Middle Ages with its chaos ...*
    This sentence was incomplete in texts (a) and (b) and was made
    up from texts (d) and (e).

19. *as can even be proved by literary means*
    Rudolf Steiner was obviously referring here to the saga of 'Poor
    Henry' composed by Hartmann von Aue (1165–c. 1215), a
    contemporary of Wolfram von Eschenbach. (See also Note 13.)
    Rudolf Steiner often referred to this poem later in his lectures.

20. *Cain, by contrast, had offered something which he had himself
    won from the earth by his own labour, as the fruit of effort.*
    This sentence only occurs in text (a). Reebstein's text (d), on the

other hand, is the only text to contain this sentence: 'Abel is the one who in the future will have the power to create [what is] holy through [the forces of] his soul.'

21. *This joint force (communal force)*.
Text (a) has 'communal force' (*Gemeinsamkeitskraft*). In Seiler's fair copy it is 'joint force' (*Gesamtkraft*), but in Seiler's shorthand copy, *Gemeinsamkeitskraft* can be read. The whole text, including the preceding paragraph, is rendered in Reebstein's text (d) in the following way: 'Objective love was present in the Gods who created the cosmos. Something superhuman is stirring, which today is understanding, which later will be love. Manas, buddhi, atma is a joint force which gives power over the Cross.'

22. *And of what use is it if a corporate body possesses the power of the Cross?*
Text (a) has the word 'Christ' instead of the word 'Cross', but on the other hand, Seiler's shorthand and fair copy, as well as Reebstein's text (d), give 'Cross'.

23. *Wolfram von Eschenbach's* Parzival.
Composed around 1200–10. First printed 1477. Forgotten then for many years and only came to be known again about 1750. First critical edition by Lachmann (1833) followed by numerous others. English translations: J.L. Weston, *A Knightly Epic*, 2 volumes (London, 1894), in verse; Mustard and Passage, *Parzival*, Vintage Books (New York, 1961); A.T. Hatto, *Parzival*, Penguin Classics (1980).

24. *Bulwer Lytton in his futuristic novel* 'Vril'.
The Right Hon. Lord Lytton, *The Coming Race*, George Routledge and Sons (London, 1870). Translated into German by Günther Wachsmuth at Rudolf Steiner's instigation (Stuttgart, 1922), under the title: *Vril oder eine Menschheit der Zukunft*.
   In an answer to a question put to Rudolf Steiner at the end of a lecture held in Leipzig, 13 October 1906, regarding the meaning of *Vril*, he said the following:
   'Everything which was previously present in the world will

return again. The Vril-force underlies something special. At present man can really only make use of the forces of the mineral world. Gravity is a mineral [force], electricity also. The building of railways we owe to coal. What man does not know how to use, though, is the force of plants. The power which causes the blades of corn to spring up in a cornfield is a still latent power, which man will press into his service just as with the power of coal. That is Vril. It is the same force which the fakirs still use. They live in atavism—the mark of an ancestral condition.'

25. *Whoever heard my last lecture about Freemasonry ...*
Double lecture on 23 October 1905, for men and women separately (Lectures 17 and 18).

26. *at the remark with which I ended last time ...*
In the lecture of 28 December 1905 (unpublished as yet), Rudolf Steiner said: 'Allow me to conclude my observations of the old year with an allusion I have made once before [in the lectures of December 1904, included in the present volume]. A major work of destruction is being carried out all around us, which could tell an observant person—even if he were not clairvoyant—that we stand at the beginning of a great work of destruction involving outer material [culture] as it has developed in recent centuries, for material development only goes up to a certain point.'

27. *Keely invented a motor ...*
The American John Worrell Keely (born 1837) caused much talk in the second half of the nineteenth century through the invention of the 'self-motor', the so-called Keely Motor. A treatise on his experiments is to be found in H.P. Blavatsky's *The Secret Doctrine*, Vol. I, Book III (X 'The Coming Force', pp. 554–56). Among the lectures of Rudolf Steiner there are several references to this subject, notably in the lecture given during the Great War on 20 June 1916: 'Cosmic Being and Egohood' (cycle C 43), where he says: 'It was a concept still. Thank God it was only a concept at that time for, if this Keely's concept had become reality then, what would this war have become!' Compare also the lecture given in Dornach on 1

December 1918, in *In the Changed Conditions of the Times*, Rudolf Steiner Publishing Company (1941).

[It has been pointed out to the translator that Rudolf Steiner, in his lecture of 2 January 1906, does actually differentiate between two phases of Keely's investigation, though Keely himself was unclear on this point—the phase when he was '... operating a force without the intervention of any will-power or personal influence, whether conscious or unconscious of the operator' (Keely's words, quoted on p. 562 of *The Secret Doctrine*) and the part in which 'my power will be generated, my engines run, my cannon operated *through a wire* (idem. p. 561). Madame Blavatsky says of this (same page): 'The "wire" is already a step below or downward from the pure etheric plane into the terrestrial ... from a generator six feet long he has come down to one no larger than an old-fashioned silver watch; and this by itself is a miracle of *mechanical* (but not spiritual) genius.' Then she quotes Mrs Bloomfield Moore, who says: '... the two forms of force which he has been experimenting with, and the phenomena attending them, are the very antithesis of each other.']

28. *This power is symbolized by the Tau sign and was indeed poetically symbolized by the image of the Holy Grail.*
    Texts (a) and (b) have: 'the Tau' of the Holy Grail. The other texts do not have this passage, the image of the Holy Grail is Marie Steiner's correction; perhaps, however, it rests on an error in copying and it should read: 'the Taube' (i.e. 'dove') of the Holy Grail.

29. *Goethe, for instance ... There are still many mysteries ...*
    See in this context Rudolf Steiner's later lectures: *The Problem of Faust*, twelve lectures, Dornach, between 13 September 1916 and 19 January 1919.

30. *a task which is incumbent on us ...*
    Rudolf Steiner is referring here to the Section dealing with cult and symbolism of his Esoteric School which he was about to found. See in this connection *The Course of My Life*, Chapter XXXII.

PUBLISHER'S NOTE REGARDING RUDOLF STEINER'S LECTURES

The lectures contained in this volume have been translated from the German which is based on stenographic and other recorded texts that were in most cases never seen or revised by the lecturer. Hence, due to human errors in hearing and transcription, they may contain mistakes and faulty passages. Every effort has been made to ensure that this is not the case. Some of the lectures were given to audiences more familiar with anthroposophy; these are the so-called 'private' or 'members' lectures. Other lectures, like the written works, were intended for the general public. The differences between these, as Rudolf Steiner indicates in his *Autobiography*, is twofold. On the one hand, the members' lectures take for granted a background in and commitment to anthroposophy; in the public lectures this was not the case. At the same time, the members' lectures address the concerns and dilemmas of the members, while the public work speaks directly out of Steiner's own understanding of universal needs. Nevertheless, as Rudolf Steiner stresses: 'Nothing was ever said that was not solely the result of my direct experience of the growing content of anthroposophy. There was never any question of concessions to the prejudices and preferences of the members. Whoever reads these privately printed lectures can take them to represent anthroposophy in the fullest sense. Thus it was possible without hesitation— when the complaints in this direction became too persistent—to depart from the custom of circulating this material "for members only". But it must be borne in mind that faulty passages do occur in these reports not revised by myself.' Earlier in the same chapter, he states: 'Had I been able to correct them [the private lectures] the restriction [for members only] would have been unnecessary from the beginning.'